W9-ABO-439

RUSSIA
AFTER
KHRUSHCHEV

RUSSIA AFTER KHRUSHCHEV

Robert Conquest

FREDERICK A. PRAEGER, *Publishers*
New York · Washington · London

FREDERICK A. PRAEGER, *Publishers*
111 Fourth Avenue, New York 3, N.Y., U.S.A.
77–79 Charlotte Street, London W.1, England

Published in the United States of America in 1965
by Frederick A. Praeger, Inc., Publishers

Second printing, 1965

Some of the material in this book has appeared in different form in *Problems of Communism* and in an essay by the author entitled "The Future of Communism."

Library of Congress Catalog Card Number: 65–15645

This book is Number 164 in the series
Praeger Publications in Russian History and World Communism.

Printed in the United States of America

For

Annabel

Preface

WITH THE FALL OF KHRUSHCHEV, the Soviet Union entered a period of profound crisis. Over the years of his ascendancy it had become clear that major difficulties confronted the regime and that it had not been able to adjust to them by seeking fully realistic solutions. The Soviet economy faces challenges that the system is ill-equipped—in some cases totally unequipped—to meet. Beyond this, and basic to it, there is a crisis of ideas: Party orthodoxy has not come to terms with the beginnings of a constructive movement toward freer thought in all fields. Intellectual and social trends are away from official standards. And a political machine originally designed to impose its decisions even in such hostile circumstances no longer manifests a clear and single will. There is an unprecedented lack of both quality and credibility among those at present best situated in the struggle for power. All this strongly implies a period of marked instability.

Other elements of Soviet reality enter into this book, as they are bound to do, but basically it is about politics. For in Russia today, politics is central. None of the great changes that are called for can take place until the political system is transformed.

My aim here has been to examine the present situation in detail and to set forth, in a more general way, the potentialities of Soviet development. Beyond the immediate crisis, immense, and possibly beneficial, changes seem to be impending. If we in the West are to cope with events, and perhaps play a helpful role in them, we must not only take a sound and reasoned view of the realities of today's Russia; we must also keep our minds open to the ranging perspectives of the possible Soviet future.

R. C.

January, 1965

Contents

Preface *vii*

1. *Russia in Crisis* 3
2. *The Evolution of Stalinism* 12
3. *Continuity of Rule* 21
4. *The Khrushchevite "Liberalization"* 32
5. *Official "Anti-Stalinism": The Dilemma of the Regime* 42
6. *The Mind of the* Apparatchik 51
7. *The Logic of Faction* 68
8. *Economic Challenges* 77
9. *Themes of Faction* 94
10. *Khrushchev: Impact and Fall* 109
11. *The Present Contenders* 124
12. *Restoration of the Fallen?* 160
13. *The Army* 171
14. *The Seeds of Change* 188
15. *Succession States?* 203
16. *Chinese and Other Communisms* 217
17. *The Role of the West* 230
18. *A Liberal Future?* 248

Index 265

RUSSIA AFTER KHRUSHCHEV

I

Russia in Crisis

BY THE AUTUMN OF 1964, people throughout the world had begun to feel that Cold War pressures were easing. A Russia gradually become stable and sensible after the troubled postwar decades seemed to be relaxing its internal dictatorship and its outward intransigence. Rightly or wrongly, these developments had everywhere come to be associated in people's minds with the rule, apparently quite unassailable, of Nikita Sergeyevich Khrushchev.

Then, on October 14, 1964, it was suddenly announced that Khrushchev had "resigned." His high positions were taken by men of whom the world knew little. Leonid Brezhnev, a longtime Party official who had been very close to the fallen leader, became First Secretary of the Party, traditionally the leading post. Alexei Kosygin, who had served in the highest bodies of the State for twenty years, became Chairman of the Council of Ministers. They and their colleagues in the Presidium had, it appeared, seized power in a secret conspiracy against their chief.

Many in the West were shaken by these startling events. Those who had, since the last major political crisis, in 1957, become used to a certain political stability and continuity, were shocked by the sudden, brutally clear view afforded them of the real tensions in the Soviet Union. Those who had formed the impression that some sort of democratizing tendency had set in in the U.S.S.R. were faced by a change of government carried out through a coup at the top, with the victors making no attempt to explain the matter to the apathetic masses. In fact, far from democracy being anywhere visible, it was clear from the pronouncements of the new regime that even rational and consistent oligarchy was by no means inherent in the system. For Khrushchev had, it was now revealed, put through a whole series of hastily prepared and ill-considered schemes, disrupting industry, agriculture, and the Party organization itself over the past few years, without the other leaders being able to do anything effective to stop him.

We usually recognize the complexity, and the idiosyncrasies, of a polity and society to which we are accustomed. But we are all too apt to oversimplify our ideas of those of which our knowledge is more indirect. We are inclined to construct models of strange political systems on too simple a basis, especially when the facts are not readily available. But it is quite inappropriate to think of Soviet politics in anything like Western terms. The most striking difference is that there is no mechanism for the social forces to express themselves. In the advanced countries, society and polity virtually coincide. In the Soviet Union, the political world is limited to a few thousand members of a self-perpetuating elite. Moreover, this elite was originally formed, and has been trained for decades, with the purpose of enforcing its will against the tendencies of society as a whole.

For the regime in the Soviet Union has its roots and traditions, its veteran personnel, and its established institutions. Brezhnev and Kosygin and the others inherit a set of principles and the machinery designed to put those principles into effect. And those who come to the top hereafter will arise from the present cadres and partake of their limitations.

The basic principles of Soviet rule may be defined as:

(a) Party monopoly of all decisions and (b) control of the Party by a self-perpetuating elite—"democratic centralism."

At present, as in the past, the essentials of power are concentrated in the Presidium of the Central Committee of the Communist Party. In the Party, as in the State, there is an elaborate "democratic" apparatus. Party Congresses assemble and "elect" the Central Committee, which "elects" the Presidium and the Secretariat. In Lenin's time, the Congresses were doubtless not truly representative, since the election of delegates to them from the Party branches was powerfully influenced by those in control of the Party machinery. But still, they were the scenes of debate and voting. The three Party Congresses held under Khrushchev's rule, including the 1961 Twenty-second Congress, were the scenes of complete unanimity. In fact, the delegates to the Congresses themselves are in practice selected by those in control in the Secretariat and Presidium. The election of the Central Committee by these Congresses has in all recent cases consisted of assent to a list presented to them by their managers. The whole machinery is, practically speaking, simply a sounding board for the leadership and a respectable method of perpetuating its grip. In 1956, to be sure, voices were raised (to be denounced in *Pravda*) urging that since Stalin and his heirs were the illegitimate beneficiaries of the illegal purges which carried away the majority of the legitimate Central Committee in the 1930's, a new and democratically organized Party Congress should take place to provide a genuine and new leadership. At the Twenty-second Congress, too, Kozlov had to denounce "certain comrades" who had urged that different factions should be allowed to state their views openly and to have them voted on. In fact, there is, as we shall see, even within the Party an element wishing for some degree of democratization. It has had no success whatever and represents as yet only an intellectual fringe quite divorced from the organs of power.

For the essential thing in Russian political life is simply this:

Power is in the hands of a self-appointed Party bureaucracy, and all institutional arrangements are designed with one of two purposes—to perpetuate, and to conceal, this fact. There are therefore two sorts of institutions in the country: those through which power is genuinely transmitted, and those which provide the shadow, though never the substance, of popular sovereignty. Both systems were fully developed in Stalin's time. Both operate in essentially the same way to this day. Moreover, it is not simply the outward forms of rule in Russia which have undergone little change. It is rather the basic principle, the essence of the whole political system.

A noted analyst of Soviet politics, Leonard Schapiro, has remarked acutely of changes in the U.S.S.R. since the death of Stalin: "Though the *method* of government has changed enormously, its basic *mechanism* is the same, because no new institutions have taken the place of the old."* Nothing that has happened since has affected this.

There are indeed disputes within the leadership. And this, to some extent, means that a given Central Committee, and a given Presidium, may be a compromise solution reflecting various trends—as is the case at present. But in any event the dispute is effectively among a few dozen people. Very occasionally, when they are closely matched, arguments may be transferred to the Central Committee, and this body may then have some voice. This, it is sometimes said, is what took place in June, 1957—and in October, 1964. The writer believes this to be a somewhat misleading description of what happened. But at least it is not impossible that in certain circumstances a struggle at the top would genuinely involve the Central Committee and perhaps even lower echelons, just as the Fascist Grand Council finally played a real part at the time of the fall of Mussolini. Meanwhile, we must regard factions and disputes, within the elite of the *apparat*, as *being* Soviet politics properly

* *Survey*, April, 1963.

speaking. It is on that narrow, confused, and often bitterly contested field, and only there, that Russia's problems can as yet find political expression.

For these problems are many and difficult. The rulers of the Soviet Union are under external constraints and pressures, beyond those arising simply out of the handling of the Party machine. They are committed to matching the United States militarily, to modernizing the economy, to solving the permanent crisis in agriculture, and so on. Such a program is beyond Russia's resources and faces its rulers continuously with the "allocation problem"—how best to allot the inadequate resources available for investment.

The industrial machine Stalin built up was based on large-scale production of steel and the more common engineering products and armaments; it was of a simple nature that made it easily administrable by a political *apparat*.

The steel-centered economies, which dominated the West until a generation ago, have often been noted (for example, by George Orwell) for their association with a true old-fashioned proletariat, as in the steel towns of Yorkshire. Orwell could already point out that the new electronic and other industries of the south of England, to which the balance of economic emphasis had shifted, were associated with a different style of life. Modernizing the economy, transferring the productive emphasis from the old muscle-power-and-slums area, has great social as well as economic results.

Russia is still a country where, to the Western eye, the consumer is treated very cavalierly indeed. Even so, the principle of incentives is now more or less accepted. Terror and the sweatshop are both difficult to apply and psychologically unsuitable to the large new productive class of technicians and semitechnicians which to some degree replaces the old proletariat in the newer industries; and this fact is gaining some recognition. At the same time, higher standards of education are technically necessary. And though "education" of this sort should not be taken as automatically meaning intellectual liberation—as C. P. Snow naïvely supposes—nevertheless, student bodies do tend to be ready for new ideas. After the brief "liberalization" of 1956, the technical institutes were as much censured as the universities proper for outbursts of "anti-Party" opinion.

In a sense, both socially and economically, Russia is becoming increasingly Europeanized. And we can add that educated Russia has always strongly felt its membership in the European tradition. Nor has this mood died out, however suppressed and silenced, in the long years of Stalinism and Khrushchevism. In Yevgeny Yevtushenko's long poem "Zima Station,"* the first thought of his provincial (indeed Siberian) uncle about the repudiation of Stalin's Doctors' Plot is that it was "a scandal before all Europe."

The potentials for great change therefore exist. The Soviet Union is on the verge of becoming, in most respects, an advanced country. Meanwhile, these economic and social forces are held back by a political integument suitable to earlier times. It is actually, in a sense, the classical Marxist situation: "From forces favoring development the conditions of production now turn into fetters on these forces. . . . Then a period of social revolution sets in. . . . Owing to the alteration of the economic basis, the whole immense superstructure is, gradually or suddenly, subverted."†

These dilemmas of the regime have expressed themselves over the last few years, equally classically, in a series of economic crises, as the political leadership has attempted to make some adaptation of the system of rule to the real problems. For it is old experience that ruling classes and castes cannot easily adapt themselves to new conditions. The vast bureau-

* Published in *Oktyabr,* October, 1956.
† Karl Marx, *Critique of Political Economy* (London: 1904).

cratic machine that rules Russia is deeply imbued with traditionalisms, prejudices, and a corporate chauvinism which are not easily to be shaken off.

A basic question for the next decade or two is whether the Soviet Union will be "liberalized," as it needs to be. We shall see that there is little prospect of anything but resistance to real liberalization from any faction significantly represented in the Central Committee, from Brezhnev as well as Kosygin, from Mikoyan as well as Suslov. Nor do any of the younger cadres of the inner Party, such as Shelepin or Polyansky, show any signs of being influenced in this direction. Liberal feeling exists as a powerful aspiration among the intelligentsia and other classes excluded from effective political life, just as it did under the autocracies of the nineteenth century. It then formed the seedbed for change, but the actual changes did not come until the ruling groups were at the very least highly disorganized.

Such disorganization in the *apparat* is quite conceivable. But it could only follow a whole series of crises and power grabs that would shake both its self-confidence and its solidarity to the degree that a faction within it might feel bound to attempt alliance with something in the nature of a genuine democratic force. This cannot be excluded. For, even when we go on to deal with day-to-day politics, we need not lose sight of the fact that they are ephemeral, transitional. We are all liable to exaggerate the stability of that which exists. In spite of the great and obvious weaknesses besetting it, the Austro-Hungarian Empire was not thought to be facing disintegration at the beginning of this century. With all the signs of change visible in 1780, the idea of the collapse of Bourbon rule in France would have been thought laughable.

But when the stability of a regime depends on the formal power of the government in being, when it is evident that the social, economic, and intellectual tides have set in firmly against the system, then, in the long run, the apparent and visible stability is misleading. The Soviet Union must now be regarded as being in a most unstable condition and subject to extreme change over perhaps quite a short period.

It would be generally agreed that the Soviet Union is passing through a transitional stage. What the transition is *from* is clear enough, though there may be various views about the other end of the process, set as it is in a not easily determinable future. In any case, we may accept the fact that transitions of this type, although they may later appear to have been comparatively smooth at some basic level, are marked by a great political instability at the top. Even on short-term political moves, as the events of the past ten years in the international Communist movement should perhaps have taught us, we should not expect a smooth and easily predictable development. One may keep an entirely open mind and try to consider the remotest possibilities as carefully as those which appear to be more probable, but it is still only too likely that one will end up saying, as Euripides does at the end of the *Bacchae:* "The things I expected did not come to pass, and the end of the path which I could not discern led to this."

We cannot "predict" even the immediate Soviet future. But we can examine the nature and tendencies of Soviet politics and of Soviet politicians as they are today, and the various possible results to which the play of these forces may lead.

The power of individual leaders actually to impose policy directions is one we are inclined to underestimate. If Stalin had died in 1933 or 1934, it seems virtually certain that a Stalinist Russia in the sense we know it would not have emerged. (Just as, perhaps, we may feel that if Theodore Roosevelt had survived and regained leadership of the Republican Party in 1920, American—and international—history might have been very different; and similarly in Britain, if Curzon rather than Baldwin had become Prime Minister.) This is not, of course, to say that the leader operates in a vacuum: but neither is he a mere locus or projection of social forces. Thus it is important to gain a sound view of the nature of the leading figures. Yet we need not regard them or their ideas as fixtures. In such periods, all sorts of crosscurrents and reversals, contradictions and compromises must arise.

Although Khrushchev, with his erratic and changeable policies, has to some degree shaken the old solidarities and certitudes of the Party, he nevertheless provided the main element of political stability and continuity in the recent period. For the regime was at least centered and concentrated on one man of long experience and political credibility. With his removal, we see a Russia in which the disintegration that has long beset the economic and intellectual spheres has broken through into the political. Although it would be going too far to say that this is irreversible, it seems probable that the Soviet system has thereby entered into a general crisis from which it can only emerge, if it emerges at all, transformed out of all recognition.

As I have suggested, the social structure, the economic problems and perspectives of Russia are not in themselves so alien to our whole habit of thought as the political side is. And Russia's development now depends in the first place on the possibility of changes in political attitudes and in the political system. Therefore, to arrive at an understanding of what is going on, it is necessary to begin by examining how the present ruling elite developed and the nature of its special attitudes. We can go on to consider the style of Soviet politics and factions, and the way in which the basic problems of the country have presented themselves in political and factional terms. In this context, we can take a close look at the present contenders for power in the Kremlin and other possible interveners on the political scene. And we can conclude by considering, beyond the present crisis, the broader potentialities of Russia's future.

2

The Evolution of Stalinism

THE CHARACTERISTICS of the present ruling elite arose historically, in the long development of the unique Party which it represents and leads. The Communist variant of Marxism evolved on the basis of the special conditions of Russia. It was necessary, or at least convenient, to have a small, highly centralized, conspiratorial organization in Czarist times. Lenin originally thought of this as mere temporary tactics and looked forward (as Marx had) to a large, democratically organized, legal party like the Social Democrats of the West. However, the Bolsheviks seized power in 1917 long before a working class adequate to support such a party had evolved in Russia. They won the Civil War and maintained their grasp on the country as a result not of their popularity—which sank to a low level even among the workers—but of those qualities of will power, discipline, and organization they had learned in conspiracy.

Yet the evolution of totalitarianism was gradual. In the first months of Bolshevik rule, opposition papers were allowed to appear. Other party organizations were not suppressed, and the Left Social Revolutionaries even entered the Soviet Government. These freedoms disappeared in the process of the Civil War. But even then there was a considerable and open ferment of ideas *within* the Party. "Oppositions" were openly organized. Those of the early 1920's—particularly the Democratic Centralists and the Workers' Opposition—publicly accused the Party oligarchs of substituting bureaucracy and decisions by the leadership for genuine Party decisions. It was not until 1921, when the worst was over, but famine was rampant and the first worker and peasant revolts (in Kronstadt and the Volga basin) were giving evidence of the population's dislike of the regime, that Lenin introduced the regulations, still in force to this day, forbidding the formation of oppositions. (It was in the same period that he broadened the scope of this new "Leninism" to apply to the entire world. It was laid down that Communist parties, on precisely the Soviet model, were to arise everywhere in place of the great democratic bodies Marx had worked for. A totally new principle was thus exported to the entire movement, and when a Communist Party came to power it was already set in neo-Leninist ways.)

Yet even these provisions did not at once produce the rigors we associate with Stalinism. In fact, both in the Party and in the intellectual life outside, there was much more freedom during the 1920's than there is now in the 1960's. The expression of opposing opinions was allowed in the Party, even if the organization of opposition groups was not. And the writers were not subjected, or only halfheartedly so, to Party rule.

But the antirational, antidemocratic results of the early decisions had a fatal effect. The Party fell increasingly into the hands of the professionals, headed by Stalin. But the development of political Stalinism was gradual; it did not spring into existence fully formed simply by a logical process. As Marxists point out, general ideas bear the impress of unconscious political and other forces. And present-day Soviet ideology shows many signs of being the product of the triumph within the Party of the Party machine. But let us for the moment consider the *operational* characteristics of the ideology, rather than its form or its origins.

The basic points are first, that it considers all other political and economic ideas and actualities as fundamentally and irrevocably hostile. There is no prospect of evolution by or within other social systems that could lead to the peaceful development of a world acceptable to the present Soviet authorities. Secondly, there is no room for discussion or democracy in any significant sense within the Party itself.

From a Marxist point of view, Lenin's revolution, made in a country with inadequate industry and proletariat, was justifiable only as part of an expected European revolution. When this did not occur, the proletarian party should logically have abandoned power or shared it with bourgeois democrats. But of course the Communist Party does not abandon power, and it was thus left the alternative of creating ex post facto the local proletariat and industry to justify its rule. Or, to look at it another way, the Party had to re-create its links with the people. Bukharin and the Rightists saw this, and their program can be defined as an attempt to combine industrialization and the creation of a proletariat with reconciliation with the people —that is, both the peasantry and the proletariat. From this point of view, the criticism of Stalin's policy is that it did not work. The peasantry was totally alienated and the new proletariat very largely so as well.

While insisting on the primacy of economic forces, Marx and Engels stressed that noneconomic action could in turn influence the economy. Although Engels speaks of the "economic movement being by far the strongest, most elemental, and most decisive," he is careful to make the point that "force [i.e., state power] is also an economic power."* Marx in fact recognized one state form (the "Asiatic") where a state bureaucracy took the place of a ruling economic class. He recognized the increasing strength of the state in the nineteenth century—and it was precisely those advances in the tactical

* Letter to Conrad Schmidt, October 27, 1890.

organization of state power which made him regard a violent revolution as necessary in most countries. He might have foreseen that further massive advances would be made in this field, so that state power by Stalin's time was actually capable of meeting the economic forces head on and thwarting them. In fact, as we shall see, in one aspect Stalinism is a Marxism that depends on holding together by brute force an economy that would otherwise disintegrate for lack of popular consent.

Only from the vantage point of a complete commitment to the idea that Soviet-style Marxism is genuinely "scientific" could one credit any real rationality to the policies and acts of Stalin and his associates, especially in regard to their motives for the economic policies of the early 1930's.

The standard of intelligence and the level of political thought among the Soviet leadership from 1929 onward were hardly very high, and many of their policies, although they may have been put forward in language reflecting deduction from theoretical principles, were actually slapdash and ill-considered improvisations (as indeed were some of Khrushchev's in more recent times). It seems most implausible that Stalin launched his major campaigns of the 1930's simply, or even mainly, as a result of rational choice between competing ideas. But it is not merely as a political maneuver against the Rightists that crash industrialization can be seen as a matter of internal power politics. More basically still, we may consider the result of the Party's adoption of the new urban and rural tactics: violent collision with the people of Russia. As in the Civil War, organization and will power became the Party's main weapons. In this artificially created crisis, the leadership could demand absolute solidarity and use extreme rigor in stamping out weakness among its own followers. Stalin had, in fact, launched a civil war for the same reason that dictators wishing to create an atmosphere of hysterical militarism have launched foreign wars. In both cases, waverers can be disposed of, opponents shot, voices of moderation silenced. Far from being necessary for industrialization, the Stalinist economic methods were necessary as the preconditions of pure political Stalinism. An industrialized Russia could have been achieved by other means; Stalinist despotism could not.

It may be true that you cannot make omelets without breaking eggs, but you can break eggs and still fail to make omelets. It is a common myth that Stalin and his methods were necessary if Russia was to be industrialized, but there is no reason to accept this. In the first place, the pace set was far too great. In 1931, 40 per cent of the national income was going into capital investment. This was almost ludicrously excessive, and it was quite clear that it led to enormous distortions and losses. The Rightists, who would have set a slower political pace, would most probably have achieved more. The wastages in industry are, of course, well known. As a result of dilution, inadequate incentives, and erratic allocation, labor was very inefficiently used. Grandiose plants were preferred to smaller and economically more suitable units. In the resulting disillusion, the skilled engineer force was decimated before the firing squads for "sabotage." Of course, collectivization proved to be a total failure. And it is obviously an economic disadvantage affecting more than just the countryside to have the food supply reduced catastrophically—to say nothing of the reduction of the rural population, which was to provide the labor reserve for the towns.

As a result of the agricultural collapse, industrialization was in fact attained *without* anything like the full peasant contribution that was the *economic* basis of the original scheme. From this one can presumably argue that at least as good results could have been attained without touching the peasantry at all. Moreover, the long-term result has been that collectivization, *because* it is rationally unjustifiable, has become a dogma; an ideological albatross, it still hangs around the necks of the

Soviet leaders and continues to inflict incalculable damage on the country's economy.

The first wave of collectivization met with disastrous defeat; there were concessions to private ownership by the peasants, remnants of which survive to this day. Moreover, it has since been proved that a Communist regime (for example, Yugoslavia) can maintain itself and make striking economic progress without Soviet-style collectivization. But even so, only the most tentative of moves to a more rational agricultural policy has yet proved possible even in post-Khrushchevian Russia. Moreover, the idea of rural cooperation on a more voluntary basis, which might surely have made some progress in thirty years, has probably been made less rather than more feasible by the Soviet treatment of the peasantry.

One common retrospective justification for Stalin's policies is, of course, that the industrialization attained enabled Russia to survive World War II. Certainly, this industrialization was a major factor in Soviet resistance to the Germans, but, as we have already argued, a comparable level of industrialization could have been attained by non-Stalinist policies. And surely it is not irrelevant that it was as a result of the congeries of policies that made up Stalinism that the German Communists were forced to pursue tactics which helped make it possible for Hitler to get in, and that half of Russia's hard-won productive capacity was overrun by the Germans at an early stage, again as a result of Stalin's military and political miscalculation (or so we are now told).

In fact, the circumstances of despotism are liable to produce a particular sort of misjudgment. In foreign affairs, for example, the man who has won control by trusting nobody and using every trick will not realize that democratic states are, up to a point at least, unable to conduct truly Machiavellian policies and are hence unwilling to sign documents whose provisions they are not prepared to observe. Although they are restricted by ideological imperatives in their general policies, despotisms suffer another, and rather curious, handicap when it comes to tactics—the *absence* of inertia in the machinery of political decisions. Politics can be totally reversed from day to day. A quite inadequate review of the circumstances, or even a mere whim or a suddenly accepted notion that seems a bright idea at the time, may produce catastrophic results.

Already in 1956, Khrushchev cited a number of instances where Stalin showed a complete lack of realism: Stalin placed a totally unjustified faith in the Nazi-Soviet Pact; he made a grotesquely inaccurate estimate of the military situation; he wholly misunderstood the position in Yugoslavia; and he produced chaos in agriculture—even to the degree of proposing taxes on the peasants which would exceed their total income. And Khrushchev himself is now accused of hastily and poorly conceived policies in agriculture, light industry, and economic organization which he was able to put through only because the system of rule still gives the leading figure (or figures) the opportunity to act without adequate debate.

Stalinism produced inefficiency in other ways. The almost total absence of reliable (or even unreliable) statistics was obviously a fearful handicap to a modern economy. The necessity (still found) for factory directors and collective farm chairmen to fake their results was a major nuisance. The absence of any tolerable distribution or marketing method, particularly for raw materials, led to the vast, unofficial economic underground.

But Stalinism was not simply a case of conscienceless power. There is, as we have said, the other side of the coin: ideology. In this aspect, the main role of ideology is to provide justification and self-justification for an "elite" method of rule.

Even this is not a new phenomenon. We may compare it with the autocracies of the Metternich period in Central Europe. In the 1830's and 1840's, the Austrian Empire and other states were ruled by a bureaucracy and police devoted to the principles of legitimism, a conservative political theory providing most of the comforts of a modern ideology—and approved by Marx's predecessor, Hegel. The Metternich type of state was not, indeed, totalitarian in the modern sense. But this was partly a result of primitive techniques. In principle, the police claimed rights of thought control not much different from those seen in the Soviet Union today.

A further parallel at once presents itself, in that all the progressive and healthy elements in the legitimist states of the time—the writers, the students, and, in a less conscious and obvious way, the workers—were more or less opposed to the controllers of political power. So were the minority nationalities: Russian troops putting down the national and democratic revolution in Hungary in 1849 in the interests of a super-authoritarian, antiliberal idea must remind us very strongly of the events of 1956.

Marx had spoken of the "simple laws of ethics and justice by which individuals must be guided in mutual relationships and which must be the supreme laws of conduct between states." This now gave way to the theory that anything weakening the Party's grip was bad—a formulation justifying the terrible excesses in which Khrushchev tells us Stalin indulged. Intellectual life moldered: A single philosophy was taught in the universities; rules were laid down for literature; crackpot doctrines were enforced on scientists by decision of the politicians of the Central Committee. And at the same time, it became impossible to discuss political and economic questions properly.

In fact, this grasp of absolute power, and the belief that the teaching on which the Communists based themselves was infallible and wholly inimical to all other types of thought, led to totalitarianism. It does not seem that this was particularly a fault of Marxism, or even of Communism as such. One can well imagine dogmatists of any party behaving similarly once they found themselves with limitless power. It is not so much the particular doctrines of the Communists that cause the trouble here as the fact that the Communists were actually empowered, and believed themselves entitled, to enforce them in every sphere of life. The supremacy of political criteria, the idea that a Party decision overrides all others, is firmly established. It remains a basic principle of the Party of Stalin and Khrushchev, of Brezhnev and Kosygin, and of their probable successors.

3

Continuity of Rule

WE HAVE SEEN that Stalin's rise to power was the occasion for repressions against the humanist element that still remained in Communism. The war mentality was again introduced into the Party by the process of launching it on what might be called the second civil war, in 1929. Not only was the opposition to Stalin crushed outside and inside the Party; even those who supported him merely as the result of political arguments were all executed, to be replaced by those whose devotion was unreasoned. This evolution to ruthlessness and thoughtlessness had its roots. The men who rose to the top were a special selection from the Party's past.

Lenin had constantly complained after the Revolution that Party members were inclined to be insufficiently ruthless, particularly toward their former comrades, the Mensheviks. He put before them the example of the Jacobins (although Engels had powerfully condemned the terror of 1793).

In these circumstances, two things happened: Those whose ruthlessness needed no encouragement flourished, and those who had a milder side gradually began to give the violent side of their nature a freer hand. (Those who remained in any degree loyal to humanist theories, even though prepared for temporary violence under the conditions of the Civil War, became the Workers' Opposition and the Democratic Centralists.) But it is worth noting that the effective Stalinists came up for the most part during the late 1920's. Their experience was not simply of *ordering* executions, as Zinoviev and other leaders had done, but of actually carrying them out. They were not in the top circles already as a result of revolutionary work in the underground and in exile. They rose precisely on account of their ruthlessness in the post-Revolutionary period. The Stalinist cadre, which held most of the Party positions by 1930, faced in the collectivization campaign a further test of its ability pitilessly to impose the ruler's will. By now, most of its members doubtless thought nothing about the physical destruction of "class enemies." The kulaks had just been declared such a class. But it must have been obvious that the terror in the countryside actually fell on the peasantry as a whole, and at the same time that the whole policy was quite disastrous from the point of view of the national economy. Those who ran the cities were similarly engaged in imposing backbreaking labor, severe military discipline, and hunger rations on the proletariat itself. At this time, any who had qualms about terror—not against Mensheviks or kulaks, but against the very "people" they were supposed to serve—fell by the wayside.

Yet there was a further test, even for this hardened cadre. Particularly after 1934, they had to turn the same weapons against the actual Party membership, and more often than not against men they knew perfectly well to be innocent in every conceivable sense, even politically. Once again, the process of natural selection drew from the already hard-bitten terrorists of the Party *aktiv* the minority whose enthusiastic fulfillment of the dictator's murderous orders never wavered. It was not simply a question of killing Party members with different views. For it began to involve the Stalinists themselves. The

Seventeenth Party Congress, in 1934, was virtually free of opposition representation; but more than half the participants were shot, together with 70 per cent of the Central Committee elected at that time. The new Stalinist promotions to the Politburo went through a similar winnowing. It follows that the survivors were of a highly specialized type. Only three important provincial secretaries lived through the Yezhov terror—Khrushchev, Zhdanov, and Beria. (Meanwhile, the other veterans of an earlier Stalinism were being replaced by a younger generation—those who were to rise to the top in the 1950's and 1960's.) A hypertrophied sort of politician to whom humanist ideas counted for nothing was being bred by a process of natural selection. The struggle for power, which in any political regime must be an exceedingly potent force, became an all-consuming passion.

This bias suited the rule of terrorist bureaucrats rather than politicians proper. In the early days of the Party, and indeed right up to Stalin's attainment of power, prominent Party officials did not play a more important part than that of leading figures in the propaganda or administrative area. The same applied to the industrial and economic managers (for whom a claim to a full share of influence was openly put at the time of the Twelfth Party Congress, in 1923). But Stalin's control of the Secretariat put an end to all that.

Through this he gained control of the supposedly elective bodies of the Party and, through them, of the government apparatus. Finally, he and his private Secretariat formed the center of the State and the Party, above and in control of all the organs of power in the country. In the late 1940's he had concentrated most of the power and prestige on the governmental side. Just before his death, however, his preference was again turning to the Party machinery. None of these changes were of any basic importance, though they often reflected changes in policy—since certain machinery was more suitable for the implementation of certain policies; for example, ideological terror (as in 1946–48) was best exercised through the Party. In fact, there were occasional reorganizations in Stalin's time, but the essence remained the same.

In the same way, changes of detail, sometimes of quite a striking nature, have occurred in the past few years. The leadership exercises its control over the country through a variety of institutions, some Party, some State, and some public. The kinds of reorganization that have taken place—in Stalin's time as well as now—have involved no essential change.

As a case in point, one of the most striking of the 1962 organizational changes was the setting up of a single Committee of State and Party Control under Shelepin. In effect, the control organs have always been part of the police side of Soviet life. That is, they had powers of investigation and, in effect, of dismissal, though not of arrest and punishment. Even without changes of form, their significance and power have varied. For example, for many years the Minister of State Control was Merkulov, a close associate of Beria, and a secret police veteran. This meant that the organ was, in effect, a subsidiary arm of Beria's Ministry of the Interior (MVD) and Ministry of State Security (MGB)—the police organs. After Beria's arrest, it was transferred to the charge of a nonentity and became a routine operation. In 1956, during a period of Khrushchev's weakness, Molotov took over. During the following year, as was later complained, he made it an agency for conducting his own inquiries toward discrediting his opponents. (It was even said that it "terrorized" other State organs.)

The 1962 merging of this Ministry with a Party body appears to be a revolutionary move. But from the point of view of the country as a whole, it represents, if anything, simply a strengthening, an improvement of efficiency in the ruling organs. Indeed, the very move points up strikingly the absence of any absolute difference, and any distinction in principle, as apart from convenience, between the apparatuses of Party and State.

It is sometimes implied that the transfer of duties from the State to the Party apparatus, or vice versa, may be a sign of democratic progress. Why this should be thought is hard to understand. For whichever organ passes down the decisions, the decisions themselves are those of the ruling oligarchy, under whose control *all* the various apparatuses come. (Changes of this sort may have political significance, in indicating changes in the balance of power between sections of the apparatus, but that is a very different point.)

Administrative and economic difficulties that have beset Russia over the past decade have led to all sorts of such experiments in the organization of the ruling machine. But there has never been any concession of power to the ruled. The rider is riding his horse less brutally, with less use of spurs and whip, but he is still in the saddle.

It has sometimes been suggested that the occasional experiments (as in 1957) with granting greater local initiative to local authorities represent in some way an extension of democracy. But on examination one finds that these were always completely compatible with the principle of dictatorship. The comparison to be made is with an army. In World War II, the high commands of all armies granted, in fact insisted on, much greater tactical responsibility in lower formations than in World War I. Many more decisions on local matters had to be taken by platoon, company, battalion commanders, and so on. But this in no way meant that they were less disciplined, less restricted to the carrying out of the intentions of the commanding generals than before. Nor, if it comes to that, were they any less "militaristic" for such reasons. In this, as in many other ways, the Soviet Communist Party is quite comparable to an army.

Russia (and, following it, all the other Communist countries to varying degrees) has been for decades and still is ruled by professionals of the political machine in a way that has not been the case in any other form of state. The closest parallel description from the West of what political life is like in Russia is to be found in James Farley's *Behind the Ballots.** Farley gives a brilliant account of how what the Americans call ward politics is conducted in the big cities of the United States. He shows how the controllers of the city machine prevent ambitious local leaders from becoming too powerful by raising up against them "rank and file" revolts in their own wards, and in general the techniques that are bound to prevail in such organizations. The difference is that in America the type of thing Farley describes is only a part and not the decisive part of political life: The De Sapios do not rise to the Presidency, and it is rare that any but the lowest courts and the most local of law-enforcement authorities are in the hands of the machine. So that, in general, the struggle cannot be conducted in the uninhibited fashion that the more extreme political toughs would perhaps like. If we imagine a super-Tammany, given a political monopoly and provided with full control of the press, the police, and the courts over the entire area of the United States, we may begin to envisage *something* of the Soviet situation.

As a basic reality, the Soviet polity consists of three elements: (1) a ruling oligarchy of *apparatchiks* and (2) a bureaucratic machine for transmitting its orders to (3) the population. Every organization in the U.S.S.R., operating in every area of life, is in principle, to use the Communists' own expression, a "transmission belt" for Party policy.

Certain changes have been made in the actual machinery of transmission. And orders and decisions are not enforced with the same brutality. But the basic principle remains today what it was under Stalin. The trade unions are, overtly, a means of

* New York: Harcourt, Brace & Co., 1938.

controlling the workers. The autonomous regions and republics represent a method of controlling the minorities. And so on.

As to the size of this *pays légal* of the Soviet Union, although the various sources are not in complete agreement, they are adequate to yield the round number that is all we require.* These show that if, as seems most realistic, we limit ourselves to the bureaus of the provincial committees and higher organs (including candidate members), there are about 2,600 men involved. To these must be added a good many Party workers in the Army and elsewhere, but if we doubled the figure we would be making a liberal estimate. Between 5,000 and 6,000 thus seems the limit of real participants in political life in the U.S.S.R. There are in addition about 8,000 Party workers who are attached in a professional capacity to these bureaus and doubtless have some minimal influence. If we are to count the full membership of provincial committees, we get a figure of about 20,000, and again doubling this for reasons similar to those given above, we may talk of 40,000 being in some way involved in political discussion around the extreme periphery of power.

It is also important to understand the continuity not merely of institutions, but also of personnel from the Stalin epoch to today. One sometimes sees the Russian political leadership divided into three categories. The first consists of seniors like Mikoyan, who served throughout the Stalin period, but had memories of other and better things and were not, so to speak, molded simply by the old dictator. The second, with men like Suslov, is the "middle generation," assumed to have risen simply as Stalin's creatures and to be thoroughly set in its ways. The third, the "later generation"—or "Young Turks"—is assumed to be forward-looking and comparatively untainted by the stamp of Stalinist training.

It is this third group which might, fairly soon, inherit

* See especially *Party Life*, No. 20 (1957), pp. 89–93.

power. But just who are these young men? Their careers started with years of intensive indoctrination and Party politicking in the Stalin school. Let us look at the careers under Stalin of three of the most prominent among them:

Polyansky (*now a member of the Party Presidium*)

Born 1917	
1934	Komsomol work
1939	Joined the Party
1939–40	Komsomol work in Kharkov
1942	Attended the Higher Party School attached to the Central Committee of the CPSU
1942–45	Head of the Political Department of a Machine Tractor Station, then Secretary of a Party Raikom Committee in Novosibirsk
1945–49	In the *apparat* of the Central Committee of the CPSU
1949–52	Secondary Secretary of the Crimean Provincial Committee, CPSU

Shelepin (*now a member of the Party Presidium*)

Born 1918	
1940	Joined the Party
1940–43	Instructor, department head, then Secretary, Moscow City Committee of the Komsomol
1943–52	Secretary, then Second Secretary, of the Central Committee of the All-Union Komsomol
1952	First Secretary of the Central Committee of the All-Union Komsomol

Semichastny (*now head of the Committee of State Security* [*KGB*])

Born 1924	
From 1941	In leading Komsomol work
1944	Joined the Party

1945–46	Second Secretary, then First Secretary, Donets Provincial Committee of the Komsomol
1946–50	Cadres Secretary, then First Secretary of the Ukrainian Komsomol
1949	Member of the Central Committee of the Ukrainian CP
1950	Secretary of the Central Committee of the All-Union Komsomol

And these are the young hopefuls!

As to the older leading cadres of the present comparatively "progressive" regime: Ideology is in the charge of Stalin's editor of *Pravda*, Ilychev, and international relations are run by a veteran of the Comintern from the 1930's, Ponomarev. Again, let us consider some of the other men in less publicized key posts in the central apparatus. The present head of the Political Administration of the Army and Navy, Epishev, followed Khrushchev from Kiev to Moscow in 1951, to become Deputy Minister of State Security during the Doctors' Plot period, 1951–53! Mikoyan's chief deputy, Ignatov, was an NKVD operative. Shvernik's chief deputy, Serdyuk, supervised the crushing of the West Ukraine's postwar resistance. Andropov, Secretary for Soviet-bloc affairs, presided, as Ambassador, over the destruction of Hungary's revolution. The Deputy Head of the Party State Control Committee, Churayev, also followed Khrushchev to Moscow in 1951 and worked in the central *apparat* through the worst period.*

There are among the present Central Committee members and candidates twenty who were in it as constituted in 1939–41. There are forty-two men who were members of Stalin's 1952 Central Committee, and six who were candidate-members of it. Six full members of the present Presidium (out of ten) and two candidate-members (out of six) were among those

* See *Deputies of the Supreme Soviet of the U.S.S.R.* (Moscow, 1962), and the *Large Soviet Encyclopedia, Yearbook for 1962.*

forty-two. This is a fair indication that the old cadres remain the main sources of leadership—particularly when we consider that the Presidium's present candidate-membership includes decorative figures like Mzhavanadze and Rashidov. Of the ten full members of the present Presidium, four—Mikoyan, Kosygin, Shvernik, and Suslov—were among the fourteen who formed Stalin's Politburo and Secretariat fourteen years ago. Another, Brezhnev, was on the Secretariat (and was a candidate-member of the Presidium) selected by Stalin twelve years ago in his last, maniac, phase. Shelepin was in 1952 a full member of the Central Committee and First Secretary of the All-Union Komsomol; and Voronov was also a member of the Central Committee and First Secretary of the Chita Provincial Committee.

Of the four full members who were not on Stalin's last Central Committee, in 1952–53—Polyansky, Podgorny, Kirilenko, and Shelest—Podgorny was a member of the next ranking body, the Revision Commission and was First Secretary of the Kharkov Provincial Committee; Polyansky, having worked as a Central Committee official, was Second Secretary of the Crimean Party Committee; Kirilenko, having served since 1939 as a Provincial Committee Secretary in the Ukraine, was First Secretary of the Dniepropetrovsk province; and Shelest had, since 1941, served in minor Party and economic posts. Of the candidate-members of the present Presidium, Grishin was a full member of the 1952 Central Committee and Second Secretary of the Moscow Provincial Committee; Rashidov was Chairman of the Supreme Soviet of Uzbekistan; Mazurov was First Secretary in the Belorussian capital, Minsk; Mzhavanadze had served since 1935 as a Political Officer in the Army and was a member of the Ukrainian Central Committee; Efremov was a full member of the 1952 Central Committee and First Secretary of the Kursk Province; and

Demichev was working in the apparatus of the Moscow Provincial Committee.

In fact (and the same applies all the way down the line), every one of the present leadership, and all the subordinates of any significance at all, held posts of trust, higher or lower, in the Stalinist political machinery. And, in general, the youngest group of all were just entering the dictator's service in the particularly bad years preceding his death.

Thus, the leading personnel of the present regime are the product of the Stalin era, just as its institutions are. To make this clear is not by any means to imply that all progress is impossible under the Soviet system as it now exists. Improvements, and important ones, have taken place. But they are neither complete nor irreversible. If we consider them soberly, we shall be able to distinguish between what has been done and anything resembling a genuine democratization.

4

The Khrushchevite "Liberalization"

THE PRESENT REGIME IN RUSSIA IS *sui generis*. But we can usefully define it in terms not so dissimilar to those used for certain other types of rule in the past. On the one hand, it is a bureaucracy of a special kind that could be particularized as "apparatocracy." On the other hand, it has its theoretical justifications, to a degree previously seen only in regimes thought of as theocratic. Theocratic is obviously an unsuitable description, but it will not confuse us if we think of the U.S.S.R. as an ideocratic apparatocracy.

It might be thought that a ruling group with such a background is an unlikely instrument for the "liberalization" of the U.S.S.R. which is now so much spoken of. The possibility indeed exists that, over the long term, democracy, the rule of law, and the end of centralized, all-pervading, self-perpetuating oligarchy may be in store for Russia. But the idea that these sweeping changes are likely to be achieved by the efforts, or at the desire, of any faction within the present ruling hierarchy is another matter. And still less sense can be made of current assertions that something of the sort is already taking place.

A good deal of confusion results from the indiscriminate use of the word "liberal" with regard to Communist (and particularly Soviet) politics. We must here make an important—indeed, an absolutely basic—distinction. When it is said that the present system of rule in Russia is more "liberal" than Stalin's, this is perfectly true in one sense: The population is far better treated. Arbitrary arrest is now the exception rather than the rule. And, in general, the consumer, the minorities, the writers, the peasants are all subject to less stringent regimentation. But to equate this with anything approaching democratization is completely erroneous. They are still subject to regimentation.

Even within the Party, there have been only very slight signs of a devolution of authority, certainly going no further than the provincial committees. The effective elite may thus have expanded from a dozen to a hundred people, or perhaps even a couple of thousand. This, however, is not an increase in democracy, but merely an expansion of oligarchy. The enlargement of the Roman ruling circle from the few scores in the Senate to the thousands in the Praetorian Guard brought no democratic advantage.

To seek and expect any significant changes from the present rulers of the Soviet Union is to be unjustifiably sanguine. H. G. Wells, dealing with a future oligarchical society in which a leader has made use of popular pressures to oust his immediate rivals, has one of his characters express such hopes:

> "But there has been a revolution," he said. "All these things will be changed. Ostrog . . ."
>
> "That is our hope. That is the hope of the world. But Ostrog will not do it. He is a politician. To him it seems things must be like this. He does not mind. He takes it for granted. . . ."*

Meanwhile, we may consider the central problem of true liberalization. As one observer commented when the current

* *The Sleeper Awakes.*

relaxations were mentioned, "Yes, but what about yesterday —and tomorrow?" All the "liberalizing" steps depend on the will of the leadership and can (in principle, at any rate) be retracted. In the past few years, there have been periods of tough reaction on cultural and other "fronts," and although these have never led to action on a Stalinist scale, the atmosphere of threats and pressures in, for example, 1957 and the first quarter of 1963 was enough to remind one forcibly that there are no guarantees.

Yet we find the London *Observer** flatly asserting: "Under Khrushchev, a start has been made on dismantling the machinery of dictatorship by the regime itself—an almost unprecedented event in history." No facts whatever support this statement. The horrors of Stalin's regime were such that anything less bad must seem, and actually be, a great and welcome improvement. But if Khrushchev's Russia or the Russia of his successors were judged by any standards operating before the rise of Hitler and Stalin, it would be considered an oppressive dictatorship. Even now, if political justifications and partisanships are put aside, one must judge it very much more oppressive than the dictatorships of Salazar or Franco or Tito—although it is true that, disregarding China, there are several regimes in Eastern Europe that are less liberal still.

Nevertheless, it can be argued that it is the direction in which a regime is evolving that counts. Going from worse to bad, it is felt, may be a vector pointing toward good. And Western journalists and visitors, particularly those with some experience of the U.S.S.R. of earlier times, are quick to remark on the improvements. The new Soviet image of Khrushchev's time, which has carried over into the post-Khrushchev era, is the product of such reports, inadequately related to their background and strengthened by the dynamic and purposeful tone of the speeches and "plans." At the same time,

* In an editorial on August 23, 1964.

the dramatic exposure of parts of the foul Soviet past that were not wholly known before is combined with the hint that there are still forces of darkness abroad that would like to restore such a regime—a "Brand X" that makes the present rulers shine by comparison.

The question to be considered is how far the post-Khrushchevite reformers are willing to go toward really satisfying the inchoate aspirations of the Soviet public. We can perhaps arrive at the probable answer by asking how far they have gone already. First of all, it may be worth listing the areas in which the "permanent" characteristics of Stalinism remain in evidence:

1) Most important, a self-perpetuating Party bureaucracy remains completely in charge. No sharing whatever of its power with any other part of the population has taken place.
2) The peasant, in spite of improvements in terms of tenure, continues to be a collectivized serf.
3) The trade unions remain, in practice, simply adjuncts of the Party and governmental machine. Wage decisions are still imposed on the worker.
4) The consumer, though to a lesser degree than formerly, still has to put up with low standards because of the channeling into capital goods and defense products of a proportion of the national income far higher than he would freely grant.
5) "Socialist realism" remains the official law of the arts. Truly heterodox work is still banned.
6) Control of all organs of information remains a Party monopoly. Even foreign books are admitted only as selected by cultural bureaucrats.
7) The minority nationalities continue to live under strictly centralized control from Moscow. Great purges, carried out in reprisal against an extremely mild degree of nationalism, have swept away the party leaderships of republics from

Latvia to Azerbaidzhan and Central Asia; the influx of Russians has led to the virtual partition of Kazakhstan.

8) Travel abroad is permitted only to a limited number of citizens.

9) The labor camp network, though much shrunken since Stalin's time, continues to function. The laws against political opposition remain draconic.

10) Soviet political history, including the record of collectivization and the purges, is still taught in an entirely false and misleading fashion. So is foreign history.

A formidable list! And what can be set against it? That all the same basic policies were imposed in a more intolerable and rigid fashion under Stalin.

For someone who has been chastised with scorpions for any length of time, it is no doubt quite a relief to have the chastiser go back to whips again. And it would be quite false to ignore the change for the better in Soviet conditions. Yet a double objection still remains: First, whips are unpleasant enough. Second—and in some ways a more cogent objection—Soviet society remains divided into the whippers and the whipped, and the whippers retain the right to decide what form the relationship between the two shall take in the future.

In so far as the new image of the Soviet Union obscures these facts, it is a dangerous mirage. We may welcome the improvements already made and we may hope for new ones, but to delude ourselves serves no useful purpose whatsoever.

Again, one must recall that certain innovations of the post-Stalin regime, especially in the social field, amount to an actual increase in repression. The death penalty, whose scope is usually regarded as a test of liberalism in other countries, has been continually extended since Stalin's death. In May, 1961, it already covered treason, espionage, sabotage, murder in the first degree, and banditry, and it was then introduced for large-scale economic offenses, forgery, and violent behavior in prison by habitual criminals. Then, in July, 1961, it was extended to cover serious infringement of currency regulations (and applied retroactively to two offenders previously given long prison sentences). In February, 1962, it was extended further to attempts on the life, health, or dignity of the police and members of the volunteer guards as well as to certain cases of rape and of bribery. Executions have been reported almost daily in the Soviet press.

Another rather widely publicized measure of Khrushchevian "liberalization" was the encouragement of extralegal action by "popular" organizations—sometimes represented as a step toward the withering away of the state. Actually, the supposedly "spontaneous" meetings of residents in a neighborhood to condemn the behavior of certain of their number are Party-sponsored on all occasions and amount in practice to a sort of official lynch law. The same can be said of the action of Komsomol groups that are now encouraged to harass people for what they regard as antisocial behavior. The Soviet press itself reports dozens of ludicrous instances of young prigs making nuisances of themselves by trying to suppress Western hair styles and so on. Nevertheless, the groups continue to operate on a very large scale; and just as the popular meeting is even less responsible than a Soviet court, so the actions of the Komsomol are considerably more of a bother than those of the militia. The hard-working police official in the U.S.S.R., as has often been pointed out, does his best to avoid involving himself in minor social troubles like illicit distilling, let alone patrolling dance halls to see that the bands steer clear of the more decadent forms of jazz. Not so the little horrors of the youth organizations.

Moreover, these young zealots are used to prevent activities the Party disapproves of but is unable to take legal action against. For example, the poetry recitals around the Mayakovsky statue, which became such a rallying point for students and other young progressives, were broken up by bands of "young workers" whose action was represented as a spontaneous "democratic" demonstration. Detestation of the Komsomol activist is, of course, widespread in Russia.

Stalin's last years were bad and showed every prospect of getting worse. But, strictly speaking, the present should not be compared with that time so much as with the immediate post-Stalin period, when those now denounced as Stalinists were the most powerful figures in the State. The political climate of 1953–54 may indeed be regarded as Stalinism with its extreme acerbities removed, and if the present and immediate past are compared with that period, the improvement is not enormous. That time was no more marked by Leningrad Cases and Doctors' Plots than is the current one. A policy of greater emphasis on consumer goods and a literary "thaw" were both under way in 1954—and indeed were both wrecked later on with the aid of Khrushchev himself. Thus, one might reasonably feel that recent contributions to the betterment of Soviet life have been somewhat exaggerated. And it is difficult anyway to estimate to what extent the improvements since 1954 have been due to the positive policies of the regime and to what extent they merely represent concessions that *any* Soviet government would have felt bound to make.

It can be argued that as a country becomes more and more politically developed and technically educated, a demand for something in the nature of the beginnings of political liberty is bound to arise. It is true that demands can arise without the rulers taking any notice of them; for example, Nazi Germany was just as developed industrially and technically as modern Russia. The first thing to emphasize is certainly that there has been no extension whatever of the *positive* political responsibilities of the Soviet people. There is no real consultation with them. Nor are they allowed access to any information deemed undesirable by the authorities. Popular desires have always had some influence in Russia. Even Stalin never thought it possible, as Mao does, to run the country like an army. But if this influence is now noticeably increasing, it is less through any positive political advance than through a relaxation of certain of the negative political pressures on the citizen. He may still have no effective vote, but he is very much less likely to be physically silenced at the whim of the bureaucracy.

Nevertheless, as Togliatti commented in his posthumously published "memoir," in 1964: "The general impression is of slowness and resistance in returning to the Leninist norms that guaranteed, within the Party and outside it, a broad freedom of expression and debate in the field of culture, of art, and also in the political field. This slowness and resistance is difficult for us to explain."

Perhaps it is not so difficult to explain. There is no reason whatever to believe that the changes produced by Khrushchev and his successors in Russia could have been sold to the Central Committee (or, indeed, to the leaders themselves) except on the basis that they would, in one way or another, help to consolidate the power of the ruling apparatus. In so far as they fit the aspirations of the newer generation, they can be seen only as concessions and not as acceptance in principle of the idea of genuine liberalization. Nor has there been any notion of admitting the right of outsiders to comment, let alone take part in political life. As Khrushchev said sharply to the Writers' Congress in May, 1959, "If anyone is to relieve and lay bare faults and shortcomings, it is the Party and the Central Committee."

We shall never determine to what extent Stalin could have improved the Soviet economy while retaining his repressive methods intact. So there is no way of divining how much the post-Stalin relaxations are the result of the economic changes and how much they can be credited to the simple fact that there has been no one with Stalin's concentrated power. Every time the will power of the Soviet leadership is divided or confused, the population is bound to benefit, at least in the short run.

One aspect of political liberalization should perhaps be viewed as follows. It is completely normal, in any society, for those wishing to effect a simple political revolution—that is, to place themselves in power—to involve the popular masses as well, by means of various promises and slogans, only to return them to their normal position of organized obedience when the new regime is properly established. (In the long run, the Russian Revolution itself may be looked at in this way, although the revolutionaries were of course not wholly conscious of this side of the matter.) And, similarly, if the populace can be employed by the rulers against their rivals, it is natural for this to be done.

In present-day Russia, there is no sign that things could go anything like so far. Even so, certain factions may be playing with fire in their willingness to make some sort of limited gesture toward the populace, or toward students and other intelligentsia (who may be regarded as harboring the populace's first stirrings toward political liberty). The rulers have unparalleled experience in quenching flames of this sort. In fact, while there is a bitter struggle for power within the ruling group, it nevertheless remains in the interests of all of them to preserve the divine right of *apparat* rule. And we may be sure that "liberalization" will be kept within definite limits unless the rulers miscalculate. But it cannot be denied that they are, indeed, capable of miscalculation. And any faction might be compelled in the end, even with the intention of only doing so temporarily, to seek support from emergent social forces outside the Party.

It would be absurd to look on the new men so sanguinely spoken of in the West as "convinced anti-Stalinists" as if they had the slightest desire to alter the system of rule in a democratic direction; yet the intensity of the struggle at the top may lead them to seek it and to use *any* weapon against the opposing faction. It is true that they may—like Kadar—find themselves faced with an even more difficult struggle against a vastly strengthened democratic movement later on. But in a political struggle, the natural tendency is to win the current battle first and worry later about future ones brought on by the victorious tactics.

These considerations are of the greatest importance, because if a democratization, a true "liberalization," is to occur in Russia, it can do so only as a result of some sort of breach in the solidarity (solidarity, that is, against outsiders) of the ruling group. We may come to the conclusion that the Soviet regime must evolve or perish—must, in fact, either disintegrate or explode. But if the breakup were of an explosive type, it would be likely to be so only too literally, involving the world in a nuclear war. Any prospects of a more peaceable evolution would be welcome.

5

Official "Anti-Stalinism": The Dilemma of the Regime

STALINISM! A vague term indeed. But before going any further one should point out that, whatever is meant by the term, it would be misleading to think of "Stalinists" and "anti-Stalinists" in the Soviet leadership. A more realistic view would see a conflict on tactics between half-Stalinists and three-quarter–Stalinists, or perhaps between those oscillating from being two-fifths Stalinist to three-fifths Stalinist and those whose gamut is from three-fifths to four-fifths. This is an important division; and the oscillations are quite understandable, for no logical compromise has yet been found.

The ambiguous and hesitant attitude of the regime toward Stalin is typical of the facing-both-ways position in which it has found itself. The denunciation of the old dictator in Khrushchev's "secret speech," in February, 1956, striking and dramatic in its revelations as it was, nevertheless contained quite a few reservations: Stalin was "one of the strongest Marxists," having looked at matters "from the position of the interest of the working class," and so on. The first public statement—the Central Committee Resolution of June 30, 1956

—was even more restrained. And by January, 1957, Khrushchev was saying "the term Stalinist, like Stalin himself, is inseparable from the high title of Communist."*

The account of Stalin in the 1958 *Large Soviet Encyclopedia* was critical, but summed him up favorably: "His name is inseparable from Marxism-Leninism." The new *History of the Communist Party of the Soviet Union* that appeared in 1959 gave a generally positive picture, even praising the Stalinist *Short Course* history of the Party, which Khrushchev had particularly attacked in the "secret speech." Then, in October, 1961, came the Twenty-second Congress, with its powerful assault on Stalin by Khrushchev, followed by outbursts of execration from various other figures, and culminating in the removal of his body from the Red Square tomb. (Observers might have recalled Gibbon's comments on the Emperor Commodus: "These effusions of impotent rage against a dead emperor, whom the senate had flattered when alive with abject servility, betrayed a just but ungenerous spirit of revenge.")

Even at the height of this 1961 attack, Khrushchev added, in passing, "Of course, Stalin had great merits in the Party and the Communist movement, and we give him his due." And during the short period of "reaction" in the early part of 1962, Khrushchev again backtracked: "Stalin was dedicated to Communism with his whole being. Everything he did was for Communism."† The last half of that year saw powerful attacks starting up again, such as Yevtushenko's officially approved poem "Stalin's Heirs." The swing to conservatism in the first months of 1963 again saw an easing-off of the attacks, with Khrushchev indignantly accusing Beria of actually rejoicing at Stalin's death. After the return to a more liberal line of general policy in June, 1963, there was still another oscillation and attacks again became frequent and far-reaching.

But, even then, how far-reaching? We may take the extraor-

* *Pravda*, January 19, 1959.
† *Pravda*, April 27, 1962.

dinary situation that has existed in Russia since 1956 regarding what could be called the key to the whole of Stalin's political rule—the great trials of 1936–38. A number of individuals implicated in these have been more or less quietly rehabilitated.* Accusations against the oppositionists have been explicitly or implicitly revealed as unjustified. Stalin's big lie has been undermined, but it has not been replaced by any coherent story at all, true or false. Most striking of all is the treatment of the crux of the whole "Trotskyite conspiracy," the murder of Kirov in December, 1934. In his "secret speech" Khrushchev strongly implied that it had been organized by Stalin himself, and he promised an inquiry. Five years later, at the Twenty-second Congress, he was still unable to go further. On February 7, 1964, *Pravda* published an article by L. Shaumyan implying even more strongly that Stalin had ordered the murder to break up an attempt to depose him. But *still* nothing has been said directly.

A great problem facing the regime is that it must confirm the political legitimacy of Soviet rule from its beginnings until now, asserting the continuity of policy over the entire period. While blaming Stalin as much as possible for those aspects of the past particularly detested by the Soviet populace, the rulers must nevertheless represent them as being peripheral and accidental. So, wholly aside and apart from the responsibilities of the current leadership for the terror, they are politically unable to repudiate the Stalinist past effectively. The pressures to repudiate it are intense. But so are the pressures to legitimize it. An uneasy compromise is the result—not merely between factions, but within the policies of *any* given Soviet leader.

* Bukharin and Rykov were briefly acquitted of being "spies or terrorists" in the *Stenographic Report of a Conference on Measures to Improve the Training of Scientific-Pedagogical Cadres* (1964)—a notable improvement, but as yet something short of full justice. And so far not even this much has been done for Zinoviev—let alone Trotsky, whose widow's plea for his rehabilitation, in 1961, was of course thoroughly justified.

Logically, there are only two solutions for the Russians (not that strict logic always prevails in politics, or that various make-shift solutions involving a long and muddled transition period full of setbacks are impossible): Russia can find another Stalin, or it can evolve to sanity.

"Anti-Stalinism" has not yet gone very far. The rehabilitations have been strictly limited—to military men, to certain writers, to Stalinist figures whom the dictator tired of, and to a trickle of lesser oppositionists. The major massacres of the Stalin period have barely been touched: neither that of the kulaks nor that of the old Bolsheviks. It is still publicly asserted, with equally transparent absurdity, that Beria was an "imperialist agent." And if we wish to seek a further notorious example of Stalin's actions, Soviet responsibilitiy for the Katyn massacre of Polish officers has not yet been accepted.

Obviously, until false charges not only against Stalinists but even against non-Stalinists are repudiated, it is quite impossible to talk in terms of real justice being at issue in the anti-Stalin campaign, and one must seek instead for political motives. No regime in Russia can really get the weight of the Stalinist past off its back until it truly repudiates *all* the repressions of the late dictator and rehabilitates *all* its victims. It is true that the "period of mass repression" has been condemned and that, at least implicitly, this rehabilitates millions who suffered because of pseudo-political charges. Yet, when Kaganovich was accused at the Twenty-second Congress of shooting hundreds of railwaymen, he was being singled out for the kind of incident that was repeated everywhere in industrial plants, offices, universities, and army units under the direction of many of the present leaders. It is true that the responsibilities of some of those who had minor Party positions in the 1930's are proportionately less than, say, Molotov's. But when one learns anything of these minor characters, it becomes clear that their activity was just as terroristic. For example, we happen to know a good deal about Korotchenko (until 1961 a candidate-member of the Party Presidium and still Chairman of the Presidium of the Ukrainian Supreme Soviet and member of the Central Committee) because the Smolensk Archives fell into Western hands by chance. The documents reveal a truly horrifying story of his misdeeds as Party Secretary in the area in the early part of the Stalin epoch.

Whatever its oscillations, the Party line in connection with the attack on Stalin has remained one of confining it to a limited target. A clear definition, typical of the whole period, is that "Unrelenting struggle against . . . manifestations of the personality cult does not of course imply making concessions to petty-bourgeois liberalism or countenancing any attacks by the revisionists."*

To put it into Western terms, no real liberalization was to be permitted. Nor was there any prospect of revising the basic doctrines of the Stalin era. The present leaders of the Soviet Union must inevitably approve the general political line Stalin followed against the opposition—the crash programs of industrialization in the First Five-Year Plan and, above all, collectivization. The collective farm system as established has been an enormous handicap to Soviet agriculture. In *Doctor Zhivago*, Boris Pasternak was able to write that it was a failure as well as a mistake, and that it was refusal to allow this to be said that produced the terror. But such an analysis is probably impossible for the present leadership: Collectivization is a dogma that no one dares dispute. In general, praise of all Stalin's major policies has to be coupled with denunciation of the terror. And the terror must be regarded as peripheral, an excess totally unrelated to the economic and social aspects of his regime. As the Italian Communist leader, Togliatti, pointed out in 1956, this leads to the attribution of all excesses to the personal faults

* *The World Marxist Review*, December, 1961.

of a single man; and nothing more un-Marxist than this can be imagined. It is, in fact, a cult of personality in reverse.

Other very apt comments have been made on the new line from within the Communist movement itself: These may perhaps be taken as representing ideas that cannot yet be made articulate, yet exist even within the Soviet Communist Party. At the meeting of the Central Committee of the Italian Communist Party held in November, 1961, one delegate, Senator Secchia, said that the Russians had "not come to executions without a long process, which started neither in 1937 nor in 1934, but much earlier, when minorities were deprived of the right of expressing their views and then were isolated and kept under suspicion, and eventually expelled and imprisoned. This is why we should not be satisfied by the mere fact that today there are no more opponents of the regime in prisons. This is in itself not sufficient." Garavini pointed out a contradiction between the "highly articulate and rich economic balance" in the U.S.S.R., to which there was "no corresponding political balance—that is, a similarly articulate balance of Socialist democracy."

The signs of any such beginning of inner-Party democracy in the Soviet Union are as yet negligible. But at the Twenty-second Party Congress, Kozlov's rebuff to inner-Party democracy showed that some Party members had raised the possibility of going back to the position as it had been before the repressive moves of 1921 and of reintroducing some measure of Party democracy. He said: "In the course of the discussion of the Draft Statute, the following questions were raised: Does the monolithic unity of the CPSU and the whole Soviet society not exclude the possibility of any dissenting activity within the ranks of the Party? Are any formally stated guarantees against factionalism and clique formation necessary in present conditions? Yes, Comrades, such guarantees are necessary." He went on to raise the Anti-Party Group issue as exemplifying the need for the "monolithic approach." In fact, at least one of the motives for now attacking the Group appears to be to convince those who desire a measure of Party democracy that nothing of the sort is feasible while such enemies can still raise their heads. Yet the demand evidently exists, and while the leadership is (as it inherently must be) split into warring groups, there is always the possibility that one group may break the rules and appeal for the support of this democratic trend—just as Kadar and the anti-Rakosi faction in the Hungarian *apparat* found themselves in uneasy alliance with Nagy and the democratizers in 1956. The Kadar wing miscalculated the strength of the new force and could only dispose of its powerful allies by calling in foreign armor, a recourse that would not be possible in Russia itself (unless we are to see Chinese troops in action in Moscow!).

Stalin's reign as supreme ruler was succeeded by the leadership of men with neither his single-mindedness nor his grip. Yesenin-Volpin, the heretical poet and philosopher imprisoned under both Stalin and Khrushchev, has written:

> Even the relative freedom which we have gained (a level of freedom which would seem to a person from another country to be the most shameful slavery) was not won by our society itself but was granted to it . . . as a sort of cat-and-mouse game with the people, rather than for the sake of more civilized rule, and then only because Stalin's successors have lacked the imagination and courage to follow in the footsteps of their leader.*

Be that as it may, an oligarchy, or even an apparent oligarchy, is likely to be able to command less ready submission than one man. The natural attitudes are those implied by Macauley: "Shall we, who could not brook one lord, crouch to the wicked Ten?"

* Aleksandr Sergeyevich Yesenin-Volpin, *A Leaf of Spring*, trans. George Reavey (New York: Frederick A. Praeger, 1961), p. 5.

In any case, the possibility of a certain reversion to Stalinism is even recognized in the new Party Program of 1961. One of the great theoretical accusations against Stalin, from as early as the time of the "secret speech," has been that he erroneously introduced the view that the class struggle becomes more intense as Socialism becomes more firmly established, thus giving a theoretical justification for the terror. Nevertheless, the Program, having it both ways, says:

> The general trend of class struggle within the Socialist countries in conditions of successful Socialist construction leads to consolidation of the position of the Socialist forces and weakens the resistance of the remnants of the hostile classes. But this development does not follow a straight line. Changes in the domestic or external situation may cause the class struggle to intensify in specific periods. This calls for constant vigilance in order to frustrate in good time the designs of hostile forces within and without.

This is, in effect, a charter for terror, even though we may have reasonable hope that it can not easily be implemented. Meanwhile, we would scarcely accept the idea of a de-Nazification that left in control of Germany a group of the most faithful of Hitler's accomplices. De-Stalinization, to the degree it has been carried out in Russia, has not affected any members of the present leadership, all of whom occupied posts of trust under the old dictator. Nor can we ignore the fact that their whole training, and the actions of their earlier careers, were based on acceptance of the principle that every form of falsehood and violence is acceptable if it serves the ends of a political party.

For we may still compare Russia with such polities as the Machiavellian states described by the Swiss historian and economist De Sismondi in his *History of the Italian Republics:* "Venice was governed by secret councils, where the voice of the people was never heard. Its foreign policy was administered by the Council of Ten, which, in its mysterious meetings, took interest only as a guide. The decemvirs dared unblushingly propose to their colleagues deliberating under the sanction of an oath, and animated by the same spirit as themselves, the sacrifice of what was honest and just to what was useful."

6

The Mind of the Apparatchik

WE HAVE SEEN that the origins of the ruling elite were morally and politically selective. Certain standards and attitudes alien to the European culture—and indeed to most other cultures—have been successfully cultivated. But there is a further aspect to this. It is not simply that the cadres show an attachment to dogma that would strike others as irrational. It is also the case that the *apparatchiks* exhibit eccentricities of thought, habits of mind not directly and logically derivable from their principles, but dominating them through the accidents of their cultural and historical background.

The ruling caste was not selected on a basis of innate intellectual ability. The qualities needed for survival and promotion were not those associated with mature thought. Full-time political operators, indoctrinated with unquestionable but increasingly low-grade teaching put together by an increasingly low-grade lot of apologists, could only develop their thinking, if they did it at all, in a half-baked way. Crank academics and theorists, even in areas where there was no evident political justification, seized the attention and allegiance of the *apparat* for long periods: "Linguists" like Marr and "biologists" like Lysenko received support they could never have got in other circumstances. Generally, this defective thinking is basic to the *apparat* mind. In considering the Russian Communist, we are in the presence of a definite irrationality. It colors and characterizes the whole of the active Party, from the oldest Stalinist to the newest Komsomol bullyboy. It is something that comparatively rational elements in the Party leadership must cope with; and so must we. For, in fact, it is a part—and an important and well-established part—of the present Soviet reality.

When we refer to the *apparat* of the Party, technically speaking we mean its paid permanent staff—full-time employees of the Party machine. At every level, these amount to about a quarter of a million people. They do not wholly overlap with the Party *aktiv*—those members who are always busy with Party duty, even though employed in other posts; but for practical purposes, except when it is a question of rivalry between institutions, we need not make much distinction. Full-time top-level politicians, too, may or may not be employed in the Party machine, or may go to and fro between jobs in Party and State, or even hold jobs in both simultaneously. But again, with the same reservation, we can regard them, too, as permanent members of an elite best described as the *apparat*. For above all is the fact that the Communist Party in Russia has long been dominated by its permanent machine, which gives it so many of its special characteristics, and these pervade the whole of the top echelons.

The fact that oppressors need, and obtain, justification both in their own minds and in the support and solidarity of their accomplices is an old story. Gibbon remarks: "Persecutors must expect the hatred of those whom they oppress; but they commonly find some consolation in the testimony of their conscience, the applause of their party, and, perhaps, the success of their undertaking."

"The testimony of their conscience . . ." During the Hungarian Revolution, the crowd lynched a notorious AVH (Hungarian secret police) officer. Having begged for mercy, and seen that he could expect none, he shouted out as he was being killed, "Long live world Communism!"

This man's behavior is more horrifying and more significant than that of the many other AVH men who, like him, had for years been torturing the bodies and destroying the minds of the best people in Hungary and were now being brought to rough-and-ready justice. For justice it certainly was. Few more horrible deeds than those of the AVH have ever been recorded. Few more horrible places than the AVH torture cellars (which were thrown open to the public and to foreign correspondents for a few days) have ever been seen. That criminal organization contained thugs and sadists by the hundreds—the filth of society given power over its citizens. But loathsome though their behavior was, there is something even more compelling in the exclamation of this man. For he was, at least in part, not simply a torturer for torturing's sake. He sincerely believed, or so it seems, that what he was doing was justified by a high ideal. It is not simply a question of a crude loyalty to some group or a bold defiance of his enemy; these elements were as well or better exemplified at the public hanging in Prague of Josef Frank, the former Nazi oppressor of Bohemia, who similarly defied his executioners with a cry of "Heil Hitler!" But the Hungarian went further, into a mental dissociation which one might think impossible but which is obviously only too typical. Not only did he believe himself to be acting rightly, even morally, but he associated his crimes with the eventual achievement of a classless and stateless society in a unified and peaceful world. He considered it right, in the name of an idea with humanist roots, to torture even members of his own Party to extract from them admissions of crimes he knew to be false. He had perhaps started off many years before as an idealistic young worker or student, and originally become a Communist because of a hatred of injustices. He was now practicing far worse ones himself; nor was the society that throve on his deeds more popular, more prosperous, or more promising than its predecessor. Yet he was able to absolve himself by the ritual repetition of the slogans of his youth, apparently without realizing that any change had taken place.

I do not mean to urge any simplified view of such people as this. Certainly it takes a man with a peculiar psychological makeup to be capable of believing, up to and beyond the point of its public refutation by a populace in arms, that terror and lies can be justified as the means to a worthy end. At the same time, only a man with at least some intellectual capabilities and some rudimentary sense of humanity would require an ideological apparatus to justify his misdeeds. I do not think that this necessarily makes him better than the ordinary thug. In a sense, it makes him worse, for, at least partly, he is sinning against the light. But it makes him incomparably more significant. It demonstrates the power of that apparatus of ideas which uses the language of Socialism and of humanism to justify lies and terror, not merely to the masses it might hope to dupe, but actually to the tyrants and terrorists themselves.

If Stalin was only marginally rational—rational as a paranoiac is rational, that is—his assistants shared his manias to varying degrees. But quite apart from any character defects that may accompany it, the political talent in an underground party of a few thousand members, or even in a revolutionary party of a few score thousand, is likely to be limited. The ineptness even of men like Zinoviev was truly amazing. And by far the majority of the most active and intelligent of these revolutionaries were eliminated by 1934. And the purge struck even more heavily at the replacements produced by a now exceedingly narrow strip of the political spectrum. If most members of the U.S. Congress, of the state legislatures, and on down to the town councils, the university professors, etc., had been shot in 1937, and the top posts recruited from the few survivors of the lowest echelons, we might expect that this would be reflected in a remarkable deterioration of quality among the American leadership—particularly when we consider that the qualifications for survival would have included total suppression in the survivor of any signs of independent thought. It is true that politics is not such a high and difficult art as all that: As the great Swedish statesman Count Oxenstierna remarked, "Do you not know, my son, with how little wisdom the world is ruled?" Yet we might feel justified in expecting that the main skill to be found in the next generation would be the attainment and preservation of power rather than the ability to decide sensibly on policy.

It is difficult for Westerners to rid themselves of the notion that there are certain principles of common sense and of "natural justice" accepted by almost everyone. We see the habits of mind of democracy, of freedom of thought, as sentiments natural in themselves and only to be overcome by the temporary and special pressures of paranoid fanatics. There is doubtless a sense in which all this is not unreasonable, as regards the great majority of ordinary people if given ordinary opportunities. It is certainly the case that mass indoctrination has nowhere in practice produced a high level of Party-mindedness in the people as a whole, or even perhaps in the Party as a whole.

Nevertheless, we can extend this much too far. The idea that once Stalin and certain of his main accomplices had been removed, the dominating element in the country's politics and culture would more or less automatically come around to democracy was perhaps not really believed in the West. But the idea of at least the basic rationality of the *apparatchik*, of his acceptance, even in his determination to maintain his interests, of the general conclusions of our culture is also to be rejected. Over the past few years, it has become perfectly clear that not merely among the political leadership but even in the lower ranks of the cultural bureaucracy and elsewhere, there is a cadre of men with closed minds, wholly saturated with the prejudices, the illusions, and the inordinate pretensions of a low-grade and limited dogma.

We may accept not merely that there are elements different from our own in Soviet political habits of mind, but that they are of a particular type associated with their Russian roots and, more important still, deriving from the nature of the Stalin-type despotism. In any country there are doubtless antisocial elements readily available for the right moment and the right regime. The Eichmann mentality existed in suspension, as it were, in Germany until it was given its head by Hitler. The particular canting scum who rose in Rakosi's Hungary were already there, even though they received their final impress and style from the Rakosis and Farkases. A morally and intellectually half-educated stratum exists, in varying form, everywhere in the world.

Stalin's Russia, like Rakosi's Hungary, had preserved the justifications of the *apparatchiks*, at the same time that the regime was actually habituating them to the most disgraceful real activities. As Yevgeny Yevtushenko notes in his *Precocious Autobiography**:

> Now that ten years have gone by, I realize that Stalin's greatest crime was not the arrests and the shootings he ordered. His greatest crime was the disintegration of the human spirit he caused. Of course Stalin never himself preached anti-Semitism as a theory, but the theory was inherent in his practice. Neither

* New York: E. P. Dutton & Co., 1963.

did Stalin in theory preach careerism, servility, spying, cruelty, bigotry, or hypocrisy. But these too were implicit in Stalin's practice.

The effect upon society of the Byzantine Emperor Michael Palaeologus has been described by the historian George Finlay in terms very appropriate to Stalin: "He was selfish, hypocritical, able, and accomplished, an inborn liar, vain, meddling, ambitious, cruel, and rapacious . . . his reign affords a signal example of the extent to which a nation can be degraded by the misconduct of its sovereign when he is entrusted with despotic power." In fact, we must not underestimate the simple *moral* corruption emanating from the old dictator.

The Byzantine allusion may remind us, too, that the special characteristics of the political culture of Russia are not merely a matter of the possession of institutions different from those of the West. We cannot be too careful in emphasizing to ourselves at all times that the Soviet leadership in action is not simply something deviating from, but still not essentially distant from, the norms of our own polities. If one wishes to avoid this almost unconscious aberration, to which we are all naturally subject, one needs the broad perspective of political possibilities and attitudes that a regular reading of the historians of other epochs—Tacitus and Abulfeda, Gibbon and Clarendon, Finlay and De Sismondi—affords. I make no apology for quoting such writers; if any, theirs is the true "comparative politics" for the Soviet era. There are many differences between the nature of Soviet politics and that of the Byzantines or the Tatars, but there are points of resemblance, or at least of comparison, which are at least as striking as the more "modern" elements in this very idiosyncratic subculture. Political customs to which we ourselves have become unaccustomed produce certain similarities in all oligarchical and autocratic systems, and these have been investigated and illuminated by keen minds long before our own era.

One of the components of the State and Party which Stalin created in his own image was, indeed, the whole momentum of Russian history. The end of Beria much more strongly resembles the actions of the highly placed assassins of the Emperor Paul—"Over the Kremlin's pavements bright / With serpentine and syenite"—than it does any Western event.

We do not need to exaggerate this specifically Russian element in the political attitudes of the ruling caste. Yet it can hardly be denied that a deep-seated political tradition different from that of the West subsists in Russia; and, on the other hand, conditions have always been suitable there for the flowering of wild-eyed millenarian sects. Engels once wrote: "Moreover, in a country like yours where the great modern industry is grafted on to the primitive peasant commune, and where all the phases of intermediary civilization are represented at the same time, which besides is more or less surrounded by an intellectual wall of China erected by despotism, it is not astonishing that the most peculiar and extravagant combinations of ideas come into being."* The conditions still apply.

On the Russian tradition in politics, Marx himself has written revealingly:

> A simple study of names and dates will prove that between the policy of Ivan III and that of modern Russia there exists not similarity, but sameness. Ivan III, on his part, did but perfect the traditional policy of Muscovy, bequeathed by Ivan I Kalita. . . .
>
> Open force itself could enter as an intrigue only into a system of intrigues, corruption, and underground usurpation. He could not strike before he had poisoned. Singleness of purpose became with him duplicity of action. . . .
>
> Peter the Great is indeed the inventor of modern Russian policy, but he became so only by divesting the old Muscovite

* Letter to Plekhanov, February 26, 1895.

method of encroachment of its merely local character and its accidental admixtures, by distilling it into the overthrow of certain given limits of power to the aspirations of unlimited power.*

Another Marxist observer, Rosa Luxemburg, noted, long before the Revolution, the transfer of this tendency into Lenin's Party:

> Knocked to the ground, almost reduced to dust, by Russian absolutism, the "ego" takes revenge by turning to revolutionary activity. . . . But here is the "ego" of the Russian revolutionary again! Pirouetting on its head, it once more proclaims itself to be the all-powerful director of history—this time with the title of His Excellency the Central Committee.†

We may also remember that there are, in lands long subjected to Oriental or quasi-Oriental despotism, certain habits and standards of conduct different from our own. Rokossovsky, who was arrested and badly beaten during the early purge of the 1930's, could be released and given a high command later on. Moreover, he even retained his affection for the system under which he had suffered—not just Communism, but Stalinism, which he defended in the Polish Politburo against the majority of the Party's leaders. We may be reminded of the treatment by the Byzantine Emperor Theodore Vacates of his logothete George Acropolita, whom he had publicly beaten in the presence of the troops, only to recall him a few days later to his seat on the council. Such an act would not have been possible in the Western countries, then or later, any more than it would have been in Classical Greece.

* "Revelations on the Diplomatic History of the 18th Century," *Freie Presse*, August, 1856–April, 1857. The "Revelations" were eliminated from Book I of the eleventh volume of the Russian-language edition of Marx's and Engels' *Works*, published in Moscow in 1933, which contains all their other known writings of 1856–57.

† *The Russian Revolution and Leninism or Marxism*, ed. Bertram D. Wolfe (Ann Arbor, Mich.: University of Michigan Press, 1961).

The Soviet *apparat* is a multicellular organism with a very low intelligence in certain respects, but it is extremely tenacious of life and well endowed with the cunning and skill needed to cope with the conditions of its ecological niche. As far as international circumstances are concerned, it does seem, on the whole, to have developed a healthy fear of the hydrogen bomb. In fact, one might almost be grateful that modern nuclear weapons are so overwhelmingly devastating in nature. For the existence of the hydrogen bomb, perhaps even without the current American superiority, is a threat so palpable and clear that it cannot be evaded. An adventurist Soviet regime could possibly have misinterpreted in optimistic fashion, as aggressors always have, the military possibilities of a conventional war. It is much less easy for them to do so regarding a nuclear war. The 50-megaton blast is just about the power required to penetrate the ideological carapace—the "bone curtain" around the *apparatchik* mind, a greater nuisance to the world in its way even than the Iron Curtain by which it tries similarly to isolate the minds of its subjects. (That even the H-bomb was barely sufficient is indicated by the fact that it has not penetrated the consciousness of the *apparat's* even more primitive counterpart in Peking.)

The Soviet rulers have always made pronouncements on their actions, from sensible ones like the test-ban treaty to paranoiac ones like the Doctors' Plot, in one of the political dialects familiar to us: Marxism, whatever semantic shifts it may have suffered since, is a product of Western culture, and its employment provides an appearance of assent to the humanist and scientific elements in our own polities. How far the appearance accords with the reality is a matter for examination, and not to be taken for granted. In certain circumstances, the rationality, if not the humanity, may be present in adequate proportions, but we must preserve at least a modicum of vigilance and skepticism.

The particular style of irrationality with which a numerically large and politically important section of the Soviet is possessed can be illustrated in many fields. There is much that could be said, and we can only give a few examples. Let us take the medical area, always a favorite stamping ground for the irrational layman. Lenin, in a well-known letter to Gorki (in November, 1913), advised him to avoid Bolshevik doctors: "But, really, in 99 cases out of 100, doctor-comrades are asses. . . . To try on yourself the discoveries of a Bolshevik—that's terrifying!" He realized, in fact, that the intellectual likely to be attracted to Bolshevik political theory was only too likely to be "advanced" in crackpot fashion in other fields. The same applies, even more, to the politicians proper. During the great "show trial" of 1938, it came out in evidence that a number of high Party officials had been receiving treatment from one of the accused, Kazakov, who was evidently a complete quack. During their campaign for birth control, the Chinese Communists recommended to the whole country the ancient Chinese method of swallowing tadpoles. From 1957 to 1962, the Leningrad Party leadership was sponsoring and permitting a quack cancer cure called the Kachugin method, which the medical profession proper was only able to put a stop to as the result of a turn in the political struggle. (But the victorious faction had its own quirks—specifically, Lysenkoism.)

Again, the extravagance, from our point of view, of the whole Party attitude is illustrated with particular vividness in artistic matters. One overt sign of this is the quite open rewriting of literary works—even of poems—to suit political lines. Yevtushenko's "Babi Yar," the celebrated attack on anti-Semitism, had to be amended to make the point that the Nazis had killed Russians as well as Jews. After I had included a translation of a gloomy war poem by Margarita Aliger ("The rifle regiment . . .") in my collection of "thaw" poetry, *Back to Life*, the authoress (a Party member) attacked me in the Soviet literary press for omitting two lines. I checked and found that the translation was exact as to the version of the poem given at the time, but that two extra lines, providing the moral and political uplift previously missing, had been *added* in a later version.

But it is not in the censorship and manipulation of work with some sort of political implication that the Soviet attitude appears at its most unique and ludicrous. The outburst of Party rage against the intellectuals in 1962–63 was not directed against such work as Alexander Solzhenitsyn's extraordinarily frank and politically risky exposure of Stalin's labor camps, *One Day in the Life of Ivan Denisovich*, but against abstract and nonrealist art forms—"the filthy formalist mess," as Khrushchev, not the most illiberal of the leaders, put it. His tirade on March 8, 1963, to the assembled artists made it clear that the objection was to anything that could not be used by "the people . . . as a tool of their ideology." Such work, as the noted Sovietologist Victor Erlich has pointed out, is worse than useless, because it is impossible to understand and control, let alone use. In fact, any work that either sets up a non-Party standard of moral authority or seeks methods outside the canon, is to be greeted with rage and horror, and suppressed. The new regime has made its adherence to this principle clear in a lengthy denunciation, in *Pravda* (January 9, 1965), of the "so-called progressive trend" in literature.

The clearest example of all is in science. In particular, in the biological field we have long seen a major element of the *apparat* dedicated to ideas neither valid in themselves nor of any benefit whatever to the regime even as useful falsehoods. It is of course true that some Communists are more rational than others. But here we should again be careful. It is not necessarily the case that the more "moderate" and "liberal" factions are by that token the more rational. Lysenko, in fact, is a great check on this. His triumph in 1948 came as part of the defeat of the extremist Zhdanov wing. This was not generally realized in the West because the biology decree of 1948 had been preceded in 1946–47 by the various cultural decrees associated with Zhdanov, and it was thought that it represented just one more step in the Party's control of thought. But the cultural decrees, though tyrannical and absurd, were not formally opposed to the principles of reason and science. Lysenkoism was so opposed, and it flourished and has continued to flourish during periods of control by "moderate" leaders. Stalin permitted attacks on Lysenko only in his last, most murderous, months.

In 1963, it was *Neva*, of "conservative" Leningrad, which came out very strongly against Lysenko, only to be rebuffed in the Khrushchevite *Kommunist Ukraina* (April, 1963). With the movement against conservatism in the summer of 1963, the genetic controversy was swung heavily in favor of Lysenko again by an article in *Selskaya Zhizn* (August 18, 1963) by M. A. Olshansky, President of the Academy of Agricultural Science: The article in *Neva* was denounced as "slanderous," and Olshansky most strongly and uncompromisingly attacked the anti-Lysenkoites and defended the 1948 decrees. The main points of this article were republished in *Pravda* (August 21, 1963), thus giving it the highest Party sanction during the period of "moderate" triumph. This is a lesson to us in not prejudging alignments on unsuitable abstract grounds.

And surely it is time we heard the last of the notion still occasionally repeated in the experience of this writer, even at meetings of advanced political research groups, that Khrushchev and others have supported Lysenko and his erroneous science because of his "green fingers": that is, that the leadership was not really fooled by Lysenkoist theory, but was going along with it for practical reasons. The objections are obvious. A rational man faced with a good plant breeder who is a bad scientist has open to him the perfectly simple alternative of allowing the fellow to breed plants and ignoring his scientific claims. Moreover, Marxism has at least enough respect for science and concern for the future to see that the acceptance of erroneous theories is bound to have bad effects, however green the fingers that hold the pen that writes the falsehoods. No, to take such a view is to hold that the Party's attitude was even more absurd than it really was. We must pay the leaders the compliment of assuming that they really believed a lot of arrant nonsense rather than that they were consciously attempting to ruin the country's agricultural science by imposing on it theories of whose falsehood they were well aware.

It now appears that Lysenkoism is being completely repudiated—although it is not yet certain how permanent this reform will prove. There was a long period in which Communist doctrine did not have a Lysenkoite excrescence. What concerns us here is simply the revelation of the Party mind we get from the long, stubborn, irrational attachment to this nonsense which has characterized a large section of a generation of cadres. Marxism being what it is, the leadership always finds theorists to show that any notion is a logical development of the official ideology, and thus it can arrive at a spurious air of coherence, which may impose even upon those who disagree.

A curious sidelight on the impression of semi-education so often made is that a large number of members of the Central Committee are shown as having primary education and "higher" education, but not secondary education. That is, they missed the solid background of instruction in their teens, and went through technical (usually) or political "higher" education without it. Moreover, they have normally been selected for this secondary part of their education precisely because they were *bien pensant*.

From such examples, we can easily reach conclusions about

the general quality of thought in the Soviet elite. It seems to resemble the half-baked mishmash of general ideas that prevailed in the Viennese semi-intellectual cafés of Hitler's formative period, before World War I.

Such levels of discussion are no more productive of humanist than of intellectual attitudes. It is perhaps more than a coincidence that anti-Semitism, as the distinguished Soviet author Konstantin Paustovsky has pointed out, is one of the components of the hard, shallow-minded, cold-blooded operator who typifies the Russian ruling circle. Even Western Communists—including the hidebound French Communist Party—have criticized outbursts of Soviet official anti-Semitism over recent years. The report of the five-man international Socialist Study Group, consisting of leading officials of the Scandinavian and Dutch Socialist parties and the British Labour Party, summarized a closely documented report issued in April, 1964, in these terms: "There is discrimination against the Jewish population of the Soviet Union as a national minority group, as a religious community, and as individuals." The harassment, extreme even by Soviet standards, of the synagogues; the discrimination against Yiddish, as compared with other minority languages, in publications, theaters, schools, etc.; the effective *numerus clausus* against the nationality in academic, administrative, and other posts: all these have lately taken an even more sinister turn with the execution, after public denunciation, of a much higher proportion of Jews than Gentiles for the economic crimes which have become capital offenses in recent years. Over a period of two years ending in August, 1963, more than 55 per cent of the death sentences were passed against Jews, who constitute only 1.09 per cent of the total population. (It is true that the proportion of Jews in commercial occupations is higher, but they are estimated at no more than about 10 per cent of the total employed in these sectors.) Particular public scandals from time to time—the allegation by the Party newspaper in Dagestan that Jews drank the blood of Mohammedans, or the booklet issued under the auspices of the Ukrainian Academy of Science containing, in addition to gross slanders, a picture of a hook-nosed Jew licking a Nazi jackboot, with a caption stating that the Zionists supported Hitler—are doubtless the result of excessive enthusiasm on the part of local officials. But in these cases it has always taken months of continued foreign pressure to secure any sort of withdrawal, and the perpetrators have not suffered.

Russia is perhaps the only country where it is not recognized that the Jews suffered particularly at the hands of Hitlerism. We have already mentioned the compulsory rewriting of Yevtushenko's poem, "Babi Yar." Babi Yar was the scene (in the Ukraine) of one of the most frightful of the massacres of Jews by the Nazis. Yevtushenko complained in his poem that this site is marked by no memorial (having been turned into a rubbish dump and a football field). The poem aroused violent attacks and had to be amended to imply that there was no exceptional persecution of Jews by the Nazis. The attitude toward anti-Semitism has long been regarded as a touchstone of rationality and humanity. The *apparatchik* comes out badly in this test.

All this should be borne in mind when we go on to consider the Soviet leaders. It is not necessary to exaggerate the point. Nor should we go to the opposite extreme and deny that it is possible to be rational within certain limits while falling for absurd notions outside those limits; in certain spheres of practical politics, the flat-earth proponent may be as sensible, or almost as sensible, as anyone else—just as there is a rational element of sorts in the politics of even the most barbarous society. Nevertheless, this sort of attraction to the irrational, and attachment to it against all good sense, cannot be entirely irrelevant to our judgment of the degree and nature of the attachment of the leadership to its political myths. And, above all, it characterizes the average *apparatchik* very clearly.

Not only ideology, or rather stubborn habits of mind, but also interest forms a strong and tenacious element in Party conservatism. "The fact that the Party has for a long time headed the government has given it a great attractive force for all kinds of careerists"*: This comment was indeed made about the Swedish Social Democratic Party, but it might just as easily be applied to the CPSU.

In Soviet political circumstances, the only possible reservoir for the next generation of rulers—leaving out of account any question of an unprecedented revolutionary political upheaval—lies in a limited number of Party officials with considerable experience. And this in turn dictates that a certain continuity in policy and in the personality type of the ruling cadre is inevitable. Whoever is at the top must either purge all the cadres that rose under Stalin, on the face of it an impossible task—or, whatever his own views, he must share or endure their habits of mind and the limitations of their ideas to a considerable degree.

The irrationality of the *apparatchik* mind should not be underestimated. Except in certain tactical matters, it is formula-bound and inflexible, and on a wider variety of subjects and policies than has often been seen. The Soviets are facing a highly changeable and crisis-prone situation. This is the formula for trouble!

* *Voprosy Istorii,* June, 1958.

7

The Logic of Faction

"IN THE WEST . . . there is a lack of knowledge about the different situations in different Socialist countries. . . . Some situations seem difficult to understand. In many cases one has the impression that there are differences of opinion among the leading groups, but one does not understand if this is really so, and what the differences are." So Togliatti wrote shortly before his death—and not long before the overthrow of Khrushchev. His basic conclusion was right; so, however, were his feelings about the difficulty of following the course of the political struggle in the Soviet Union.

For seven years no absolutely open and definite political crisis had occurred. It is true that in 1960 the number-two man in the Party, Alexei Kirichenko, was suddenly removed without explanation. And many observers saw what they took to be continual signs of friction. But, for want of declared hostility, some commentators took it as proven, or at least highly probable, that no real friction could exist.

Not long before the overthrow of Khrushchev a serious American journal* published a letter from A. Allison stating

* *Problems of Communism.*

flatly assumptions that in a vaguer way still seem to affect many students. He held that the view of Soviet political life as one of conflict relies on "inferential and selective evidence while heavily discounting what appear to be simple and obvious realities." Such "realities" included the public appearance of harmony in the Presidium, which must be taken to disprove the existence of faction and struggle! But it is ancient history that public figures are capable of public behavior—indeed, of private behavior—that conceals their political aims. An example among thousands that come to mind is to be found in Lytton Strachey's *Elizabeth and Essex:*

> Raleigh himself was utterly unsuspecting; there seemed to be a warm friendship between him and the Secretary. . . . His earlier hopes had been shattered by Essex; and now that Essex had been destroyed he was faced by a yet more dangerous antagonist. In reality, the Earl's ruin, which he had so virulently demanded, was to be the prologue to his own.

In other words, a skilled operator was capable of deceiving not merely the public but even fellow members of the Council! In any event, we *know* that similar practice has long been common in the U.S.S.R. Malenkov and Beria were in public—and perhaps in private—notable cronies until the moment of truth arrived; and the same was true of Khrushchev and Bulganin. But their public solidarity was in no way affected. No, to take such superficial observance of the conventional amenities as meaning anything at all in any political society reveals a certain naïveté.

For the view we take of Soviet politics is to some degree a matter of opinion, dependent not so much on particulars of evidence as upon standards of judgment, historical scope, and political sense. There are, indeed, wholly divergent treatments of the political history of past periods by competent, and even great, historians, each taking all the facts into account and none easily susceptible of proof or refutation as such. So it is impossible to say that what follows is indisputable. Having made this reservation, if we wish to define the condition of Soviet rule at the moment, we may think of it in the following terms: Khrushchev was the effective leader for some years. In Soviet politics, a leader who can hope to keep his grip must be a man with skill, experience, and allies in the Party apparatus, and at the same time with political weight and prestige. Khrushchev was the only one among the leadership at that time to combine all these qualities. But, if he was to maintain the system to which he was devoted—that is, reliance upon the Party rather than any revisionist innovation involving going to the people—then he had to depend on the *apparat*. And the leading cadres of the Party constitute a clumsy, unwieldy body with all sorts of built-in inertias—"like a squadron of slow old battleships." It was unlikely, as things stood, that he could rule against this force. He could cajole, prod, and generally influence it into courses not wholly to its liking, but the mule was liable to balk and, if he went too far, to throw him. Stalin in the 1930's was able to restaff the *apparat* almost completely. But he was a much younger man; he was dealing with a far less conservative, routine, and veteran Party; and, even then, it took him several years of the most unremitting terror, a course not open to Khrushchev. Khrushchev's alternatives, therefore, were either to have his own *khvost* of followers in isolation at the levers of power or to have there men more generally representative of the *apparat*, collaborating with him far less fully and yet, in a sense, more effectively. Khrushchev did, indeed, try an approach to the first solution. But in 1960 members of his *khvost* were driven from many of their positions, and he had to come to terms with other forces. In 1963, he reinstalled his men, but the victory was still hardly a Cannae, and other elements remained in the Presidium.

The Soviet Union thus had a leadership composed of Khrushchev himself; a few senior figures like Mikoyan without access to the levers of power, whose role could be regarded as mainly advisory; enough representatives of Khrushchev's own *khvost* to keep a balance and—he must have hoped—at least thwart any serious attempts to overthrow him; and a group the old *apparat* could consider as adequately representative of them and their ideas.

To argue about definitions is often misleading. But if we were to call Khrushchev a "dictator" as is sometimes done, we would have to qualify it immediately by saying that he was not a dictator as Stalin or Hitler was. And to say this is at once to concede that his single will could not necessarily prevail over other voices among the leadership, and that the Party *aktiv* had not either by habit or by terror come wholly to accept the role of a mechanism for fulfilling his orders. If we wish to avoid a not very fruitful controversy, we should probably agree to call his system either a dictatorship modified by oligarchal elements or an oligarchy modified by the primacy of a single personality.

As we shall see, only some of the members of the present leadership have depended on Khrushchev for their careers. But even if all the present Presidium had emerged from the various machines controlled earlier by him, this could not constitute a guarantee against friction—as is apparent when one considers the frequent purges of Stalinists by Stalin.

So long as unquestioning obedience could not be exacted, it is plain enough that not all the policies proposed by the First Secretary would automatically be accepted by his colleagues. Since he was a great proposer of new and startling policies, it is clear that the potential sources of friction were frequent and powerful. Before going into the nature of policy disagreements, we can venture a general idea of the probable state of affairs.

The logic of Soviet politics requires that the established

leader seek absolute power (even though he may have to settle for less at any given moment). For if any independence is left to his colleagues, he can never be entirely safe. He initiates and carries out policies. If they fail, those below him are in a position to hold him responsible, unless the power to do so has been completely withdrawn from them.

But if the logic of his position tends to force the leader into attempts to break—or at least reduce as far as possible—the independent power of his fellow members of the Presidium, the logic of their position requires them to oppose all such attempts and, as far as possible, to limit the power of the leader himself. None of this is to say that stalemates, even long-lasting ones to which the contenders are apparently resigned, may not ensue (and *rien dure comme le provisoire*). But it *is* to discover the essential dynamic of Soviet politics.

In his *L'Esprit des Lois,** Montesquieu writes "*C'est une expérience éternelle que tout homme qui a du pouvoir est porté à en abuser: il va jusqu'à ce qu'il trouve des limites.*" ("It is invariably the case that every man who has power is led to abuse it; he goes on until he finds limits.") These limits are fairly well defined in democracies. But there is no such specificity, no properly established institutional bar, in the Soviet Union. The ruler goes as far as he can until *ad hoc* opposition is mustered in sufficient strength to stop him.

Thus it is necessary to envisage the matter in nonabstract terms. It is not simply a question of collaboration or opposition. Similarly, there is no simple contrast between ambition and loyalty to the cause, or between motives of power and of policy in the sponsoring of, or opposition to, particular moves. We may (*mutatis mutandis*) compare the Soviet Union to a Western company or corporation. Until twelve years ago, it was a family concern, and all the shares were owned and voted by the president, who was at the same time chairman of the

* Book XI, Chapter 4.

board. On his death, the shares were distributed among the various directors and vice-presidents. An attempt eight years ago by a group of these to take over control was thwarted by another group, whose leader became chairman and president. But he did not have the full control that the old man had.

If we consider, in such circumstances, the motivations of an ambitious vice-president, we may be getting close to what goes on in the mind of a member of the Presidium. When a new invention affecting production, or a new sales scheme, is proposed to him, he does indeed think in terms of its probable benefit to the company. But it would be asking a great deal of human nature if he did not also consider how it could be turned to his advantage. Similarly, when schemes proposed seem dangerous, he will think not only of the results for his firm, but also of the results for himself. The question of the security of his own tenure on the one hand and of the chances of his advancement on the other will always be before him. Benjamin Franklin saw that "while a party is carrying on a general design, each man has his particular private interest in view. . . . That few in public affairs act from a mere view of the good of their country, whatever they may pretend; and though their actions bring real good to their country, yet men primarily considered that their own and their country's interest was united, and did not act from a principle of benevolence."

It may well be that at a given moment, when things have settled down, he has no scheme for ousting the president and taking his place; but this hypothetical vice-president could be forced into attempting some desperate measure in that direction by either of two things: The president might try to gain total control, and either remove his junior or cut down his power and security to nothing; or the president might sponsor policies so risky from the point of view of the firm's profits that his junior might feel it necessary to block these policies and have a showdown, in the interests of the firm as a whole. The directors and executives of a corporation can indeed be seen as loyal collaborators in one sense, but at the same time as competitors involved in permanent opposition to one another.

In a one-party state, the term "opposition" cannot be conceived in the same way as it is in the democratic West. Yet even in the West, there are occasions when a clear-cut distinction in words does not suit the real situation. Was Dr. Erhard a collaborator or an opponent of Dr. Adenauer, or Mr. Brown of Mr. Wilson? The answer, of course, is both. And the same must be taken as applying to the relationship between Khrushchev and members of his Presidium—and, by the same logic, between his successors.

In this context, we must nevertheless make an important distinction between Soviet and Western politicians. As we have said, the Soviet leaders are all machine politicians rather than what we would regard as politicians proper—i.e., Carmine De Sapios rather than John Kennedys. But so are their supporters. Their skills and appeals are basically a matter of handling the committees, not the electors. A different type is required in a democracy. It is true that the West is not quite immune to control by machine men, exercised through powerless nominees. Vachel Lindsay may have been wrong in his estimate of President McKinley as "Mark Hanna's McKinley,/His slave, his echo, his suit of clothes." But fear of such control over the executive by representatives of party machines is a reaction to a danger that is rare and liable to provoke effective revulsion. In Russia, the machine is the actual and overt source of rule, and there is no political force to oppose it.

Although it is reasonable to see competing factions in the Soviet Union as filling the role of competing parties in the West, this parallel should not be pressed too far. Party loyalty and party discipline are much stronger and more enduring than their factional equivalents, simply because they are more institutionalized. For similar reasons, it is seldom possible to think of a Communist faction "platform" as being anything like as general and comprehensive as that of a Western party. On the contrary, if we thought in terms of majorities and minorities on given issues within the Presidium, we would probably see a continuous gradation between matters about which groups of members vote together frequently or always, and others which on a single occasion divide the Presidium along quite different lines. Again there may be, and probably are, different regular majorities on different types of issues—on de-Stalinization, on international affairs, on Party reorganization, and so on, as we shall see. This is not, however, to deny a general polarization on many essentials between a "forward" and a "conservative" attitude.

And here we must make a distinction. The Party and its Central Committee contain, in positions of influence, those whose general views may be described as "conservative" (or even "Stalinist") together with others ranging beyond Khrushchev in the direction of concession to reality. They do not include—or only as isolated individuals, such as those occasionally denounced in the student or scientific branches of the Party—any true radicals or progressives. The range, for purposes of practical power, runs from extreme neo-Stalinist "left" to, at most, right center. In the cultural quarrels of 1962–63, for example, we can identify a "leftist" reactionary policy aimed at bringing the writers to heel as in Zhdanov's time and a centrist policy of making concessions to the writers and giving them some rope; but the notion of freeing them from Party control, the notion that abstract sculpture is really to be tolerated, has no effect at the serious levels of politics. In fact, generally speaking, the current *political* (as against economic and administrative) disputes among officialdom may perhaps best be labeled as between "repressionist" and "concessionist" forces, each equally devoted to the notion of the divine right to rule of the self-perpetuating Party leadership, but each convinced that its own recipe is the best way of perpetuating that rule.

This is a real policy dispute. But again, sheer power considerations often produce intense struggles in which actual policy divergencies may play a minor, or decorative, role. In the great struggle for power in 1957, the Party was not split between progressive and reactionary, right and left. Both the victorious and the vanquished factions contained elements of either political background. Malenkov's foreign-policy proposals were evidently more "liberal" than any Khrushchev was able to put into effect for several years; the same applies to his consumer-goods policy. Shepilov's line on literary freedom was at least as advanced as anything that has succeeded it.

Similarly, Khrushchev found himself, after 1957, relying on a combination of dependents and semi-independent allies. No unity of views was to be expected. The crucial issue remained that of power. Meanwhile, he went ahead to strengthen his own position and to impose, increasingly, a personal selection of policies on the Party.

8

Economic Challenges

ANY POLITICAL MOVEMENT HAS, between its more or less apathetic and commonsensical rank-and-file supporters and its leaders who have to cope with the problems of the real world, a stratum of party militants who hold the political doctrine concerned in a much purer, more fanatical, and less sane fashion. When these militants impose their simple-minded certainties on the leadership, the result is always disgraceful or disastrous, as with the British Labour Party vote for unilateralism or the Goldwater Presidential campaign in the United States. The leadership's normal concern is to make use of this *simpliste* following, to keep its members happy, to placate or persuade such spokesmen of theirs who must be admitted to the top levels of the party, while at the same time shading doctrine off as far as possible to meet the facts.

In the U.S.S.R., doctrine in any case plays a far more overt and important role than in the West, and the leadership itself is much more dogmatic than the norm—since the State is organized precisely to give its leaders the power to force through policies neither acceptable to the population nor suitable in terms of the facts. But, with that important amendment, the same principle applies. The leaders, or such of them as have had to cope with the real difficulties, are more inclined to see the need for a changed approach than is the *apparat* as a whole. And the same problem has to be faced in political maneuvering at the top level.

Stalin succeeded in thoroughly institutionalizing his regime. The men who came up in it were as conditioned both consciously in ideology and unconsciously in political habit to a particular form of state as the bureaucrats and theorists of legitimism had been in the 1830's and 1840's. Among them there were some more and others less susceptible to the impact of facts that no longer accorded properly with their prejudices; but in all of them there was at the least a considerable amount of this heavy ballast from the past.

After Stalin's death, the political leaders were faced with definite problems, for some of which previous solutions clearly would not serve. The agricultural and—to a lesser extent—industrial progress of the country was evidently hampered by methods that were no longer appropriate (if they ever had been). For example, the hard facts of grain and livestock production, which were put frankly to the Central Committee in 1953–54, gave little encouragement to any who might argue that the old methods would do with not more than minor changes. Economic-reform policies in the U.S.S.R. evidently had considerable support in the Central Committee right from the start, after Stalin's death. Malenkov could not have undertaken his measures, or at least announced his program, in 1953 without reliance on like-minded allies and dependents.

The problem now facing the Soviet economy is comparable to that which faced the capitalist economies of the West twenty to thirty years ago. Pre-Keynesian capitalism produced frightful economic debacles, not because of any absolute or inherent defects in the capitalist system as such, but because of attitudes it would be reasonable to call "ideological"—an attachment to laissez-faire theory, combined with a power-motivated shortsightedness, the wish of the capitalist to prevent limitations on his control. The West learned its lesson, or most of it. And in the last twenty years the great economic breakdowns have been not in the "capitalist" but in the Communist countries. In the 1950's, Poland and Hungary were in a condition that Poland's top economist, Professor Oskar Lange, described as "leading to a disintegration of the national economy."* The Soviet Union has not experienced such an extreme situation, but there, too, plan after plan has ground to a halt; and agriculture was revealed by Khrushchev himself in his reports to the Central Committee in September, 1953, and February, 1954, to have become less efficient than it had been in 1914, when operated by the backward muzhik. Nor has there been sufficient improvement since then.

We need not get into a debate about the essential superiority of any economic system as such. It has been clear that many Communist failures have been due to practices not in themselves necessary to the maintenance of the system as a whole, but rooted in the ideological prejudices of the conservative operators of the machine. The main flaws have been:

a) Absence of a rational price, exchange, and distribution system; and, as a corollary, the absence of objective market data in planning considerations.
b) The doctrine of the primacy of producer-goods production and, in effect, the principle of ignoring the well-being of the consumer as an important factor in an expanding economy.
c) The collective farm system in agriculture.

Unfortunately, the dogmas behind these flaws are deep-seated. Moreover, while in the capitalist world Keynesian (and Socialist) views were much in evidence, and the capitalist

* *Zycie Gospodarcze*, No. 14 (July, 1956).

could not help recognizing at least the existence of debate all around him, under the peculiar Soviet conditions the advocacy of a serious change in the agricultural system simply did not occur. Party prejudice against change was greater, because more theological, than capitalist prejudice against change; and at the same time the relevant arguments were simply not available to the *apparatchik*.

Even in the rather freer capitalist circumstances, a major economic shock had been required—the Great Depression—to undermine the old, unthinking notions. Similiarly, we find that when extreme crisis has afflicted the Communist countries, they are more likely to show economic sense—as in Poland with the breakup of the collective farms, or (in less critical but doctrinally freer circumstances) the setting up of market relationships among the nationalized factories in Yugoslavia.

There are two sides, therefore, to the modernization of the Soviet economy. Although the removal of various superficial defects of the Stalin-style economy has produced notable improvement, economists in the U.S.S.R. have seen clearly enough that more radical moves are necessary. Meanwhile, the experience of the economic leaders has taught them that all sorts of manipulations and experiments within the old framework are insufficient, and they are prepared, to an extent determined by their own dogmatisms, to listen to the economists. In a pure one-man dictatorship, this would be sufficient. The changes could be put through by sheer power and by the belief of a party purged for that purpose that the leader's will is indisputable.

However, lacking this possibility, the currently installed oligarchy has to take some account of the prejudices of the Party as a whole. And the average *apparatchik* has the preconceptions of his leaders in a still more primitive form, unqualified by the experience and study of economic facts which they have had thrust on them by their very positions.

A much more gradual, tactful, and careful program of persuasion and pressure must therefore be undertaken. This is particularly the case since any step likely to produce revulsion in the ordinary Central Committee member would automatically be of use to one or the other faction among the leadership which, however convinced of the need for change, can on the basis of the record be expected to think of power first and correct policy later (as in Khrushchev's own case, when he swung to the pure Stalinist view on heavy industry in 1955, in order to dethrone Malenkov).

When we look at the changes that have been introduced, under the auspices of Khrushchev and men of his faction who have *seemed* ready for drastic action, we can see that the supposedly enormous switches brought about have, in fact, only looked revolutionary if compared with the even more conservative projects of some of their colleagues. Neither the Virgin Lands scheme (a huge crash program of exploiting marginal land in Central Asia) nor the reorganization of the Machine Tractor Station system—not even the increased incentive schemes for collective farms—really touched the main crux of Soviet agriculture. This is one (if a basic) example of the policy orientation of the kind of mind now in control of the Soviet State. Nevertheless, the economic realities must press hard upon the ideological unrealities, and over a period of years great improvements in at least the industrial sphere have gradually been introduced.

We must, in any case, distinguish very definitely between clear-headed and progressive ideas about the modernization of the Soviet economy and ideas of *political* "liberalization."* The first comparatively rational and forward economic program after the war was put forward by Voznessensky, who belonged to the most Leftist of the Party factions of the time.

* This point is well developed in Zbigniew K. Brzezinski, *Ideology and Power in Soviet Politics* (New York: Frederick A. Praeger, 1962).

An economic modernizer may be a political authoritarian of the most unbending type.

We see that the self-perpetuating elite are latter-day legitimists, conservatively devoted to maintaining their divine right to rule at all costs. But within the stratum, and particularly at the highest level, where the problems have to be faced, there are elements who are more flexible than others in their tactical approach: We have spoken of "repressionist" and "concessionist" tendencies in purely political matters. A similar (though not necessarily coincident) division occurs in economic matters. It is probable that the entire leadership has some realization of the unsatisfactory state of the Soviet economy, particularly when considered within the context of the economic and military competition with the United States. But there are various divergent approaches to the solution of the problems.

It seems to have become clear to at least a section of the leadership that the Soviet economy cannot support simultaneously a modern-style arms race and a peace economy that has any chance whatever of "catching up" with the United States. As Khrushchev himself said: "If the international situation got better, if we could achieve an understanding and shake off the burden of arms, this would multiply the possibilities for a great upsurge of the economy."*

But even when it is admitted that the Soviet economy has over the past few years been set tasks that are beyond its capacity, the question of allocating resources more realistically naturally produces disputes among the various physical and ideological interests that might have to face cuts in their favorite sectors. This is complicated further by the question, now becoming urgent, of modernizing the Soviet economy, which thus faces not only trimming but also transformation. Certain subsidiary disputes fit themselves into this general controversy.

* *Pravda,* February 28, 1963.

The economic problems, moreover, overlap into the highly sensitive field of foreign affairs—since any abandonment of the effort to match the U.S. militarily more or less automatically involves at least a period of *détente*. This, too, is controversial under Soviet conditions.

For (as Khrushchev implied in the passage quoted above) one of the main causes of strain on the Soviet system has been the excessive demands of military (and space) production. There seems no doubt that intense and basic controversy was taking place during 1961–63 about the resources to be put into war production and economic expansion, respectively. Khrushchev said that in this field there were "difficult puzzles to be solved frequently."* The Party traditionalist would prefer the Stalinist economic structure of an exaggerated arms production and heavy industry with the rickety props of the remainder of the economy held together by main force. And in this dispute, the military naturally has a strong interest.

Questions of modernizing the Soviet economy were debated with unprecedented freedom in the Soviet specialist press during 1962. The celebrated Liberman Proposals (especially Professor Liberman's article in *Pravda* on September 9, 1962) on the use of a profit index for checking the efficiency of enterprises were, in Soviet conditions, highly novel. That Khrushchev took them seriously can be seen from several remarks in his first speech to the November, 1962, Plenum. While rebuking "certain economists" for failing to make the distinction that under capitalism profit was the aim while under Socialism goods were produced "not for the sake of making profits," he asserted plainly: "Without considering profit, it is impossible to define the level at which the enterprise's economy is conducted and what contribution it makes to the national funds."†

* *Pravda*, February 28, 1963.
† *Pravda*, November 20, 1962.

This seems to have aroused resistance at the time. For example, Ilychev, writing in *Kommunist* in January, 1963, attacked the economist L. Leontiev for market-type suggestions as "throwing out all economic science, basic law, and also other laws of the political economy of Socialism . . . throwing doubt upon the whole political economy of Socialism."

Yet immediately after Khrushchev's fall *Izvestia* paid notable tribute to a "Liberman experiment" conducted in a Gorki factory, and on November 1, 1964, it was announced that the system would be introduced on a large scale.

The reason for the Liberman Proposals, as given by Liberman himself, was that all other industrial financing plans—except the one, not yet tried, based on profits earned on capital assets—produced active damage: overemphasis on quantitative fulfillment, striving for an "easy" plan, holding unnecessarily high stocks, hoarding labor, ignoring technological advances, and faking the books. Liberman proposed that factories should simply be given a basic production plan—and that even this should be based on commercial orders. Apart from the allotted plan, the factory itself should determine its own wages, costs, and profits plan. A proportion of the profits should be put into an incentive fund paying bonuses to directors and workers. Although Liberman made many qualifications, this did seem to amount to the suggestion that industrial enterprises should operate in a competitive market for a profit incentive.

Of course, the market exists regardless. After a careful examination of the whole of the semilegal and illegal economic practices in the U.S.S.R., Dr. Margaret Miller concluded that "taking a conservative view, it would be by no means unreasonable to estimate that something like one-fourth of all forms of economic activity in the U.S.S.R. is in private hands or moves through nonofficial channels."* In this, as in many other

* Margaret Miller, *et al.*, *Communist Economy under Change* (London: André Deutsch, 1963), p. 73.

fields, we see the facts at odds with the official system. The present acceptance of a measure of realism certainly represents an advance. It should be emphasized that there is nothing truly hostile to basic doctrine, let alone practical Party control, in the Liberman Proposals. It was simply petty quasi-doctrinal habits at a rather superficial level that proved a stumbling block to this slight advance—and may yet bring it into disrepute.

If we consider the progress that has been made after eleven years, we find that the question of genuine industrial pricing (with its market-type implications) has come to the fore; that the dogmatic primacy of heavy industry has been sniped at and eroded; but that no serious attempt to alter the practice, let alone the theory, of collective farming has been made (although there have recently been a few attacks on the actual process of collectivization in the 1930 period, which may imply the beginnings of a slight breach in the structure of dogma). It seems reasonable to conclude that the collective farm principle is the more deeply embedded in the Party mind, and in the minds of the leaders.

But even the advances already made have been achieved only after hard political struggle. As we shall see, the economic disputes developed *pari passu* with purely political and ideological disputes. Dissension about the allocation of economic resources had evidently been going on for some time. At the January, 1961, Plenum of the Central Committee, Khrushchev attacked "some comrades" for "an appetite for metals that could only unbalance the economy," and said that too little attention to the consumer would have "dangerous results."* Various pronouncements on the same lines† did not produce results at the Twenty-second Party Congress in October, 1961. At the November, 1962, Plenum of the Central Committee, Khrushchev complained again that steel was be-

* *Pravda,* January 21, 1961.
† See, for example, *Kommunist,* No. 4 (1961).

ing overproduced and argued in favor of the chemical as against the metal industries.*

In February, 1963, during the period of reversal of the concessionist cultural and other policies, Khrushchev retreated on the "metal" issue in his election speech and spoke more strongly in favor of heavy industry and defense.† As in previous periods of an evident loss of momentum in Khrushchev's general policies (e.g., June, 1960), a strong move was made to recentralize the economy—this time by the formation on March 13, 1963, of a Supreme Council of National Economy with D. F. Ustinov, the old armaments chief, significantly appointed to head it.

The swing back coincided beyond the probability of coincidence with the swing away from "conservatism" on culture, Yugoslavia, and other issues. On April 24, Khrushchev attacked wastage in heavy industry,‡ and by the June, 1963, Plenum the priority of the chemical industry had become the general line. Meanwhile, Ustinov's Council completely failed to become the great striking center of the economy that it seems to have been envisaged as. And it is worth remembering, too, that the Seven-Year Plan originally called for the production of 86–91 million tons of steel in 1965. This had meanwhile been increased to 95–97 million tons, but the budget announced on December 16, 1963, reduced it to 89.3 million tons. At the same time, the military budget was cut by 4.3 per cent as against the previous year. All this quite evidently signified sharp dispute.

We can see forward-looking Soviet economists, followed gradually by an element in the leadership, grasping the idea that if the economy is to become modern, there must be a great transfer of weight into the chemical and electronic in-

* *Pravda,* November 20, 1962.
† *Pravda,* February 28, 1963.
‡ *Pravda,* April 26, 1963.

dustries, into plastics and light metals rather than steel, into technique rather than tonnage. (This was dramatized in the *Soviet Statistical Report for 1963*, which for the first time listed the chemical industry before the steel industry.)

In 1964, it at last became possible to strike a major theoretical blow for modernization of the economy—by a flank attack on the old dogma that producer goods had indisputable priority over consumer goods in a Socialist economy. In 1955, the main public allegation against Malenkov at the time of his fall from the Premiership had been precisely that he had ignored this principle. Khrushchev himself, in his speech to the Central Committee on that occasion, had spoken of a "belching forth of the Right deviation."* In June, 1957, during the Anti-Party Group crisis, Malenkov was reported by the Polish press† to have thrown the same accusation at the First Secretary. In any case, whatever the practical policies being undertaken, the dogma itself had remained unimpugned, a powerful talisman and one evidently reflecting the minds of the Party veterans.

Again, in 1958, the dogma was announced, with formal condemnation of the Polish economic heretic Bronislaw Minc, who had expressed doubt about it at a meeting of bloc economists in November, 1957. A. Pashkov, in an article that was to remain a doctrinal document for years, said that Minc had "raised a kind of question which is beyond any discussion."‡ Minc had said that the producer-goods priority was only a relative notion, that the more advanced an economy became, the less true it was, and that it was not necessarily applicable today. Pashkov asserted, on the contrary, that it was "a law of Socialist production" and universally valid.

But then, on February 24/25, 1964, *Pravda* published a set-

* *Pravda*, February 3, 1955.
† *Trybuna Ludu*, July 9, 1957.
‡ *Voprosy Ekonomiki*, No. 6 (1958).

piece article by the economist A. Arzumanyan, "Topical Problems of Our Economy," which modified the doctrine. He said:

> Stalin believed that one could rapidly develop industrial production by systematically leaving behind production of goods of popular consumption. . . . Stalin's dogma was a deviation from the Marxist-Leninist theory and was harmful to both the national economy and the people's welfare. . . . However, even now some of our economists stick to the erroneous tenets on the correlation between production and consumption. . . . In the past it was correct to start planning from metal, which at that time determined the development of other branches and the general plan of capital investment. But by now our economy has been lifted to such heights that these methods are no longer suitable.

It should be noted that this view is not formally opposed to the doctrine that basic priority must go to heavy industry. It simply calls for adequate attention to the economy as a whole. Thus, after political vagaries lasting eleven years, we find a decision to tone down one of the most harmful of the special dogmas of Stalinist planning, though not the more basic principles of the Stalinist economy. The advance had clearly met with opposition, as Arzumanyan himself states. And in general, it is clear that economic reform remains deeply dependent on the political struggle.

During 1963–64, there were also many signs of disagreement over agriculture, which tied in with the chemical theme because Khrushchev's last great attempt to solve the agricultural problem was by an immense investment in artificial fertilizer. Like his previous schemes, this evidently proved to be a failure, and simply disorganized a large sector of industry as well as the rural economy.

This dispute, too, became manifest before the crisis of October, 1964. Not all the figures to which Khrushchev committed himself were followed. A target of 77 million tons of fertilizer for 1970 was announced at the Twenty-second Congress. In his speech at Krasnodar on September 26, 1963, Khrushchev named a target of 100 million tons by 1970 and criticized "some comrades" in Gosplan who thought this too high. At the December Plenum of the Central Committee (in his speech of December 9, 1963) he cut it down to "70–80 million tons." Moreover, this discussion was conducted to some extent in the open. On November 17, 1963, *Pravda* and *Izvestia* published a letter from a group of agricultural scientists to the Central Committee querying even an 86-million-ton target which had then been worked out by the Ministry of Agriculture.

In his speech to the February, 1964, Plenum of the Central Committee, Khrushchev again defended the decision to develop the chemical industry. He said that it in no way marked "a retreat from the general line of priority for heavy industry." "Only hidebound dogmatists" could think this, as chemicals go not only to the consumer but also to the producer industries. He added that some of the Gosplan leaders had tried to leave chemicals in a secondary position because of departmental attachments to the older branches of industry; and he attacked inertia and bureaucracy in general.

A further agricultural issue, not vastly significant in itself, but interesting from the point of view of evidence of economic faction, has been a long dispute about ley-farming. Khrushchev consistently opposed this during the past decade (for example, in his speech to the Central Committee of February 23, 1954). But at the Twenty-second Congress, it was still necessary to attack the practice. Voronov spoke of those in Kostroma and elsewhere who "still cling to the ley system." And Polyansky strongly censured the provincial chief agronomist in Yaroslavl, as typical of many in, significantly enough, the provinces of European Russia, for open and shameless addiction to and defense of the system. He also blamed the Academy of Agricultural Sciences and the Ministry of Agriculture of the U.S.S.R. This does not mean that even Polyansky and Voronov were necessarily great anti-ley enthusiasts at heart: Polyansky accepted criticisms of his R.S.F.S.R. Government and the Party Bureau for the R.S.F.S.R. for inadequacy in the matter.

After the Twenty-second Congress, there were further attacks by Khrushchev himself on scientists still "obstinately" putting forward the idea of ley-farming; for example, in his speech of December 14, 1961, at the R.S.F.S.R. Non-Black Earth Zone Agricultural Conference and again in his Report to the March, 1962, Plenum of the Central Committee. In the Soviet context, "obstinate" defense by scientists of views impinging on policy matters means almost inevitably that they are receiving political protection—just as in the parallel case of writers who print or defend politically controversial literature.

Khrushchev overtly made agriculture a political issue in his speech of December 9, 1963, by arguing against "some people" who had criticized him for buying grain abroad—a move that had never before been necessary, even during the times of the worst harvests. He said that this was the case only because Stalin and Molotov had been willing to let Russians starve to death—in 1947, for example. Of course, Molotov, then Foreign Minister, had little to do with grain in 1947; all this really signified was an attack on current agricultural conservatives as adherents of a fallen faction. It is perhaps significant that V. V. Grishin, candidate-member of the Presidium, in a speech to the Soviet Trade Union Congress on October 28, 1963, had flatly stated about the year's harvest that it was enough "to give full satisfaction to the needs of the population"—precisely the view Khrushchev later attacked.

Although any formal attack on collectivization as such has

not arisen, there are many elements in the agricultural situation that have created conflict. Over the years from 1954 to 1963, Khrushchev's own great contribution to the solution of agricultural problems was the opening up of the Virgin Lands of Kazakhstan and Siberia. This highly controversial effort at no time came up to expectations.

Kommunist, in the issue of September, 1963, contained some striking admissions about errors in the Virgin Lands in 1954–60, and the revision in 1959–60 of some of the "distortions" of the earlier period. In November, 1963, at a Plenum of the Kazakhstan Central Committee, the local First Secretary, Yusupov, gave the grain yield for the Virgin Lands territory as 3.6 centners per hectare* for 1963, as against 6 in 1962 and 6.7 in 1961. *Novy Mir,* in 1964, published a dramatic description of dust-bowl conditions produced by the plowing of these marginal lands, with comments like the following: "In the reports the area of arable land had increased. But in reality thousands of hectares are by now so eroded that they could not even grow a crop of weeds." There was even praise for a local agronomist who had saved lands from this by putting in false returns.

On February 23, 1964, the Italian Communist paper *Unita* published an account of an interview given by Khrushchev to the Italian publisher Giulio Einaudi. He described the Virgin Lands scheme as a stopgap "maneuver" undertaken only to "overcome the most serious food difficulties faced in 1953. When agriculture of other regions reaches a more intensive character, the Virgin Lands too could be restored essentially to cattlebreeding." On February 24, Moscow Radio gave its version of the interview: Khrushchev had spoken of "the Virgin Lands . . . which are to be transformed once more to achieve intensive cultivation there too, but on a basis more

* The metric centner equals 220.46 lbs; the hectare equals 2.47 acres.

suitable to the soils and areas, developing pastures and stock-breeding organized on intensive lines."

At the same time, *Pravda* (February 24/25, 1964) was publishing the fundamental, authoritative article by Academician Arzumanyan, referred to above. This described the Virgin Lands project in the same terms as Khrushchev—as "a certain economic maneuver" necessary as a temporary measure until the Party had achieved the mechanization neglected by Stalin and required for intensive agriculture (a dubious proposition in itself). Arzumanyan added that "the Party has not forgotten for a minute the task of securing the conditions for intensive agriculture . . . at present the country has reached a level at which the problem of full intensification can be fully posed."

This confusion and disintegration of policies was to be condemned by Khrushchev's successors. What their solution would be remained unclear. The first three months of their rule produced in agriculture a relaxation of pressures on the peasant's private plot which Khrushchev had been applying, and a condemnation of the disastrous overinsistence on maize which had been one of Khrushchev's personal crazes. In industry, there was an extension of Liberman-type operations in the consumer-goods production and some moves to tighten up on an excessive decentralization of control associated with the old leader. But, apart from such trimming off of the more striking irrationalities of recent years, no real reorientation of the economy was yet seen. And in January, 1965, the rulers were still calling on the planners for adequate information and guidance.

Meanwhile, we may note that not all the issues were primarily between Khrushchev and the remainder of the leadership. While agricultural and organizational disputes were largely concerned with his personal policies, this is not so true of most of the essential industrial questions, on which the surviving leadership seems to have been basically divided. Nor, of course, does opposition to Khrushchev's agricultural policies mean any automatic unity on a particular alternative line. If we see the recent coup in economic terms as a blow at Khrushchev's erratic agricultural, chemical, and administrative measures, it seems that attention to light industry, skepticism about steel, and Liberman-type improvements in price organization will be maintained by a majority of the present leaders. Whether they can persist against those who evidently put up a hard fight two years ago remains to be seen. It seems probable that the elimination of an economically conservative faction, perhaps formerly headed by Kozlov in the name of a backward section of the Central Committee and of the Army leadership, may be necessary. But there are political considerations which may cut across such a straight economic fight. While the political setup remains as it is, there is no guarantee that this partial attempt to modernize the economy will not meet the fate of its predecessor in 1953–55.

9

Themes of Faction

These economic disputes were, up to a point, concerned simply with practical matters—the best adjustment of the economy to urgent problems of organization and production. But, at a more basic level, they were also ideological. For it is not sufficient in the Soviet Union to propose policies suitable to the actual problem; they must also be compatible with the organized prejudices of *apparatchik* doctrine—and, of course, with the full maintenance of *apparatchik* power.

In fields not directly impinging on the economy, and thus not objectively as pressing and critical, dispute and disarray have been equally evident. We have noted, for example, the extraordinarily inconsistent attitudes toward Stalinism. It can be shown that in all sensitive fields of purely political content, these conflicts prevail, as they always have. Indeed, in a sense, although the economic problem is more urgent, matters more purely concerned with power and doctrine are commonly at least as central to the Soviet political scene, and usually lie in the most sensitive area of discussion.

The Soviet oligarchy, like most oligarchies in the past, is self-perpetuating and does its own recruiting and training of suitable members. The rulers of Russia, so long as there is any continuity with the present regime, will be nurtured in the long-service Party apparatus. Again, like all oligarchies, the Soviet oligarchy has a conviction of its own right to rule. We sometimes hear of a drift from ideology; this is a vague conception, but in so far as it concerns the marrow of the CPSU's ideology—this self-justification—there is little to be said for it. At present, all ranks appear to exhibit the same certitude of political mission. When and if ideology really does begin to disintegrate on a large scale—which is to say, when the *apparatchik* begins to think for himself—we shall probably be in sight of disintegration of the whole system.

For the Party is united under a discipline of hierarchy, but also under a discipline of doctrine. The two chief departments of the Central Committee are Party Organs and Agitation and Propaganda. The former ranks highest, and power is always the bedrock of Party attitudes; but Agitprop also holds great sway. Faction involves both a contest for key positions and an argument about policy and doctrine. The struggle *must* have some sort of ideological theme, and *may* have, on the face of it, a purely ideological appearance. Policy disputes are never simply on policy, but on policy interpreted in ideological terms.

We may begin to consider the faction struggle in the U.S.S.R. in its political aspect by examining a passage in Yevtushenko's poem "Stalin's Heirs":

> Some heirs, in retirement, cultivate roses,
> And secretly believe
> That their retirement is temporary.
> Others abuse Stalin from the platforms,
> But they themselves at night
> Are longing for the old times.*

* Published in *Pravda*, October 21, 1962.

A perfectly explicit announcement, sponsored by the Party's own organ, that a "conservative" element hostile to Khrushchev's line and leadership remained in active politics.

Overt political polemics within the CPSU are confined virtually to attacks on dead or fallen leaders and their views and actions. Since these are often not directly relevant to current affairs, it might appear to reveal an unrealistic obsession with the past and neglect of the essence of the matter. But Soviet conventions forbid open political quarreling among the leaders still in power and about policies still in operation. Silence or tepid approbation from one leader on a subject arousing enthusiasm in another is about as far as participants can go under the long-established rules.

So when Stalin or the Anti-Party Group is attacked, when their wrongdoings become the central *political* theme of a Congress or Plenum, we are entitled to surmise that it represents merely the visible part of the iceberg. In fact, the varying intensity and nature of such polemics are most significant.

In examining the issues that have evidently divided the leadership, we may first note that they do not always divide it along the same line, that no straightforward formula can give us easily opposable and clear-cut factions.

In the past, of which we know more, this was already patently the case. It can clearly be seen from the Resolution of the Central Committee of June 29, 1957, that even the three leading victims then condemned—Malenkov, Kaganovich, and Molotov—were not in agreement as against Khrushchev on most important policy matters until his economic decentralization scheme of the early part of that year at last brought them together. In fact, over the previous four years a variety of majorities had existed in the Presidium: for example, Molotov voting with Khrushchev against Malenkov's consumer-goods policy, and Malenkov voting with Khrushchev against Molotov's Yugoslavian policy. We have less information concerning events of more recent times, but it seems reasonable to assume that similar conditions have accounted for otherwise unexplainable moves in recent Soviet politics.

The issue most directly and publicly debated recently has been the attitude to be taken to the Anti-Party Group, as it was raised at the time of the Twenty-second Congress and for some weeks afterward. Examination of the speeches at that Congress shows that those attacking the group most strongly were themselves divided. As at the Twenty-first Congress, the most violent attack came from Spiridonov, the First Secretary of the Leningrad Provincial Committee. He, and certain others not closely connected with Khrushchev, directed their primary attack against Malenkov and confined themselves for the most part to the criminal rather than the political errors of the Group. But the majority of the speakers directed their main attack at Molotov, whose promotion to the first-named in the Group was now wholly formalized.* But among the speakers who stuck to this general line, there was a major divergence between those alleging criminality and those denouncing political error in comparatively moderate tones.

In an earlier book of mine,† I pointed out that at the December, 1958, Plenum, the distinction had been openly drawn (by Kolushchinsky) between those who attacked the Anti-Party Group's political views and those who emphasized the "criminal" way in which the Group had sought to implement them. It is interesting that the point was again made explicit at the Twenty-second Congress in the speech of N. N. Rodionov (another Leningrader), who said: "The participants in the Anti-Party Group are called dogmatists. That is correct. But what they tried to do in June, 1957, that is not dogmatism,

* See the change between the 1959 and 1962 editions of the official *History of the Communist Party of the Soviet Union:* Malenkov is almost invariably the first-named in the former, and Molotov in the latter.

† Robert Conquest, *Power and Policy in the U.S.S.R.* (New York: St Martin's Press, 1961), p. 369.

that is banditry." Of those who spoke at the Twenty-second Congress, thirty-four urged the expulsion from the Party of the Group, forty-two failed to do so, and fourteen made attacks that either carried the implication of criminality or hinted in general terms that members of the Group "should be held to responsibility." Some of those who attacked the Group most strongly—N. G. Ignatov, for instance—were men who were evidently pursuing old feuds within the *apparat* rather than trying to eliminate the Group in order to ease the way for Khrushchev's political plans. Mikoyan, who has most uncompromisingly opposed the political platform of the Group, has been most obviously unwilling to press the case to extremes. In fact, the leadership has appeared to be divided, on this issue, in ways that do not necessarily reflect its other disputes. It is also the case that some of those who urged the expulsion of the Group from the Party did so on grounds of policy alone.

The confusion at a lower level can be seen from the fact that of the meetings of Party activists held in the republics after the Congress only half came out explicitly for the expulsion of the Group from the Party. *Pravda* on November 15, 1961, omitted from its account of a meeting of Moscow city activists a call for the expulsion of the Group which had been printed in the report of the same meeting carried the previous day by *Vechernaya Moskva;* and on November 17, *Pravda* failed to mention a similar call made by "the entire Moscow Provincial Party organization" reported the same day in that organization's own *Leninskoye Znamya.*

The issue remained unresolved. And with the evident failure of Khrushchev's policies, people began to remember the criticisms advanced by the Group. *Izvestia* on March 1, 1964, called attention to people who for some reason felt it necessary to stimulate "an unhealthy interest in the extinct political 'stars,' as some people depict the chief figures of the Anti-Party

Group." This hint at support for Khrushchev's worst enemies was soon followed by the publication (in *Pravda* on April 3) of Suslov's speech attacking the Chinese, which referred incidentally to Molotov, Kaganovich, and Malenkov as having been "thrown out of the ranks of our Party."

The circumstances reveal not simply long dissension but also confusion, and indicate, as much as anything, that this was an issue on which it seems to have been difficult to find a majority for any policy at all. At best, one can perhaps say that two different groups of "expulsionists" were attempting to put the issue in different ways, one for "conservative" and one for Khrushchevite ends, while a large element preferred no action at all, a course followed for some time.

Nevertheless, for our purposes it is useful to note that at the Twenty-second Congress of the leading figures we are chiefly concerned with, Kosygin, Mikoyan, Suslov, and Voronov took a moderate line, and that Brezhnev and Polyansky were also comparatively moderate. Podgorny and Shvernik were notably immoderate, the latter particularly with reference to Malenkov.

Thus, even on an issue on which the evidence is to some degree baffling, and on which confusion evidently prevailed in the CPSU itself, we are able to extract certain information. We can see that divisions have existed and that they are important. And we can note, of certain figures, a stance relevant to all the disputes of the time.

There are, indeed, issues on which the point in dispute is clearer, and which are both more recent and more *directly* relevant to the factional lineup. For example, the treatment of "liberal" writers during 1962–63 was quite clearly a focus of Soviet *political* interest and struggle throughout the period.

In May, 1962, there was a "liberal" capture of the Moscow Writers' Organization, and through that year the more outspoken writers pretty much had their own way. On October

21, *Pravda* published Yevtushenko's poem "Stalin's Heirs." In November, Solzhenitsyn's *One Day in the Life of Ivan Denisovich* appeared. Khrushchev is reported to have revealed in an unpublished speech of November 23 to the Central Committee Plenum that he had authorized the book's appearance in its present form, although other leaders had suggested cuts.*

This was the high point of "liberalization." At the November Plenum, a number of reactionary intellectuals presented a petition to the Party to act against "formalism." A campaign of attacks on the "liberals" now went into high gear; the tone was set in a strong address by Ilychev to a meeting of Party leaders with writers and other creative artists on December 17. The liberals, or at least their defenders, were still able to answer back—for example, Fedin in *Literaturnaya Gazeta* on January 3, and K. Chukovski in *Pravda* on the same day. By the end of January, attacks on the writers had become fiercer.† February saw a truce of sorts, since the moderates had refused to withdraw and it had presumably become clear that they could not be suppressed except by very strong measures indeed, which many of the leadership must have been reluctant to take. On March 7, a new impetus came from another meeting between Party leaders and intellectuals in which Ilychev again made a sharp attack on Ilya Ehrenburg and other writers.‡ At the end of March and the beginning of April, the leaderships of the Moscow Writers' Organization and the Writers' Union of the R.S.F.S.R. were purged, as various editorial boards had been earlier. On March 18, Khrushchev made a speech strongly aligning himself with the attacks on Ehrenburg and others, but remaining comparatively moderate about Yevtushenko. (It was noticeable that, as in all periods of retreat on such matters, he spoke more friendlily of Stalin

* See *The New York Times,* November 29, 1962.

† See *Izvestia,* January 20; *Pravda,* January 27; *Izvestia,* January 30 and 31.

‡ *Pravda,* March 9, 1963.

than he had for over a year.) Further attacks followed through April. The Moscow literary world was expecting still harsher measures at the forthcoming Plenum of the Central Committee. However, by the end of April, the campaign began to peter out. And by May 19, *Pravda* was announcing, quite contrary to the line that had been taken through the winter, that there was "no need to watch over every step" of the writers.

As to the relevant pressures, it must first of all be said that the true "liberalizers" in principle do not constitute much of a political force. (We must go far down the Party hierarchy finally to meet a representative of "liberal" opinion proper—Alexander Tvardovsky, candidate-member of the Central Committee.) In the Presidium there is no one who can be identified, even tentatively, with so advanced a program; or, at most, one might say that a single man, Mikoyan, leans rather in that direction, although even here we can judge only by his speech at the Twentieth Congress and certain other moves. When a literary relaxation occurs in Russia, it must be enforced from the top. The publishers, the Science and Culture Department, the officials of the Ministry of Culture, manned as they are by second-level bureaucrats, do not give permission for heterodox work unless specifically told to do so. And again, it is at the center that decisions about transferring literary journals from "Stalinist" to "liberal" editorship or vice versa are taken.

This is not to say that the "liberal" opinion on this issue on the part of the great mass of Soviet writers and artists lacks all political significance. It is certainly a pressure that has been taken into account by all factions in Russia for the past generation, whether for purposes of appeasing the writers with a view to using them more efficiently, or of suppressing them with a view to making them write more orthodoxly. On the other hand, if we are to take such pressures into account, it would be appropriate to mention other and more important ones—the whole political interest represented by Party members in general, in their thousands in all the influential positions in Russia, including those not holding any decisive political power, and, secondly, the philistine opinion of the great Russian bourgeois public, as part of which may be added the *ofitserstvo*, with their frequently expressed preference for rousing patriotic literature.

Taking all these points into account, we are likely to conclude that a conservative group in the Presidium secured the adoption of its literary policies in the first quarter of 1963, with Khrushchev's more or less unwilling consent, and that he was later able to reverse the decisions. This view is rendered more probable by the fact that it fits in with the remainder of evidence in other fields where similar processes can be seen.

In November, 1962, Khrushchev intruded a most sensitive political issue into his economic schemes by his splitting of the Party into two sections at the provincial level, the agricultural and the industrial, on the grounds that "economics comes first" —that is, that every resource, political and otherwise, must be deployed for the economic struggle as its main objective. The result was to disintegrate the Party machine. The successors were later to imply that Khrushchev forced this through against their will, and even at the time there were rumblings. *Pravda** attacked "dogmatists" who would undoubtedly object to the new system. *Party Life*† similarly criticized "the fears expressed by certain comrades." And the chief editor of *Kommunist*, V. Stepanov, wrote a long article‡ dealing with objections that had been raised. More important, Kozlov expressed the reservations of the Presidium when he said that the

* December 9, 1962, in an article by P. Fedoseev.
† No. 2 (1963).
‡ *Izvestia*, February 7/8, 1963.

prospect of the reform leading to a split between the urban and rural Party "cannot be allowed in any circumstances."*

Such organizational issues touch very closely on sensitive power considerations. However, they can be reversed comparatively easily. When it comes to matters of general political interest, we find, as in the economic field, problems that cannot be settled by a quick decision and thus may be expected to play their part in the post-Khrushchev struggle as much as they have in the past. The main "permanent" themes of this type are the Anti-Party Group, Stalin, ideological control, China, and foreign policy. We have dealt with the first three and shall consider the last two at more length later on. Meanwhile, it will be useful to summarize their general effects.

The Anti-Party Group divided the conservative (and non-Ukrainian) elements of the Party; stern measures were urged, mainly by the Leningrad organization† and against Malenkov. But it also divided the more progressive elements; Mikoyan, for example, consistently spoke in favor of dropping the matter, and even certain Ukrainians showed little enthusiasm. It is therefore a difficult issue to turn to political advantage. On the other hand, it carries with it the refractory policy problem of an unrepentant, manifesto-writing, and possibly influential Molotov.

Stalin: Beyond a certain point, "de-Stalinization" becomes unsatisfactory to an increasingly large segment of the Party cadres. The issue is a fairly simple one that polarizes reactionary and progressive attitudes. Each wave of de-Stalinization thus far has ended rather abruptly at what was doubtless a balking point for a majority.

Ideological control, particularly of the writers, is an issue that unites all the more authoritarian elements in the Party in

* *Leningradskaya Pravda*, February 27, 1963.

† Together with the other former Zhdanovite stronghold of Gorki, whose representative, L. N. Efremov, took a similar line at the Twenty-second Congress.

a fairly straightforward way. And even moderates favor relaxation pragmatically rather than in principle, and are quick to have afterthoughts when mutinous thinking shows up too clearly among the intellectuals. On this theme, as on the closely associated "de-Stalinization" moves, progressive initiative tends to lead to a situation in which the Party is thrown back into the arms of the reactionaries.

China: Here, however, the Peking leadership can be relied on to put the conservative element in Moscow in an awkward position, by an implied support for them. When this is combined with a "leftist" adventurism that even Stalin would have deplored, and with the implication that Soviet primacy must be abandoned—and even that the hard-won Soviet industrial achievement must be risked in war—it inevitably throws the conservative dogmatist in Moscow over to the defensive. No one in Moscow can be pro-Peking; but there may, of course, be divergencies on the best tactics to pursue.

Foreign-policy disputes seem in part a matter of nuances. The undesirability of nuclear war is probably recognized by all. The Cuba adventure showed that even Khrushchev permitted considerable latitude in interpretation. As a political issue, coexistence seems rather a question of ideological verbalization (conservative ideologists favoring a more hostile phrasing) and of tactics (each viewpoint finding something to criticize in individual foreign-policy decisions when they arise, as in any other polity). The issues of Eastern Europe face the Party most directly. Saving the bloc at the cost of devolution is to be judged according to the tactical possibilities as against the ideological disciplines. There must be many who now reluctantly accept the view that the best practicable result has been secured but who would be disillusioned if some fresh upset in the area led to further disintegration. And Khrushchev's Yugoslav policy, although not entirely without results, was not as fruitful as might have been hoped, and in comparable circumstances stands as a reproach against the progressive elements in something of the same way that China does against the reactionaries.

In general we can see that (*a*) there are issues on which the members of the ruling group are divided; (*b*) there are different divisions on different issues; and (*c*) there are circumstances in which a majority on a given issue becomes a minority, with both policy and personal position suffering sudden changes—indicating that faction is not fully polarized but that, on the contrary, there are intermediate or wavering positions.

Moreover, when it comes to a large section of the Presidium, we need to recall that devotion to a policy—standing and falling on a given political line—has never been the hallmark of Soviet politics. Stalin took a Right-wing line to destroy the Left opposition and then a Left-wing line to destroy the Right; Khrushchev took a Left anti-consumer line against Malenkov, only to switch later to a Right pro-consumer line. So we must bear in mind that, on the whole, as Leonard Schapiro has written, the student should not "project on to the Soviet system political principles with which he is familiar in his own experience. They very seldom apply. For example, in democracies politicians quarrel over policies and if need be resign in the hope of making a comeback. In the Politburo and the Presidium it is the other way round: politicians quarrel over power, using policies as a means of struggle."*

In fact, Kosygin was making a perfectly sound point—and one applicable to more than just the opposition—when he said in a speech to the Twenty-second Party Congress: "Often the position of members of the Anti-Party Group in the solution of economic questions was determined, not by economic or technical advisability, but by considerations of personal prestige."

* *The Listener*, May 18, 1961.

The point had been made in a different way by Bulganin in a speech to the December, 1958, Plenum of the Central Committee: "The questions were put to the Central Committee by Comrade Khrushchev. Is that not the reason Molotov, Malenkov, Kaganovich, and Shepilov came out against these proposals? It is precisely the reason they did not wish to hear of these proposals."*

We must not, indeed, go too far with this. There are certainly leading figures whose prestige itself depends, at least until such time as they might reach the very top, on identification with certain policies. Their "sincerity" or otherwise is not directly relevant, so long as they are in any case forced into this position. But one nevertheless forms the impression that in the case of Molotov at least, the reactionary policy line he stood up for at the June, 1957, Plenum, and repeated in his programmatic submissions which aroused such condemnation at the Twenty-second Party Congress, represented personal conviction. (As Lenin said of the Italian Socialist leader Turati, no one has yet invented a "sincerometer.")

With all these reservations in mind, we may make some tentative deductions from the conflicts we have noted.

First of all, there exists a "conservative" element, susceptible of attack as "Stalinist," although not necessarily advocating a full return to Stalin's ways. Members of this group opposed and slowed down some of the ideologically doubtful industrial measures. In attacks on the Anti-Party Group, they have reserved their spleen as far as possible for Malenkov the modernizer. On the other hand, their somewhat covert defense

* We should add that apparently close personal relationships or personal antagonisms are also quite indecisive. Malenkov and Beria were always closely associated, as were Bulganin and Khrushchev. And similarly with antagonisms, as Khrushchev said in his speech to the Twenty-second Congress: "Some comrades know about the unpleasant personal relations between Voroshilov and Molotov, between Voroshilov and Kaganovich, and between Malenkov and Voroshilov. And yet, despite these relations, they joined forces."

of Molotov has long saved him from expulsion. They have opposed all concession to the "liberal" writers. And they have evidently exerted a powerful influence. One may tentatively identify Kozlov and Shvernik (and probably N. G. Ignatov, outside the Presidium) as representatives of this element.

Next, there is a group of "modernizers," concerned with economic advance, but not necessarily favoring ideological concession in fields like the literary. Their main attacks in the Anti-Party Group issue have been against Molotov. Kosygin and Polyansky seem typical of them; Mikoyan shares their economic views, but inclines to riskier ideological maneuvers.

Then we come to the Khrushchev appointees proper—Brezhnev, Podgorny, Kirilenko, and Shelest—who have been attached to his policies by the requirements of dependency and interest rather than of conviction. Brezhnev, at least, seems long since to have built his bridges to the more systematic "modernizers" (perhaps followed by his old associate Kirilenko) and, possibly, further still, to an attitude of less enthusiasm for reorganization and a position comparable to Suslov's.

This leaves Suslov, Voronov, and Shelepin, whose attitudes on all these issues might best be described as "moderate."

From such a rough lineup one can see that majorities, though different majorities, could be found for (*a*) a moderate modernization of the economy, (*b*) opposition to Khrushchev's split in the Party apparatus, (*c*) opposition to excessive "liberalism" in literature, (*d*) opposition to Khrushchev's adventurism, and (*e*) opposition to "Stalinist" dogmatism and to Molotov and the reactionary element in the Anti-Party Group.

It can also be said that, besides the varying majorities, the lineup shows a certain immediate instability.

We can, in any case, see that in all spheres of Soviet policy—economic, ideological, and political—sharp divergencies of approach were manifest over the entire Khrushchev period. They manifested themselves sometimes in deadlock, sometimes in sudden shifts and reversals of official policy, sometimes in slightly veiled polemic. Their existence did not automatically produce a political battle *à l'outrance* at any given moment. But—compounded with extreme political ambitions—they formed the raw material of crisis, and from time to time were bound to produce it. They are bound to do so in the future as well.

10

Khrushchev: Impact and Fall

THE IMAGE PROJECTED by the Russia of Khrushchev was not only "liberal"; it was also "dynamic," "self-confident," "forward-looking." It was an image of a regime that had supposedly broken with dogmatism and freed Soviet economics, and politics as well, from conservative tendencies—which made it attractive both inside and outside the U.S.S.R. And there was just enough truth in this image to make it fairly easy to accept.

But to launch vast changes is not, in itself, "progressive." For instance, repeated promises some years back to catch up with the United States in meat and milk production were announced with vast *réclame*, and although all independent experts thought them impossible, they received a great deal of publicity in the West as well. Yet, their abandonment after a few years passed more or less unnoticed, particularly as it was covered up by the spectacular proposals of the Seven-Year Plan. Later on, that plan in turn was overtaken by the long-term plan of 1961. In each case, a dynamic air of self-confidence emanated from Khrushchev personally and from his followers everywhere. The plans evaporated, but the air of confidence remained, and there is no doubt that a picture of immense economic perspectives stayed in the public eye, even abroad.

Stalin's propaganda was not without its results. But Stalin's method of keeping his claims large and vague and concealing the results is worth comparing with Khrushchev's. The latter gave the figures of the plans and later allowed the fact of their nonfulfillment to trickle out, relying on each successive glorious future to distract attention from the failure of the last.

Khrushchev's political behavior was, in fact, embodied in a series of crash programs, often ill-considered and inadequately prepared—the Virgin Lands in agriculture, the decentralization of industry, the initial attack on Stalin, and the hasty reconciliation with Yugoslavia. These often ran into great difficulties in the long run, but by that time the First Secretary was usually able to destroy those who chose to oppose him on the particular issue. Nevertheless, his bullheaded methods had their dangers. To have run twenty steps successfully along a tightrope does not mean that at the next one you will not slip—and safety nets are not part of the equipment of Soviet politics.

It is a common error of observers to imagine that those who rise to the top in a state, and particularly in a despotic one, are necessarily endowed with great political judgment. Somebody has to win a struggle for power, and even in this sphere, in which no one can doubt the skill of the Soviet operators, chance must play a big part. Many commentators are still inclined to argue that Khrushchev proved himself a cleverer politician than Malenkov in 1957. But that was obviously a very close call for him, and to take this line is to commit the sin of historicism—to invest the actual winner as some sort of mystic man of destiny (as who might say that Wellington was a greater general than Napoleon).

It will be seen that in all of Khrushchev's maneuvers it was not only—or perhaps not mainly—a particular line of policy that was so striking. It was rather what the Russians themselves often refer to as his "style of leadership" (that curious, semi-aesthetic phrase). The veteran observer of Soviet affairs Boris Nicolaevsky has distinguished between the attitudes of Malenkov and Khrushchev in their periods of ascendancy as "pragmatic" and "mythopoeic," respectively. But this takes us into an area in which the comparison is not, strictly speaking, one between easily recognizable congeries of policies. And if we seek a unifying factor in the various actions Khrushchev undertook over the past decade, it is easier to note a consistency of tone than of direction. Khrushchev's "style," in fact, was an attempt to solve political problems by large-scale scheming and ill-considered moves, as with Cuba.

Indeed, even among the basically much more aggressive Chinese, we may note a far greater tactical prudence, and while there is no actual identification of the Chinese line with that of the "Stalinist" type of thought associated with Molotov, these might well have coincided on the issue of the 1962 Cuban crisis; the Chinese attack on Khrushchev for his conduct of that affair, condemning him as "capitulationist" in the last phase *but* as "adventurist" in getting into the conflict at all, seemed just what Molotov would have urged, and with some cogency. Just as, in general, power takes precedence over policy, so we may feel a leader's personal style often determines action more effectively than do political ideas.

A great propaganda success for Khrushchev personally, in the West at least, was the acceptance of the notion that he alone represented opposition to Stalinism, Chinese belligerence, and so on. This impression was strengthened by the many attacks on Molotov. But it is worth remembering that Molotov is practically alone among Khrushchev's opponents in being a more or less orthodox adherent of the policies of the 1940's. (It is true that Stalin planned to have Molotov executed in 1953, while Khrushchev was still getting on famously with the old dictator, but this only illustrates the complicated relationship between purges, doctrine, and power.)

Khrushchev's personal image, as distinguished from that of his regime, was not a complete success in the West—let alone in Russia. Yet the notion of a bouncing, uninhibited, rather clownish fellow, rough and crude in certain ways no doubt, but basically likable and honest, still has its effect abroad, particularly in Britain, where people like a certain hominess—and had once even been prepared to put Stalin's pipe in the balance against the reports of purges and labor camps and to refer to him as Uncle Joe.

No doubt these comments apply to the Khrushchev image as it reached that level of the populace who are only just conscious of international politics at all—i.e., the Khrushchev of the cartoonists. Yet the instincts and feelings of the mass of the population are an important political factor in the West. Moreover, it would be wrong to think that this sort of misapprehension was limited to the uninstructed. It may have been only with them that it constituted the entire, or almost the entire, picture of the Soviet leader. But even among the more sophisticated and politically conscious sections of the Western public such notions were present to a greater or lesser extent, even if they were partly balanced by more considered estimates.

We should compare this image with something of Khrushchev's real background. Long before Khrushchev's fall, Senator Terracini, of the Italian Communist Party Directorate, said that responsibility for the Stalin blood baths had now actually been extended from Stalin to the whole leading group of his epoch and might "engulf perhaps eventually also Comrade Khrushchev himself. In fact, it should be said that Comrade Khrushchev belonged to the leading group around Stalin which shares responsibility."

Khrushchev's actual personal involvement in Stalin's terror

is still obscure. He was not a full member of the Politburo during the Yezhov period, and he later reproached those who were formally responsible for many of the executions. But he did, after all, become a candidate-member of that body in January, 1938. And throughout the worst period he had been Secretary of the Moscow Provincial Committee. In his "secret speech" to the Twentieth Congress, he revealed that Eikhe, as Secretary of the West Siberian Territory Committee, had had the duty of "sanctioning" arrests of Trotskyites, so one can presume that Khrushchev himself had similar powers. In any case, his transfer to the Ukraine in 1938 was followed by a major purge. Even though he may not have been responsible for the arrests of Kossior and Postyshev, which (it is unofficially reported) resulted from the report of a Politburo Committee of which he was a member, he certainly had the task of the massive removal of Kossior's supporters throughout the Republic. In fact, it was officially stated that the effective smelling-out of "the Trotskyites, Bukharinites, bourgeois nationalists, and all other spying filth began only after the Central Committee of the All-Union Communist Party sent the unswerving Bolshevik and Stalinist Nikita Sergeyevich Khrushchev to the Ukraine."* And the Ukrainian Central Committee was soon suffering even heavier casualties than the All-Union Central Committee in Moscow—97 per cent! Much the same could be said of most of Khrushchev's senior colleagues. All this may have been forgotten in the West, but not in Russia. Even in the Party the tactical hypocrisies of the attitude seem to have been recognized.

Not that such considerations are likely to have played any detectable part in the resentments against Khrushchev that were building up. It was rather the extension of his personal power on the one hand, and his erratic conduct of affairs on the other, that caused the decisive revulsion. We have traced

* *Bilshovik Ukrainy,* No. 7 (1938).

something of the policy disputes that had been developing within the *apparat* over the entire Khrushchev epoch. It was during 1962–63 that these faced Khrushchev with his first serious challenge since 1957.

In his speech on April 24, 1963, to the R.S.F.S.R. Conference on Industry and Construction, Khrushchev said: "I am already sixty-nine years old. Anyone can see I cannot occupy the post I have in the Party and State forever." This was taken as a hint that a decision might have been taken to release Khrushchev from one or both of his posts.

As we now know, from 1962 onward Khrushchev was heading for disaster. Opinions in the West about his strength centered particularly around the suggestion that he was in very considerable difficulties in the winter of 1962, and that Kozlov's illness in April, 1963, coinciding with the switch back to old-style Khrushchevite "liberalism," was also linked to it causally. It is true that Khrushchev's remarks came after the probable date of Kozlov's heart attack. But a decision may already have been reached and reversal not yet obtained, or even rendered probable, by the time of this comment. Moreover, the severity of the heart attack may not then have been apparent. And a vote, if any, enforcing such a retreat on Khrushchev must have been a decisively large one, whose solidarity, however shaken, would have taken a little time to break down.

During the previous months, there had been, as we have said, a swing from literary liberalism; a recentralization of the economy had taken place at the same time. There can be no doubt that heart-searching debate had followed the Cuban debacle of October, 1962; the November, 1962, Plenum had produced the radical reorganization of the Party on an economic basis; and in general the atmosphere was one of sharp reassessment.

While Kozlov was still in full power, during March and April, 1963, the campaign against the young writers reached a crescendo, the economic line swung in favor of recentralization, and a moderately hostile view of Yugoslavia was taken. And, as a tone-setter in anti-Western attitudes, we may note that the "tough-line" trial of Penkovsky as a British and American agent was set up. *Pravda* announced on April 18 that the KGB had completed its investigations, the indictment appeared on May 8, and all formalities were completed on May 17 with the announcement that the sentence had been carried out.

It was on May 4, 1963, that Kozlov's illness was announced. In the absence of evidence to the contrary, we may take his heart attack to be genuine.* At least, one assumes that circumstances are not the same as when the entry of bullets into that organ, in the case of Ordzhonikidze, could be certified by a Minister of Health and three other leading doctors as a cardiac condition.† There is no need for us to doubt, on their records, that any of the leaders might employ such measures in case of extreme necessity (i.e., if they feared the loss of their own power) *if* they thought they could get away with it; but it does seem most unlikely that they would now think this.

But it might be possible for the other leaders to instruct the doctors as to the diagnosis. An unconscious Kozlov might awaken to find that a comparatively mild condition had meanwhile been labeled so grave as to remove him from the seat of power for a greater length of time than his actual condition would have justified. After all, there was the case of Frunze, then the leading figure in Soviet military life, who, according to one widely held view, was ordered by the Party to have an operation that was unnecessary, and, in fact, proved fatal; this took place years before Stalin had established his full power

* In Yevtushenko's poem "Stalin's Heirs" (see p. 95), one of the lines pointedly says, "Not for nothing do Stalin's heirs have heart attacks." Kozlov's first heart attack is believed to have been in 1960. It may also be significant that when interviewed by the Hamburg paper *Die Zeit* on February 8, 1963, Yevtushenko evaded a question as to whether he was referring to Kozlov as one of "Stalin's heirs."

† See *Pravda,* February 19, 1937.

and, indeed, in political conditions not too different from those prevailing in 1963. And there is a much more recent and pertinent parallel. Imre Nagy, the moderate Hungarian Communist leader, had a heart attack early in 1955 and was soon afterward removed from the leadership. In his *Imre Nagy on Communism,* he complains of "illegal and irregular resolutions of the Political Committee that attempted to isolate and silence me on the basis of the medical report *composed by that Committee* [italics added]."*

But if we accept Kozlov's heart attack as genuine, at least to the extent that it eliminated him at a moment of political tension, we are on interesting ground for other reasons. The outcome of political struggles may depend upon accident. The indications are that Khrushchev was at this time in a difficult position, and it is quite possible that victory went to him as a result of this unexpected windfall. The element of accident in history is one that respectable and sociologically inclined historians are inclined to discount. But a political victory, like a military one, has to be won on the ground, and it cannot be determined simply by analysis of the forces and the skills concerned. Chickamauga was lost through a chance misunderstanding, and perhaps the gap where Wood's division should have been may be compared with the gap in the ranks of the conservative faction in the Kremlin where Kozlov should have stood. But however the incident is treated, it must remind us that the stability of a political situation in the U.S.S.R. may be destroyed at any minute by minor, as well as by major, unexpected events. In dealing with the even more fluid situation likely to prevail during the impending crises, we must be ready for surprising turns. Our anticipation must remain flexible enough to cope with such eventualities.

The fading out of Kozlov and the end of the "tough-line"

* *Imre Nagy on Communism* (New York: Frederick A. Praeger, 1957), p. 290.

policies of the early months of 1963 left Khrushchev greatly strengthened. This was illustrated by the installation in the Secretariat of Brezhnev and Podgorny in June, 1963, giving control to the First Secretary's personal following for the first time since early 1960, when Khrushchev had had in the Secretariat three of his own closest senior supporters–Kirichenko, Brezhnev, and Furtseva–who were all removed at that time and replaced from outside his coterie.

Minor signs of friction already amounted to very much less than the moves of early 1963. With the evident weakening of the more conservative faction through Kozlov's virtual elimination, Khrushchev's primacy seemed less challengeable than ever. On May 23, 1963, he was able to deny reports of his resignation at a reception for Castro. This was after the swing away from conservatism had begun, and may be taken as one sign of it. The pressure on the writers had suddenly eased; the tough measures expected at the Plenum arranged for May but postponed until June had never materialized. The same kind of evidence was to be seen in other areas, notably the signing of the test-ban treaty. The May Day slogans for 1963 underwent a change favorable to Yugoslavia, certainly indicating a change of view on the part of the Presidium. It seems likely that the revulsion was due at least in part to resentment at Chinese attacks. If so, it shows how these attacks assisted a Khrushchevite line as against the old orthodoxy.

For the rest of 1963 and the early part of 1964, there were no signs of a threat to Khrushchev's power, despite the crashing defeat he suffered in agriculture with the failure of the 1963 crop. After all, many of his policies had obviously failed since 1955, and he had always weathered, or diverted, the resulting storms. Opposition, as ever, was to some degree hampered by the old principle "You can't beat someone with no one." It was obvious, too, that the gradualist 1962–63 campaign of "Kozlovite" opposition, fully adorned with policy arguments, had not been the way to political victory.

In any case, the next attempt was made after a period in which, although there were various signs of controversy, there were none of any danger to Khrushchev's position. The coup of October, 1964, came out of the blue. It achieved surprise—and success.

Common sense takes us part of the way in considering events like the overthrow of Khrushchev. It is obviously implausible that a great majority of the Presidium suddenly and simultaneously found themselves desiring his ouster, discovering to their surprised pleasure at the next meeting of that body that all their colleagues agreed with them. So it becomes clear that some members must have thought of it a good deal earlier than others, and then waited for the opportunity to recruit support. It is plain that such support could not be sought in a completely open manner, or the proposer would run the risk of having Khrushchev oust *him* first. A long-harbored hope on the part of one or two, maturing into a genuine plot of three or four, and finally recruiting a decisive majority at the key moment was the probable evolution.

If we consider the victorious alliance in terms of the factional divisions already discussed, we can see that the "conservative" vote was always available against Khrushchev in any case, and that an alliance of "modernizers" and "moderates" with defectors from Khrushchev's own faction came together to oust him. At the same time, no concessions were made to the conservatives, and their representatives remained among the lowest in Presidium listings. The victory seemed, in effect, to be against both "conservatism" and "adventurism."

The objections of Brezhnev, Kosygin, and the Presidial majority to Khrushchev were not, in principle, ones of policy—except in matters of Party organization and, to some degree, agriculture. They were objections mainly to his penchant for huge, ill-prepared schemes. And even then, it is very notable that by far the most powerfully urged complaints were the fact that he acted without consulting them, that he turned Central Committee meetings into crowd scenes to carry his proposals by acclaim, that he used his son-in-law, Alexei Adzhubei, as a personal agent in foreign affairs without informing the Presidium, and so on. But the crucial point was reached when Khrushchev openly proposed to them the installation of Adzhubei in the machinery of power. Here was a threat to old Khrushchevites and non-Khrushchevites alike. The former must have remembered how Stalin, too, had replaced his old followers with men of his personal entourage.

It is curious to note the parallels between the 1957 and 1964 crises. In 1964, Khrushchev was putting forward for public discussion agricultural plans that he admitted had not been cleared with the leadership—and *before* their submission to the Central Committee; in fact, he was openly prejudicing the issue. In 1957, too, he had gone ahead with public discussion on the economic decentralization plans, to which other members of the Presidium had not given their assent. The most recent moves in his policies within the international Communist movement had been producing fiascos. Although short on support in the Presidium, he retained his nominees on the KGB and at the key organs of Party power.

One difference presents itself at once. In 1957, he had, and on the record of the year's controversies could be sure of, Army support. In 1964, it seems highly probable that such support was not forthcoming; nor was there any compelling reason for Khrushchev to expect it. (We shall deal with the Army's role in a later chapter.)

This analysis is perhaps reinforced by another consideration. With the exception of Brezhnev, the members of Khrushchev's Ukrainian machine (Podgorny, Kirilenko, Shelest, Rudakov, Titov) were not very impressively represented in the top Party bodies. But when it came to the actual administration of power, they appeared to secure Khrushchev an overwhelming, even if not quite exclusive, grip. The Party Organs machinery was held, in addition to Titov, by Churayev. Other Ukrainian veterans included Epishev, at the Political Directorate of the Army and Navy; Mironov (now dead), at the Administrative Organs Department; Semichastny, at the KGB; and Serdyuk, Deputy Chairman of the Party Control Commission. In a crisis, such as an attempt to remove him from his leadership, there is little doubt that Khrushchev would have used or tried to use these cadres, unconstitutionally if need be, just as he used the Party machine, the KGB, and the Army against the Presidial majority in 1957.

This position implies that an anti-Khrushchev majority could not force the issue *unless* reasonably certain of neutralizing the Army, and perhaps the KGB, and in any case of securing a Central Committee majority of unshakable and unimpugnable quality. But the circumstances in which such a showdown could occur could only be ones involving a very considerable loss of confidence in Khrushchev at all levels, which in turn might well shake the loyalty of these lower-level Ukrainians, especially if a defecting Brezhnev (with whom such figures as Kirilenko and Mironov were closely linked in their Ukrainian careers) were to promise protection.

The manner of Khrushchev's dismissal was in itself a great demonstration of the nature of Soviet politics. It was carried through with all the correct Kremlinological trappings—almost to the point of caricature: the complete secrecy; the sudden coup; the issuing of a short and almost perfunctorily misleading statement about age and health; the simple cessation of reference to the name of the man who had been the most powerful in the country; the oblique, but obvious, attacks on his methods; the removal from his post of his closest adherent, Adzhubei, without comment or announcement until his replacement was mentioned casually a week or so later. In particular, the evident absence on the part of the new rulers of any idea that such procedures might be found odd by anyone (such as foreign Communist parties) reveals baldly a complete, unself-conscious attachment to the traditionalisms of Soviet politics.

And if we find it all rather repulsive, such is the nature of the system. As Lytton Strachey wrote in another context: "The consequences of a system of government in which the arbitrary will of an individual takes the place of the rule of law are apt to be disgraceful and absurd."

The extent to which the recent regime in Russia depended on Khrushchev's personal attitudes was clearly very great. We may see in it primarily a rather erratic general tendency to press reforms regarded as necessary with great *élan* and *éclat*, to effect large-scale, though not essentially radical, changes, and then to shift or withdraw or at least go through a waiting stage before the next flashy initiative. It is a method that was not without results. But the objections are obvious. And moreover, failures were frequent, from Kazakhstan to Cuba.

It seems unlikely in the first place that any successor will cultivate the personal style of Khrushchev. It also seems likely that it will become useful to blame certain economic and other errors of the present period on the inadequacies of Khrushchev's leadership methods. A "progressive" *apparatchik* rule would be more likely to proceed in a more careful fashion, in the Malenkovite style. Moreover, radical change may be expected to meet more resistance even than under Khrushchev, and the tempos are likely to be slower.

Khrushchev evidently saw that the problems facing Russia required radical solutions. But he does not seem to have thought out carefully what this might signify. A typical transition figure, he tried to achieve the results without being able to formulate the means. He even seems to have sensed that the

Party itself was an unsuitable organ for dealing with Soviet realities. His 1962 reorganization of it into two separate economic sections—one for agriculture and one for industry—at the provincial level disorganized the Party and confused the issue of political responsibility. Toward the end of his career, Khrushchev was planning to extend the principle to the top. As we have said, the whole scheme had met with resentment and resistance, and was one of the main points of objection to his political method by the men who engineered the coup.

For such solutions are unlikely to appeal to anyone who puts the Party's interests first. His successors have already revoked Khrushchev's reorganization of the Party and will probably restore comparative stability—but at the expense of again indefinitely postponing any of the radical moves that must in the end be undertaken. This is not to say that they will not make some progress, and even perhaps produce an economic plan that secures modest, but real, results, for just as long as the crisis inherent in the system does not become acute.

Although Khrushchev never showed the clearheadedness or took the long view that the comparison really requires, we may to some degree compare his modernization—and perhaps the modernization his successors may yet feel constrained to pursue—with that of Stolypin in 1907–11. Stolypin was backed in his policies by the autocrat, but encountered resistance from the main body of supporters of autocracy. Even when the top leaders in a regime see clearly what the situation requires, it is often a struggle to carry or force the slower-minded, more parochial, shorter-sighted rank and file along with them. Not that this is a problem confined to autocracies, but there does seem to be a greater rigidity in their cadres and a greater vulnerability in their constitutions than is the case with democracies.

In the early 1930's, many Communists viewed Hitler as the "icebreaker of revolution." They thought, that is, that Nazism so disintegrated the old fabric of bourgeois society that it would be ripe for Communism when Hitler fell. There is a sense, perhaps, in which Khrushchev himself may appear, not as a true revolutionizer of Soviet society, but as an icebreaker for real change. That is to say, his policies in recent years involved so much and so frequent rejuggling of the whole Party and State structure that a real sense of stability will be a long time in returning.

The present rulers are clearly disenchanted with Khrushchev personally, and with his general slapdash and risk-taking style, and to that extent they are more "conservative." Yet they are committed to, and perhaps see the real need for, the general "anti-Stalinist," "economic modernization," and "peaceful coexistence" policies in the struggle over which their group emerged and reached the top. How firm this association between faction and tactics has become will emerge later. One cannot exclude the possibility of panic retreat in the present crisis to the habits of their younger days, like a psychotic regressing to the foetal position when under stress.

Meanwhile, we can say that Khrushchev's style embodied the faults of authoritarian rule described by Francis Bacon in his essay "Of Empire," but that his successors are faced with something of the same difficulty: "And certain it is, that nothing destroyeth authority so much as the unequal and untimely interchange of power pressed too far, and relaxed too much." And Bacon adds, even more aptly: "It is common with princes (saith Tacitus) to will contradictories . . . for it is the solecism of power to think to command the end, and yet not to endure the mean." Such, in a phrase, is the dilemma of the regime.

11

The Present Contenders

WHEN SHAMIL, the great leader of Caucasian resistance to the Russians, asked his council who would succeed him, the answer was, "Venerated Imam, your successor will be the man with the sharpest sword."

Conditions in the Kremlin are different from those in the *auls* of Dagestan and Chechnia. It might be suggested that the knife in the back, rather than the scimitar at the breast, is the weapon more symbolic of the circumstances. But, in any case, there are certain qualities specially required of a man if he is to become, in any true sense, leader of the Soviet Communist Party and the Soviet Union in Khrushchev's place, or even meaningfully to share the succession.

In the first place, political prestige seems essential. We saw in 1957 that a great concentration of such prestige is not adequate in itself; but still there must be credibility about a man's assumption of the leading position. And he must also, in the ordinary course of events, have the necessary skill and experience in the required in-fighting and manipulation of the *apparat*.

Strictly speaking, Khrushchev was the only member of the Presidium who had all these qualities. We face, then, either a series of attempts to maintain collective leadership—a situation that is automatically unstable in Soviet conditions—*or* the calling in of fallen leaders with greater prestige, *or* the rather quick development of the necessary leadership qualities by one or other of the present contenders. Meanwhile, it is reasonable to view the succession period as one of instability.

The present situation differs in many important respects from that which followed Stalin's death in March, 1953. However, the events of that time are the only parallel we have, and some further examination of them must certainly prove fruitful. For the more the structure of power depends on one man, the more it is likely to be shaken when that one man is removed. On Khrushchev's departure, as after Stalin's, a power vacuum came into being. It is true that Stalin was by far the larger and more irreplaceable figure. But, on the other hand, there were then a number of figures of the second rank with long experience at the top and high prestige in the *apparat*, ready to move.

During Stalin's last months Malenkov and Khrushchev seem to have remained in the dictator's good books while Molotov and Beria were facing destruction. On March 6, 1953, immediately after Stalin's death, Malenkov and Beria took power. Beria, in circumstances that are not yet clear, had seized control of the police ministries from which Stalin had detached him over the previous two years, and flooded Moscow with MVD troops. There was no overt opposition to the changes in the ruling bodies which this duumvirate put through.

Molotov, who had been attacked by Stalin at the October, 1952, Plenum of the Central Committee, following the Nineteenth Congress, returned to number-three position, after Malenkov and Beria. He did not, however, have any political machine. Khrushchev suffered a notable defeat. His only close associate in the Secretariat, Brezhnev, was demoted to the post of head of the Political Department of the Navy, a derisory job. Khrushchev himself, while retaining the Party Secretaryship, was replaced in his First Secretaryship of Moscow Province by N. A. Mikhailov, who was certainly closer to Malenkov.

The Malenkov-Beria coup did not give them total power. It probably represented the maximum that they thought they could impose without producing violent attempts at resistance —if not in Moscow, then in military and political organizations elsewhere. If they had remained united, however, it is difficult to see how an opposition could have overcome them.

But the next thing to note is the tempo of development in these circumstances. The settlement of March 6, 1953, lasted a week. There is a strong presumption that Beria started at once to maneuver against Malenkov, and the settlement of March 14 in any case represented a new alignment of forces. Malenkov, while retaining the Premiership, was forced to give up the leading Secretaryship of the Party. At the same time (and only now), the cadres of Stalin's last phase were struck down. S. D. Ignatiev, who, though removed from the MGB, had been given a Party Secretaryship in recompense, was dismissed to the provinces amid obloquy. Ryumin, Vice-Minister at the MGB, was arrested. Aristov, responsible for the Party aspect of the purge, who had been head of the Party Organs Department of the Central Committee since October, 1952, and had remained a Party Secretary, was sent to a minor (and not even a Party) post in Siberia.

Thus, after Stalin's death, the operational apparatus of his direct agents was dismantled without the slightest trouble. In addition, his personal assistant, Poskrebyshev, was removed; ideologists of the period, including Chesnokov (the only one then a member of the Presidium) and Yuri Zhdanov, were dismissed to obscurity. Later, Stalin's special appointees to local power, Mgeladze in Georgia and Melnikov in the Ukraine, were also removed. The apparently strong positions held by many of these men proved quite incapable of protecting them once their patron disappeared. With the removal of Malenkov from the Secretariat, Khrushchev became the leading Party Secretary. At this stage, this did not appear to give him very great powers. The key Party Organs side of the Secretariat was in the hands of Malenkov's closest associate, Shatalin. Khrushchev was usually named fourth or fifth in the seniority listings of the Presidium. No members of the Secretariat but himself were on the Presidium, and power seemed to be concentrated largely in the State machinery.

In fine, the situation in 1953 provides us with certain lessons. In the first place, the first few weeks, and even the first few months, saw a particular fluidity, as the forces at work took stock of each other's strength and settled down to their positions for the longer pull. Secondly, during this period of instability, there was no question of any certainty as to results. All depended on individual decisions which might have been made differently. The Beria-Malenkov regime might have tried to destroy its enemies before itself splitting, rather than after. Later, Beria might well have seized power, as he was accused of plotting to do. And thirdly, there was no reason, at least until September, 1953, for making a correct forecast as to the eventual winner, Khrushchev, let alone for imagining that he would be able, within four years, to rid himself of virtually all his rivals of the moment.

The next phase of the struggle lasted until Beria's fall in June, 1953, again a short period. But the succession question as such was not settled until June, 1957; in fact, there was a long period in which various combinations (and some more beneficial than others from a Western point of view) remained possible. The prime condition for this sort of long struggle seems to be that no logical and natural successor who stands head and shoulders above his colleagues is available; that, on the contrary, the five or six leading figures have more or less equal claims, powers, and skill in maneuver. If we compare this with the present position, we shall certainly conclude that things are similar in the post-Khrushchev period.

Post-Stalin events may remind us also that the recent *coup d'état* is a normal procedure in Soviet political conditions, and that more may be expected. In the crisis of March, 1953, Malenkov and Beria presented the Central Committee with a *fait accompli* which it accepted under pressure of events. Again, in June, 1953, Beria was, if we are to credit the official account, planning a seizure of power. The latest reference to this, in a speech by Khrushchev on March 8, 1963, contained an admission that there was at the time "grave danger" of his succeeding.

Yet again, in the political crisis of June, 1957, the decisive point is said to have been an open threat by Zhukov that troops would move only in obedience to him—and not therefore on the orders of his constitutional superiors, Bulganin's Council of Ministers or the Presidium. This is plausible, and even if the report is not accurate, there can be no doubt that the Army's stand was most influential.

Moreover, Shelepin's speech to the Twenty-second Congress referred to armed maneuver on the part of the Anti-Party Group, with Bulganin ordering the Kremlin Guard to isolate the Presidium. In fact, when showdowns occur, the question of actual fighting is at least on the agenda. And even if it were not to come to that in Moscow itself, it is not inconceivable that a purely political coup in the capital might be resisted elsewhere by arms. We can by no means even exclude the notion of a group of Central Committee members, like the minority of cardinals during the Great Schism, decamping to Leningrad or Kiev and electing an anti-Presidium!

As we have implied, in the post-Stalin succession crisis, a handful of leaders had so much more experience, confidence, and prestige than the rank and file of the Central Committee that the possibility of their own early rise could hardly have occurred to any of the latter. But when the leading contenders are a Brezhnev or a Kosygin, there are a score or so, at the very least, of officials who only a few years ago ranked with them or above them and are unlikely to think of them as in any way their superiors. The thought must be natural that the way to the top is now open, or might be open, to any ambitious provincial secretary.

As Finlay, in his *History of the Byzantine Empire*, wrote of a Byzantine ruler: "He had risen to the highest rank without rendering himself remarkable either for his valour or his ability; the successful career of Romanus therefore excited . . . the ambition of every enterprising officer."

In dealing with the membership of the present Presidium and Secretariat, we should always keep in mind the fact that over the past six or seven years membership of these bodies has been precarious, and that they contain a number of men whose advancement over their contemporaries is recent and unlikely to be thought of as part of the established nature of things by either their seniors or their juniors.

Moreover, in these shifting circumstances, a condition obtains that was nonexistent in Stalin's time—the fact that a number of extremely prominent former members of the leadership are still "available," particularly Molotov and Malenkov. An examination of the prospects of their return to power leads to the conclusion that a faction engaged in a difficult struggle might possibly attempt to bring back one or the other, under control, to give itself greater weight. The other element with some perspectives is the Army—if it is again brought into play, as it was in 1953–57, as a card in the interfactional struggle, and if it can contrive this time to retain its freedom of action.

It is sometimes asserted that the generation of Brezhnev and Kosygin is the first to have no responsibility for the Stalinist terror. This is true only in the very limited sense that none of them were members of the highest bodies, bearing direct responsibility on a national scale during the Yezhovshchina of

1936–38. But even the youngest were in posts of definite responsibility during 1952–53, a period of ruthless oppression about which the very best that can be said is that it was not as bad as the blood purge of the 1930's—and the senior ones held posts in the highest bodies of Stalin's Party and Government. A Polish Communist poet, who was in Moscow at the time, called the essentials of the period "fascization, demoralization, and careerism."*

But even more significant is the fact that the present leaders obtained promotion from rank-and-file membership of the Party precisely at the time of the Great Purge itself. They were, in fact, the Stalinist generation proper. In *The Accused*,† his book on his experiences in the Ukraine during the Great Purge, Alexander Weissberg describes a situation in industry that parallels in all essentials what was going on in the Party. All the directors of the big foundries were arrested. A few months later, their successors followed them. It was only the third or fourth batch that kept their posts. "They had not even the normal advantages of youth in their favor, for the choosing had been a very negative one. They were the men who had denounced others on innumerable occasions. They had bowed the knee whenever they had come up against higher authority. They were morally and intellectually crippled." Such, in the political field even more perhaps than in the economic, was the origin of the cadre that now rules Russia.

This cadre, with all the "facelessness" that has been noted of it in its lower manifestations, presents itself at the highest level in the form of individual politicians. In fact, the Soviet Union is par excellence the country where rulers—once they are out of the way—are accused of the "cult of personality." The whole system is adjusted to one-man dictatorship, or a

* W. Woroszylski, in *Nowa Kultura*, November 13, 1956.
† New York: Simon and Schuster, 1951.

struggle for power among a handful of contestants. If we are to catalogue the possibilities of Soviet politics as they are at present, we are driven to examining, as far as we can, the records and reputations of a number of candidates for power.

When General Sherman learned, on July 18, 1864, that Hood had been appointed to command the enemy army, he called in two of his army commanders who had been in the same class as Hood at West Point and consulted them about the character of his new opponent. Their views were sound, and Sherman nearly met disaster from not realizing quite how sound they were. The question was of Hood's personal style—boldness and initiative. Strategy and politics may not be entirely comparable. But the more political decisions depend on one or a few men, the more the individual style, prejudices, and background of the individual leaders count.

Regarding the extent to which a man seems to have given to those around him the impression of possessing leadership qualities, we are dealing with what is largely an intangible. For political prestige and reputation are not things that can be easily analyzed from factual statements and public speeches. Comments like those by Nikolai Gavrilov, though only a personal opinion representing gossip in Moscow intellectual circles, are nevertheless more significant than official statements about a "devoted Leninist and distinguished fighter for the cause of Communism," which is the staple of announcements of awards to these people on their more important birthdays:

> Everyone also knows that Khrushchev is a total empiricist, a dull man, entirely engrossed in his immediate affairs; they know, too, that this is definitely inadequate for the leadership of a civilized nation. This is talked about (and what a huge difference it makes!), but nowhere, not in a single line of a newspaper, magazine, or book, not even in an unprinted manuscript, can one read anything but panegyrics to Khrushchev. As for the

> other leaders, Brezhnev is a lecherous toady, Suslov an anonymous illiterate, Ilychev a fool, and Kozlov a mean coward. Again, a lot of people know this, but no one dares mention it in public.*

This is, indeed, not an intra-Party view, which would have different criteria; but for all that, it is not to be regarded as wholly nonsignificant.

In giving the names of those among the current leadership who have to any degree established themselves as worth consideration in terms of the succession, we are registering general impressions. It is only when we come to consider the prospects in terms of affiliations and connections with the power machinery that we return from the sphere of the comparatively subjective. But this is not to say, by any means, that these general reputations lack political weight; on the contrary, they are precisely the factor that more often than not decides as between candidates for leadership in a faction or party.

The present Presidium-and-Secretariat is not in itself of such indisputably superior metal compared with the rank and file of the Central Committee as to compel the belief that its members will form the exclusive source of the regimes that follow Khrushchev. Nevertheless, it seems likely for institutional reasons that the *immediate* succession will emerge from it. So, if only for form's sake, it will be worth very briefly considering all those concerned before going on to treat the more serious contenders at greater length. And even apart from their current positions, its members form a rewarding cross-section of the Party's leading cadres.

If we simply divide the present Presidium into those who have come up entirely in Khrushchev fiefs, on the one hand, and all the remaining members on the other, we find Brezhnev, Podgorny, Kirilenko, and Shelest in the first category, and Mikoyan, Suslov, Kosygin, Shvernik, Shelepin, and Voronov

* "Letter from a Soviet Writer," *The New Leader*, December 9, 1963.

in the second. Polyansky, who began with the Ukrainian Party and later (1954–55) came under it again, may be considered a borderline case.

The front-runners seem to be Brezhnev, Kosygin, Podgorny, Polyansky, Suslov, Shelepin, and perhaps Voronov. Of the other full members of the Presidium, we may be inclined to rule out Mikoyan for his Armenian-trade background, although he is still a possible Premier in case of a deadlock, and Shvernik for age and incapacity or unimpressiveness; and we might say that Kirilenko seems rather hard to envisage at the top, as Ukrainian, junior, and generally unimpressive—and Shelest even more so. (Kirilenko has been closely associated not only with Khrushchev but also with Brezhnev, under whom he served in the 1940's at Zaporozhe, and whom he later succeeded as First Secretary at Dnepropetrovsk.*)

Of the candidate-members, V. V. Grishin has background and an increasing credibility. He was (unlike the two last named) a member of the 1952 Central Committee, and served as Second Secretary in Moscow Province (though Khrushchev passed him over for his junior, Furtseva, when it came to promotion). Efremov (though also a member of the 1952 CC) appears to be facing a threat to his position. P. N. Demichev, the latest promotion, is a man who cannot be written off. Although his background is industrial, he has penetrated high in the Moscow Party apparatus, politically speaking, and he is young.

The other three candidates may be summed up as follows: V. P. Mzhavanadze—Georgian, come-lately; K. T. Mazurov—Belorussian, local experience only; Sh. R. Rashidov—decora-

* He was made a candidate-member of the Presidium in June, 1957. At the Twenty-second Party Congress, in 1961, he was dropped, but only a few months later this decline was suddenly more than reversed, and he received a double promotion—to full membership. This was at the same time that Kozlov's closest associate, Spiridonov, was suddenly removed from the Secretariat to which he had been elected at the Congress, and it certainly reflected a turn in the struggle.

tive, Asian. Of the Secretariat, apart from those already named, we may similarly remark that the only pure politician is V. N. Titov, who has run the Party Organs Department of the Central Committee, and who comes from the Ukraine as one of Khrushchev's *apparat* administrators. Ilychev, in spite of his current prominence, is simply an Agitprop type, suitable perhaps as a successor to Suslov if required; B. N. Ponomarev and Yu. V. Andropov, too, are primarily ideological administrators (of foreign Communism); Rudakov is an economic specialist administrator, at present junior in status, capable of promotion in principle, like Voznessensky or Saburov in their time, but again an unlikely candidate for decisive political power. Of present high officials of the State machine not represented in the top Party bodies, the most impressive is Vice-Premier D. F. Ustinov; he was Stalin's Minister of the Armaments Industry and a member of the 1952 Central Committee.

Those who have fallen from power in the last six years are for the most part not to be considered seriously. But they include N. G. Ignatov, A. B. Aristov, and A. I. Kirichenko, all formerly influential. There are signs that Ignatov may be promoted again. His career has consisted of a series of promotions and demotions since 1939, when he first became a member of the Central Committee. He is a hidebound old *apparatchik*, and was a Secretary of the Central Committee in Stalin's last months. Of the Anti-Party Group, only Molotov and Malenkov merit really serious consideration, even though one should point out that Pervukhin, Saburov, and even Bulganin—the three who have not been expelled from the Party—could give weight or experience to a regime that required them. And finally, Marshal Zhukov, in his special position, reminds us that the Army is still a potential source of power.

For the immediate future, then, we have to consider only a handful of probable names. That is not to say that others may not have influence, or that surprises are impossible. It is not to deny the possibility of the sudden revival of some old veteran like Andreyev or the rise of some younger unknown. But in the immediate crisis, there is little doubt that the main roles will be played by those we shall discuss.

Leonid Brezhnev, Khrushchev's third successive nominee as heir-apparent, and the one actually to succeed him as First Secretary of the Central Committee, has long been the name most often mentioned in discussion of the succession problem. There are many advantages on his side, at least as compared with a very poor field. Nevertheless, he has made little impression on Russia or on the Party. One Russian is reported to have commented on his accession, "All I know about Brezhnev is that he has beetling eyebrows." And there is no doubt that he is continuing to produce this rather anonymous effect. He seems a main source of the feeling summed up by the correspondent of *Le Monde: "Un style pésant et embarrassé a succedé à la fantaisie desordonée qui marquait l'ancien direction.*" ("A heavy and constrained style has succeeded the disordered fantasy which marked the former leadership.")

There are various ways in which a country can be ruled, and something numbly rational would be an improvement after the paranoia of Stalin and the mania of Khrushchev. Nevertheless, Brezhnev's lack of experience in having to project a public persona, to perform even the limited demagogy that passes for "public" politics in the U.S.S.R., may be a handicap. And such considerations apply even more to the other faceless men who lie in reserve.

These are intangibles. The facts of Brezhnev's career show us another facet—the long-service Party machine man.

He was born in the Ukraine in 1906, but is a Russian. After working in agricultural administration through the collectivization terror, he became a Party member in 1931 and was sent for five years to the Metallurgical Institute. In May, 1937, as the purges struck, he was made Deputy Mayor of Dneprodzerzhinsk, and in 1938 became head of a department in the Dnepropetrovsk Provincial Committee, and in 1939 a Secretary of that Committee. We have seen how Khrushchev was purging the Party in the Ukraine at that time; Brezhnev was among his wave of promotions to the emptied posts.

From 1941 to 1945, he served in Army political posts, on Khrushchev's Military Council of the Stalingrad Front, and elsewhere. After the war he served as Provincial First Secretary—at Zaporozhe and Dnepropetrovsk. And in 1950, after a brief period in the Central Committee apparatus in Moscow, he attained one of the highest positions then within Khrushchev's gift (subject to Stalin's approval), the Republican First Secretaryship in Moldavia. This first rise, under the auspices of both the now rejected leaders, culminated in October, 1952, when he became a Secretary of the Central Committee of the CPSU, and a candidate-member of the Presidium. On Stalin's death, he had what is retrospectively to be seen as the good fortune of being removed to the junior post of Head of the Political Administration of the Navy, being unwelcome to the Malenkov-Beria regime. He made his return to power via Kazakhstan, under Khrushchev's auspices, and was back as a candidate-member of the Presidium in February, 1956, being promoted to full membership in June, 1957. Since then, he has served near the top, gradually gaining as his superiors fell.

He is, in fact, senior in Party experience and promotion to any of the post-Khrushchev leaders who have had the necessary *apparat* background (even including Kozlov). In the absence of any more impressive figure, his claims are high.

Brezhnev has a single disadvantage: His career is purely and solely a history of dependence on Khrushchev. In so far as most of the *apparat* seem to have shown themselves restive under Khrushchevite rule, there must be at least some reservations about Brezhnev among his colleagues and subordinates.

Nevertheless, he spoke with more restraint and caution than other Khrushchevites in recent years on most of the issues before the leadership. With adequate concessions, he might be acceptable. And he has evidently been making these concessions for some time now, and preparing a semi-independent position.

Brezhnev appears to be a typical product of the Party machine of Stalin's time. He has become associated with ideas of reform only through the accident that he rose in the fiefs controlled by Khrushchev and owed his advancement to this connection. This brought him, by accident as it were, into the political and economic schemes of the First Secretary. Just the same, this has had two significant effects: He has perforce identified himself with the Khrushchevite policies, and such identification has its influence on the political habits of the man concerned. Secondly, he has been put into a position where he has been able to—has almost been forced to—learn something of the economic and other necessities. How far these lessons and experiences have been effective in counteracting the normal instincts and prejudices of an old *apparatchik* remains to be seen.

The considerations affecting Brezhnev during the period before Khrushchev's removal must have been various and compelling. That he owed his career to Khrushchev is clear from the record. And there can be no doubt that in the past support for Khrushchev had been a necessary part of his career. But during the years 1962–64 other factors intervened. First, Khrushchev's policies were producing failures more frequently and in more fields simultaneously than ever. Certain other policies, which were technically not failures but indicated a frivolous attitude to Party theory and custom—such as the use of literary "liberalization" in the campaign to denigrate the Stalinist past—were arousing evident resentment among that section of the leadership which did not owe its position to

Khrushchev. While it is possible that complete solidarity of Brezhnev and the other Khrushchevites on Khrushchev's side would have enabled the First Secretary to hold power indefinitely, it could only have been at the expense of increasing ill-feeling on the part of the old-line *apparat*. This might even, given some new and particularly exasperating piece of irresponsibility on Khrushchev's part, have led to an explosion. At any rate, on Khrushchev's death, which might not have been long delayed, such feeling would very probably have proved uncontainable by surviving Khrushchevites, and might have led to their being swept away in the reaction. How much more prudent for Brezhnev to build his bridges in advance, to extricate himself from the stigma of Khrushchevism, and to arrange a settlement with the old-line members adequate to establish himself firmly for the ensuing struggle.

Moreover, we need not assume any particular affection for the details of Khrushchevite policies among Khrushchev's own faction. Any faction gets attached to the policies on which its coming to power has centered. But those of Khrushchev were so personal, and so continuously variable, that this sort of solidarity probably played a lesser part than is usual in the circumstances. And Brezhnev seems to have shown a particular restraint and lack of enthusiasm for many of the Khrushchevite policies of the past few years.

Even those with no enthusiasm for Brezhnev were in the position of needing him, at almost any price, if they were to get rid of Khrushchev. Once Khrushchev had gone, of course, the lists were open again. And Brezhnev's leading position was an advantage to him, but not one that could not be destroyed in later maneuvers by his competitors—just as with Malenkov in 1954. But that remains to be seen.

As a ruler, Brezhnev might be expected to stand for a rather slower version of the Khrushchevite method, with rational economic reform. But his position would involve instability and maneuvering at least for some years, if he lasted that long.

ALEXEI KOSYGIN was born in 1904, served in the Civil War, and joined the Party in 1927. Beginning in 1935, he went through the Leningrad Textile Institute, and then was appointed director of a factory in 1937, when he also became a member of a district Party bureau. In July, 1938, he was named to head the industrial-transport section of the Leningrad Party, and in October, 1938, was made Mayor. In fact, he made his career under the patronage of Zhdanov in Leningrad when, in the late 1930's, the old cadres had been destroyed. He served in economic ministries thereafter, but also as Premier of the R.S.F.S.R. from 1943 to 1946. He was promoted to candidate-member of Stalin's Politburo in 1946 and full member in 1948. He survived the purge of the Zhdanovites in 1949–50, but has always been regarded since then as in some degree a "Leftist." (Actually, the Zhdanovites were, it will be remembered, *economic* modernizers in their time; Voznessensky seems, even, to have in some degree anticipated the Liberman Proposals.) Although a full member of the old Politburo, Kosygin was only a candidate-member of the large Presidium of 1952–53 and lost high Party position in the post-Stalin reorganization, while remaining Minister. But even his combination of some hostility to the Malenkov attitudes and his long status as a high figure in the Party did not ensure him a very enthusiastic acceptance by Khrushchev. In June, 1957, although he opposed the Anti-Party Group, he was promoted only to candidate-membership of the Presidium; and despite his long economic experience, he ranked only as Deputy Premier, while the First Deputy Premier in charge of economic affairs was Khrushchev's protégé, the unknown, low-grade I. I. Kuzmin. In fact, Kosygin only replaced Kuzmin as the head of Gosplan in March, 1959, during a shakeup that seems to have involved changes of doubtful advantage to Khrushchev in the machinery of power. And he was only promoted to full membership of the Presidium on May 4, 1960, at a time when Khrushchev's old *khvost* were either being thrown out entirely or were losing their places on the Secretariat, and shortly before the industrial reorganization (June 18, 1960), which to a considerable degree reversed Khrushchev's 1957 decentralization plan for industry.

We seem, in fact, to find in Kosygin a politically (though *not* economically) "conservative" type whose relations with Khrushchev and the Khrushchev congeries have been at best tepid on both sides. And from the point of view of length of service and prominence in the public eye, he is certainly in a better position than most of his present-day colleagues. Nevertheless, though a member, he was never a prominent member of Stalin's Politburo. His associations have always been with light industry, notoriously a sphere carrying little weight. He has not had any serious connection with the Party apparatus. But one can certainly see him as one of the two or three most important figures over the succession period. His position is considerably stronger than those of most others at the top. His experience is vast. And his administrative and economic ability is unrivaled among the present leaders.

Nikolai Podgorny is another product of Khrushchev's Ukrainian machine, although his early career saw important absences from the republic. Born in 1903, he joined the Party in 1930, worked as an engineer in Ukrainian sugar factories from 1931 to 1937, and in 1939 was made Deputy Commissar for the food industry in the Ukraine. From 1940 to 1942, he held a similar post in the Central Government in Moscow, and remained there as Director of the Technological Institute of the Food Industry until 1944, when he went back to his old post in the Ukraine. From 1946 to 1950, he was back in Moscow as permanent representative of the Ukrainian Government with the Central Government, his first truly political post and one in which, during the dingdong struggle for power in the Ukraine in 1947, he seems to have offended no one, least of all the victor, Khrushchev. In 1950, when Khrushchev had come to Moscow, Podgorny was sent back to the Ukraine in his first Party post, First Secretary of the Kharkov Provincial Committee, a key position. He was not elected to the Central Committee in 1952, but he did make the lesser Revision Commission. In 1953, however, when Kirichenko was promoted to First Secretary in the Ukraine, Podgorny became Second Secretary. When Kirichenko went to Moscow in 1957, Podgorny became First Secretary of the Ukrainian Party. In May, 1958, he became a candidate-member of the Presidium, and in May, 1960, a full member. At the January, 1961, Plenum of the Central Committee, he was severely heckled by Khrushchev for agricultural failures, but he was then handsomely forgiven at the Twenty-second Congress, in October. Brought to Moscow as a member of the Secretariat in June, 1963, he has since figured prominently at the center, enough to put him, in principle, among the leading contenders. But this recent promotion seems to lack ballast. Neither his experience nor his general reputation seems adequate, as yet; any qualifications he may have are held, in greater degree, by Brezhnev.

There is now much talk of his power and his future. Almost anything is *possible* in Soviet politics. All the same, it is difficult as yet to see Podgorny as a serious contender for the highest posts, or at least for more than the most ephemeral tenure in them. It is true that for the moment he ranks fourth or fifth among the leading figures. And Khrushchev seems to have destined him for higher things. But Khrushchev, as we know, often made mistakes, and it seems hard to imagine the veteran cadres accepting an oldish man who did not belong to the Central Committee at all in 1952. (It should be noted that he does not thereby escape any stigma of Stalinism, since he served in posts requiring the approval of Stalin as well as of the other fallen leader, Khrushchev.) And this is to leave aside the general improbability of the *apparat* as a whole putting up with a Ukrainian pure and simple. We may note, too, that Podgorny seems to have made the last great eulogy of Khrushchev, and to have been absent from Moscow when his overthrow was being planned. We may speculate, even, that Brezhnev was particularly suspicious of Podgorny, as the Khrushchevite number-two man who was to replace him as he had replaced Kirichenko. Such a feeling might indeed have been one of Brezhnev's key motives in defecting from Khrushchev's side. However, the whole question of Podgorny's future is bound up with the future of the Ukrainian Party machine, which he is now showing signs of trying to win for the reactionaries.

ALEXANDER SHELEPIN was promoted to the Presidium after the fall of Khrushchev. At forty-six, he is its youngest member. We have already summarized his career under Stalin—one of trusted service in the Komsomol from 1940, as one of the Secretaries of that body's Central Committee from 1943, and as its First Secretary in 1952. That is, he was selected by Stalin for the leadership of an organization remarkable even among Soviet organizations as the training ground for informers and bullies. Its earlier leader, Kosarev, purged in 1938, is now officially reported to have lost his life because he failed Stalin in the task of turning his movement into an auxiliary of the secret police. At the November, 1962, Plenum of the Party's Central Committee, it was asserted that in Stalin's time "the very first task of all Komsomol education work was the necessity to seek out and recognize the enemy, who had then to be removed purely forcibly, by methods of economic pressure, organizational-political isolation, and methods of physical destruction."

To have been highly satisfactory to Stalin over a period of years, and to be appointed to such a position just in the period when the old dictator was tightening up, selecting his cadres, and generally preparing for another blood bath, is a sure sign that Shelepin's ruthlessness and devotion to the Stalin system were impeccable. It is not, of course, to say that he is incapable of adjusting dogma to the tactical and economic necessities.

He continued in the leadership of the Komsomol until 1956, when he became head of the Party Organs Department of the Central Committee, always a power post of high potentiality. In 1958, he was appointed head of the KGB, succeeding Serov. Having held these most sensitive executive positions, he was then made Secretary of the Party Central Committee, and in the autumn of 1962 he was installed as head of the powerful Party-State Control Committee. While still holding this disciplinary and administrative post, he was appointed Vice-Premier as well as Party Secretary—the only man, except Khrushchev himself, to hold high rank in both Party and State.

Shelepin is not one of those who came up in any of the machines controlled by Khrushchev. At the same time, like many others, he served Khrushchev satisfactorily and efficiently, until the moment when he presumably threw his influence to the anti-Khrushchev conspirators. His background is of single-minded devotion to the traditional methods of Party rule. He differs from the run of the higher-level *apparatchiks* in that he put in no time in provincial secretaryships, but came to the center at an early age to work in the Party's youth auxiliary. Nevertheless, he seems a typical and trusted member of the old *apparat*, and may be presumed to represent the weight of the old Party against the Ukrainian upstarts. (He is himself a Russian from Voronezh.) His youth gives him a great advantage in the succession struggle, especially when combined with experience and seniority in many ways greater than Polyansky's, for example. His skills as a second-level executive of the policies and wishes of others has long been evident, and now that he is at last in the top body, he can certainly be seen as a formidable competitor.

He has the further advantage that all his posts have been administrative. That is, unlike the careers of those who have had to deal with economic problems, there was no built-in probability of failure in any of his work, and unlike those concerned with ideology, there was at least less chance of theoretical deviation. We may nevertheless note that his first work in the Komsomol was as a propagandist, and that he is a graduate of the History, Philosophy, and Literature Institute. In other words, his training was in orthodoxy, and he showed himself a brilliant exponent of it, at a time when Stalin was carrying out his final selection of terrorists and justifiers of terror, in the late 1930's.

DMITRY POLYANSKY is widely regarded as one of the most dynamic and efficient of the Soviet leaders, as well as being one of the youngest. Although he has been described almost universally as a "Khrushchevite," we must to some extent temper this, on two counts.

First, although originating in the Ukraine, and living in the late 1930's in Kharkov, where (in 1939) he joined the Party and worked in the local Komsomol, after his discharge from military service in 1941 he served first in Siberia; then (1945–49) in the central *apparat*, where he worked in the personnel administration; and then (1949–55) in the Crimea. It is true that the Crimea became part of the Ukraine in 1954, but this second and last Ukrainian connection is a slight one compared with those of the "Ukrainians" of the Khrushchevite patronage proper. From 1955 to 1958, he was First Secretary of

Provincial Committees in the R.S.F.S.R. He became a member of the Central Committee for the first time in 1956, and may for this reason be regarded as part of the Khrushchevite promotion. But Khrushchev was at this time promoting young *apparatchiks* not only from his own direct following—potential allies rather than actual followers.

There is no doubt that Polyansky played a vigorous role in support of Khrushchev against the Anti-Party Group in June, 1957; Enver Hoxha particularly mentioned his intrigues in favor of the First Secretary.* But to have been on Khrushchev's side against that group is not in itself to demonstrate "Khrushchevite" sympathies greater than those of any others of the present leadership, who all took the same view (as, indeed, did Marshal Zhukov!). In general, Polyansky's speeches have shown a certain amount of independence—for example, on the issue of the Anti-Party Group. And, accepting the ability and skill with which he is credited as actual, it seems perfectly reasonable to think of him as one of the potential contenders—if not for the immediate succession, at least within the following months or years. His reported selection to make one of the key attacks at the time of Khrushchev's overthrow is significant. So is his age—forty-seven, far younger than any of the other major contenders except Shelepin. His present weakness is that he has no direct link to any of the Party mechanisms.

Gennady Voronov is much less of a front runner than any of those mentioned above. But he is worth considering here as representative of the second-level *apparatchiks*, whose participation or at least assent is probably required for the reasonably smooth operation of the leadership. He has never served in any of Khrushchev's fiefs. He was a member of Stalin's last Central

* Speech on the Anniversary of the Albanian Party of Labor and the October Revolution, *Zeri i Popullit*, November 8, 1961.

Committee, elected in 1952, when he was First Secretary in Chita Province. He then became Deputy Minister of Agriculture in 1955, but soon returned to the post of First Secretary, this time of Orenburg Province. His rise dates from 1961: He became a candidate-member of the Presidium in January, and after the Twenty-first Congress a full member and First Vice-Chairman of the Bureau for the R.S.F.S.R. This is the career of an old professional. The emphasis on agriculture probably should not be interpreted too narrowly. A provincial First Secretary who can produce adequate results in agriculture can, it might be said, do anything. Voronov is, in any case, a representative of the old, long-service *apparat*—a typical member, though doubtless more efficient than the ruck, of the scattered oligarchy which has ruled the great spaces of Russia proper for a generation. As with Polyansky, his speeches show a certain independence of approach. He has not, except recently, been associated with the central apparatus of power, and this is doubtless to some extent a handicap. But he is nevertheless an *apparatchik* by training, and one who might be acceptable at a high level to a large section of the old Party, while not alienating the modernizing element.

The much more important career of MIKHAIL SUSLOV has aroused a certain amount of ambiguous comment. Since 1947, when he became Secretary of the Central Committee, his interests appear to have been overwhelmingly "agitprop." That is, during this period, he has never had access to the instruments of power in the Party organization. It is also true that his very earliest role in the Party was as a propagandist and ideologist in the lesser Party organizations; in fact, he is commended in the Soviet Encyclopedia for his work in the 1930's against Trotskyist, Zinovievist, and Rightist deviationism. On this basis, he has been viewed, understandably, as ineligible for the leadership, because he is insufficiently experienced in the handling of the actual power mechanisms. Alternatively, as a presumed guardian of ideological purity, he has been thought of as a mainspring of opposition to deviation from old-fashioned rigor, and thereby a power behind the throne rather than a leader, a high priest rather than a king.

But, in the first place, Suslov has served many years in the organs of true power. In 1933–34, he was on a commission for purging the Party in various provinces. In 1937–39, through the terror, he was a Secretary of the Rostov Provincial Committee; perhaps this was as the Secretary concerned with propaganda, but in 1939–44, he served as *First* Secretary of the Stavropol Regional Committee. In this capacity, he certainly became involved in the struggle against Caucasian nationalism and the deportation of the Karachai nation for collaboration with the Germans. He performed so satisfactorily that at the end of 1944 he was named Chairman of the Bureau of the Central Committee for Lithuania—that is, the official responsible for the most ruthless reimposition of Soviet rule on a country bitterly resisting through a long-drawn-out partisan movement. These are not assignments for a merely ideological type. Moreover, it must have been success in these foul operations that led to his recall to responsible work in the Central Committee apparatus in March, 1946, and his appointment in 1947 to be Secretary of the Central Committee, a post he has held uninterruptedly since then.

Suslov, who became a full member of the Central Committee in 1941, attained membership of Stalin's Presidium in October, 1952. On Stalin's death, in March, 1953, he did not become even a candidate-member of the new, "small" Presidium, although his previous junior Ponomarenko held candidate-membership. A few anomalous listings of seniority at the time may indicate that there were attempts to promote him, but at the second reshuffle a week after the first, he was still not promoted, though retaining his ideological Secretaryship of the

Central Committee. It was not until July, 1955, that he was finally promoted to full membership of the Presidium. During the ensuing struggles, culminating in the attempt by the Anti-Party Group to remove Khrushchev in June, 1957, his position is not clear. He evidently sided with Khrushchev in the crisis in the final analysis, but there are indications that he wavered a little. The clash was far more one of rival power groups than of principle, and although there were thereafter no overt signs of any opposition on doctrinal grounds between Suslov and Khrushchev, continual rumors represented him as standing for a "reactionary" or even "Stalinist" line more or less hostile to the new course. It was noticeable at the Twenty-first Party Congress, in 1959, that he abstained from serious attack on the policies of the old Anti-Party Group, and even pointed out that the Congress had been called for economic reasons only, so that such matters were not on the agenda.

Khrushchev's reverses in 1962–63 are explicable only by the existence of a Presidial majority against his policies which must have included Suslov. But Suslov did not become an open rallying point of opposition until October, 1964, when he presented the main indictment against Khrushchev to the Central Committee. Although he took neither of the main power posts at this point, he ranked with the top four in Party listings. When his length of service in the top bodies and presumed prestige with the cadres are taken into account, it is no longer possible to dismiss his chances of leadership entirely, even granting the great handicap of his propagandist connections. In any case, he might be expected to play a significant role in forthcoming struggles.

We may note, incidentally, when the "technical" background of many of the current leaders is bruited about as though this signifies a down-to-earth, technocratic attitude, that Suslov, too, studied in the Moscow Institute of National Economy, the Industrial Academy, and similar institutions.

If Suslov's "agitprop" background is a handicap, we should add that there are other handicaps to supreme rule that are not on the face of it insuperable, but are generally accepted by students. Kaganovich's Jewish origins would in recent years have made him an impossible candidate. Similarly, it is almost universally felt that ANASTAS MIKOYAN, as an Armenian, has small chance of attaining power, even apart from his trade background. One of the strikes against Beria was that Russia could hardly be expected to bear another Georgian. Nevertheless, as we have said, it is not excluded that Mikoyan might become Prime Minister in circumstances of deadlock—and still less that he could continue to play a weighty secondary role in an unstable situation.

The ages of the potential successors is plainly of considerable relevance. If we look back, we find that Malenkov, whom Stalin had in effect confirmed as his successor in a most formal fashion by having him give the Report of the Central Committee at the Nineteenth Party Congress, was then fifty years old; he had in fact ranked as the number-two man since 1949–50, when he was forty-seven or forty-eight. Khrushchev's apparent nominations have been: in 1958–59, Kirichenko, born in 1908, and fifty to fifty-one years old at the relevant times; and in 1960–63, Kozlov, also born in 1908, and therefore fifty-two to fifty-three years old during his period as heir-apparent. For what these cases are worth, they seem to show a preference for a successor in the forty-five to fifty-five age group, with a reasonable expectation of useful ruling life. It is, of course, true that Malenkov was not able to secure his heritage; but this does not affect the argument about intent and the first chance. (Khrushchev, whom Stalin was also building up in the last year of his life, was born in 1894, and was thus fifty-nine at Stalin's death; Brezhnev was fifty-eight at the time of Khrushchev's overthrow.)

Before applying this consideration to the present contenders, we may list the dates of birth of certain relevant figures (including those not yet dealt with):

Shvernik	1888	Podgorny	1903	Shelest	1908
Molotov	1890	Kosygin	1904	Patolichev	1908
Khrushchev	1894	Pervukhin	1904	Voronov	1910
Mikoyan	1895	Pegov	1905	Rudakov	1910
Zhukov	1896	Brezhnev	1906	Grishin	1914
Malinovsky	1898	Kirilenko	1906	Mazurov	1914
Saburov	1900	Ilychev	1906	Andropov	1914
Malenkov	1902	Mikhailov	1906	Polyansky	1917
Suslov	1902	Titov	1907	Rashidov	1917
Mzhavanadze	1902	Kozlov	1908	Shelepin	1918

Taking age, then, as one of the factors involved in the succession, we can see that on this count Suslov and Podgorny are certainly disadvantaged, and that even Brezhnev and Kirilenko are not strengthened. Polyansky and Shelepin, twenty-three and twenty-four years younger than Khrushchev, respectively (Malenkov was twenty-two years younger than Stalin), are the men among the younger element who might be expected to benefit most.

Needless to say, all this is very much to be qualified by "other things being equal." Brezhnev's age handicap, such as it is, is probably more than compensated for by his experience and position. Kirilenko, the same age, would seem not to have such counterbalancing advantages. Polyansky, eleven years younger than Kirilenko, has served in the top bodies notably longer (and more uninterruptedly) than he; Polyansky's seniority and experience at the top are not perhaps sufficient yet to rank him among the immediate leading contenders, but this is a handicap that becomes less marked each year, and, even after the immediate post-Khrushchev crisis, he can afford to wait. To Shelepin, with his even greater experience, though a more recent arrival at the highest level, this applies equally strongly.

Such are a few considerations arising from the age factor. The reader might note the point as it affects other contenders, whom we shall consider in the next chapter.

Having dealt with personalities in a rather isolated manner, we should next say something more about the broader allegiances, interests, and connections affecting them.

Here we must distinguish between the post-Stalin and the post-Khrushchev crisis on another count. When Stalin died, there were various competing central apparatuses of power. Most obviously, Beria's police empire enjoyed a great measure of autonomy. And, in addition, the State machine was a force in its own right. The Army, too, though starting with less independence, contrived to build itself up into a genuine force in the land over the following years. Thus, the Party apparatus was far from omnipotent.

The Party machine under Stalin had defeated all other institutional interests by 1930. But Stalin then built up his own State machine and transferred many powers to it. This new "State" interest was defeated by 1957. But there are now some signs of a return to a balance. Anyhow, leaders have shifted to and fro between Party and State appointments, (e.g., Khrushchev himself, Brezhnev, Kozlov, Polyansky, Voronov, Shelepin), and the distinction between the two, except in certain special fields, has been blurred in a number of ways.

We should perhaps not exaggerate the effects of this unification. It does not, in any case, wholly curb the Army. Even the reduction to order of the police force might not prove complete in certain circumstances. And, clearly, something of the same argument applies to the other sides of the administrative machinery. Whether officially part of Party or State, their representatives must have a tendency to develop their own interests, and in certain circumstances might have divergent views and support divergent actions.

For within the Party apparatus, various local and personal interests have built up over the past years. Of these, Khrushchev's was much the most powerful. The removal of its founder does not automatically destroy and disperse it. Can the Khrushchevite faction, under new management, in fact survive the fall of its sponsor? As we have seen, Stalin's did not. That is, the group Stalin had in 1952 in charge of the technical levers of power—the MGB, the Party Organs Department, and the "Special Sector"—were unable to defend their positions.

Let us examine the groupings within the Party that are now a major organizational basis of faction. Primarily, we must consider local machines whose alumni have worked together over long periods.

A useful set of figures showing both the power and the prestige of the local organs can be found in the number of delegates to the Twenty-second Congress from the various Party organizations. Of the 4,408 full delegates, about half came from lower-level provinces and territories and republics of the R.S.F.S.R. Although their potential is enormous, these cannot, ordinarily speaking, be regarded as a bloc. The Ukrainian delegation of 783 can be so regarded. Moscow City, the next most powerful single group, sent 345; Leningrad, 199; Moscow Province, 124; Gorky, 87; Sverdlovsk, 86.*

The most important factor in the immediate struggle is the position of the Ukrainian machine. Until 1957, there was never more than one Ukrainian in the top bodies, and often not even one. There are now four. This is grossly disproportionate to the comparative population figures of the Ukraine and the rest of the Soviet Union (the republic has less than one-fifth of the total). It is also far from the proportion (less than a fifth) considered right for the Ukrainian Party machine in the size of its

* Report of the Credentials Commission of the Twenty-second Congress, *Pravda*, October 22, 1961.

delegation even to the Khrushchev-sponsored Party Congress. Moreover, these Ukrainians do not owe their position to seniority; it is precisely the four Ukrainians—Podgorny, Polyansky, Kirilenko, and Shelest—who are the four members of the Presidium not on the 1952 Central Committee. Nor has their interim record been more than mediocre—and certainly not so outstanding as to call for special promotion. (Polyansky, indeed, has not served in the Ukrainian Republic machine to any great extent, but even omitting him—particularly if we substitute Brezhnev, a Russian national but a veteran of the Ukrainian machine—the disproportion is remarkable.)

No, the representation of the Ukrainians was obtained because they were the cadres Khrushchev had personally built up over a dozen years in Kiev and continued to influence through his nominees thereafter. With the prospect of Khrushchev dying or resigning, the Ukrainians must have had to think of their future without his protection. During his ascendancy, he used them largely as instruments—votes in the Presidium and controllers of the lower levers of power—and often replaced them with scant amenity. Moreover, while utilizing them as a secure bloc, he did not rely on them exclusively; and by selecting or accepting Kozlov as his heir-apparent from 1961 to 1963, he showed little inclination to be too careful about protecting them after his death or departure.

Brezhnev is the only product of the Ukrainian machine with seniority and significant political experience. It is possible that he would see the difficulty of relying solely on an association that is bound to provoke hostility. And he seems over the years already to have made himself personally more acceptable to a wider circle of the Party. There is reasonable evidence or presumption that Brezhnev, Kosygin, Suslov, Polyansky, and Voronov were involved in the conspiracy against Khrushchev. There is no such evidence implicating the two other "Ukrainians"—Podgorny and Kirilenko.

On the other hand, there were good reasons to obtain Ukrainian support for the coup. The firmer the vote in the Presidium, the more unimpugnable the victory. And, more important, the lesser Ukrainians at the levers of power—especially Semichastny at the KGB—were worth neutralizing. So, even if the Ukrainians were not included in the original plot, there would be every motive to secure their acceptance of the coup.

In any case, regardless of Brezhnev's personal position, the Ukrainian alliance retains its posts and, by the logic of Soviet politics, is compelled to fight to defend itself or face reduction to, at best, its old prominence. The changes made at the Central Committee Plenum of November, 1964, saw the promotion of Shelest to full membership of the Presidium, as a balance to Shelepin. At the same time, eight candidate-members of the Central Committee were promoted to full membership of that body, and these included Semichastny and Epishev. It is true that their practical power had long made them eligible for the higher rank, but at least this post-Khrushchev promotion showed that they still came under high protection and were in political favor.

Yet how can the Ukrainians remain in their anomalously powerful position, no longer as the executives and followers of a single dominant figure, but in their own right, as it were? The natural pressures of the Party *aktiv* as a whole would certainly reduce them to their pre-Khrushchev position if allowed to operate freely. They are in the position, therefore, of being compelled to combat this tendency by political *force majeure*. Whether Brezhnev finds himself having to go along with them or not, this is clearly an element productive of great instability in the highest levels. For the moment, a balance or compromise is in being. But in the long run, severe trouble seems inevitable. For the non-Ukrainian element must wish at least for the reduction of Ukrainian representation and the removal of some of the Ukrainians at the less essential levers of power. But once such concessions were made, the Ukrainians would become so weak that they would be unable to protect themselves against further erosion of their position.

Could a Ukrainian combination grouping, relying on Titov and Semichastny at the levers, really become the dominating power in the State? It is hard to see how such a clique could rid the ruling bodies of other elements whom even Khrushchev was unable to eliminate—or, if they could, it would appear to be the most precarious and tentative of solutions. It would not be impossible for Podgorny, say, to come to power on the basis of the present strength of the Ukrainian machine. But it would be, in a sense, an act of desperation, and would leave him particularly open to abrupt overthrow. In fact, if such a Podgorny regime ever came to power, we could certainly take it as a sign of extreme dislocation at the top level, of a further disintegration of the stabilizing factors in Soviet politics.

In the short run, we may perhaps see a Ukrainian bid for power. But, despite the size and unity of the Ukrainian element, it may be doubted, for reasons of political psychology, that it could ever actually establish itself as the leading force in the CPSU. For, just as the Soviet *apparat* in general regards outside parties with hearty superiority, so the Ukrainian has always been viewed as a second-line, peripheral, vaguely unreliable Party—and, in addition, one whose claim to represent its own people is notoriously even less credible than that of any local Party in the Union, with the exception of the Baltic States. Moreover, if the swing against the Ukrainians were strong, we might find their solidarity less impressive than it now appears. For if they are held together by the extent of their common interests as against the remainder of the *apparat*, still there are evidently disputes and feuds within the Ukraine itself. If heavy pressure were being put on them and the idea of an alternative Ukrainian leadership more friendly to a new center sprang up, it is at least possible that some of those leaders who have declined any power in recent years, such as Kalchenko and Korotchenko, might offer themselves as alternatives. Moreover, to some degree the attachment of at least the older Ukrainian cadres to a particular political program is accidental—Podgorny is already showing reactionary trends.

The idea of a "Leningrad Group" in the leadership has often been put forward in recent years. It has usually been rather confused by attributing membership in it to everyone in the leadership who has ever been associated with the city—Kozlov, who worked in its apparatus from 1948 until 1957, and who really seems to have built up something of a power base there, but also Kosygin, who has not served there since the 1930's, and Aristov and N. G. Ignatov, whose connection was even more tenuous. What such men really had in common during the years after the defeat of Khrushchev's opponents in 1957 was not the positive one of an organizational allegiance, but the negative one of not having risen through machines controlled by Khrushchev.

In a narrower sense, however, we can speak of the Leningrad machine under Kozlov as providing a center for a non-Khrushchevite cadre—such as Spiridonov, Kozlov's successor as First Secretary in the city, who became Secretary of the Central Committee at the Party Congress in 1961, when Kozlov himself was taking official precedence for the first time as second man in the Party, but who fell the following spring. Certain other Leningraders were given important positions at the center at this time. N. N. Rodionov went to the Second Secretaryship in Kazakhstan, which had provided Brezhnev his springboard to power; A. I. Popov and V. N. Novikov got ministerial posts; Vorobiev became head of the Party agricultural department for the Russian Republic; Shikin went to the Deputy Chairmanship of the Union Republics Party Organs Department.

Nevertheless, such positions did not compare with the crop

reaped by the Ukrainians. More important was the ideological leadership of the conservative tendency which Kozlov and his closest allies now assumed. These men always attacked Malenkov, the more "progressive" member of the 1957 Anti-Party Group, with particular virulence, while the main emphasis of the Khrushchevite tendency was focused on Molotov. Similarly, Kozlov defended the extreme emphasis on Party control in literature which had originally been put forward by Leningrad's last significant leader, Andrei Zhdanov. In general, the Leningrad machine came to represent the resistance to Khrushchev at a time when that resistance was dominated by the conservative attitudes. A very likely "Leningrader" is Vorobiev.

In the most recent period, the Leningrad organization seems to have lost its superior position. This was partly a personal matter. With Kozlov's stroke and long illness, there was no longer a figure of sufficient seniority associated with the city. And Khrushchev's successors, as we have seen, have not taken the "conservative" line. However, Kozlov's removal in November, 1964, was conducted with great politeness. It may seem to leave no representation of the most traditionalist elements in the top bodies. But in a struggle their voices might once again carry weight.

The Moscow organization presents some queries. Khrushchev's recent control of it was far shorter than his rule in the Ukraine (1950–53), and although he purged its top leadership thoroughly in 1950, he did not do a full-scale, root-and-branch job. Various other considerations make it seem that though his cadre continues to rule the city and the province and to deliver its vote, it is not so firmly in control as its Ukrainian equivalent. Moreover, it seems to have revolted even as early as 1959, when the removal of the local First Secretary, Kapitonov, and another member of the bureau, who had evidently taken an unwelcome line at the Twenty-first Congress, showed inadequate Khrushchevization.

In any case, with Khrushchev's removal, whatever loyalty or dependency tied the Moscow organization to him no longer applied between them and the veterans of his quite different machine in the Ukraine. The promotion of Demichev in November, 1964, to candidate-membership of the Presidium brought a Moscow product into the top body (in which there is now no Leningrader) to join Grishin, though there has been no Moscow full member since Furtseva fell in 1961.

But the Moscow Party is in any case closely tied up with members of centralized organizations represented in the capital and has never had the clear-cut individuality of the Leningrad Party. So it is perhaps more appropriate to view the non-Ukrainian element as now no longer spearheaded by any particular organization or committed to any particular "conservatism" of the recent Leningrad type. Rather, it would include a wide range, both organizationally and doctrinally, who would all be united on one issue only—not to let the upstarts from Kiev maintain or increase their power.

All this is to assert again the basic point: that struggle continues. For it is clear that the frictions of the past few years were not polarized between Khrushchev on the one hand and all the other members of the Presidium on the other. There must have been some support among these even for the political acts now most condemned. In the first post-Khrushchev settlement, there must certainly be some who were less opposed to him than others. In any case, the conspiracy against him would scarcely have waited until it had attained absolute unanimity in the Presidium, but probably struck as soon as its forces were adequate; the alternative would have been appallingly poor security. So there must now be vulnerable men at the top.

But even the allies who mounted the coup, and are now benefiting from it, are united only in their opposition to Khrushchev. In the Soviet past, every group that has mustered against a rival has, after victory, quarreled over the disposal of the spoils, as well as on policy grounds. It is hard to see how the present rulers, even if they see the advantages of an agreed share-out, could possibly find a formula adequate to ending this old tendency, this law of Soviet politics.

One of the most striking things of all in the overthrow of Khrushchev was the absolute passivity of the Russian masses and the absolute inattention to their role on the part of the leaders. Their right to information, let alone participation, did not arise. The gulf between this sort of attitude and anything resembling democracy in any conceivable sense is going to be a major point as Russia faces issues which can scarcely be settled without the genuine involvement of the public. For the problems before the country can hardly be solved under the monopolistic rule of an elite of narrow, ideology-bound machine bureaucrats. As George Orwell could write flatly, as long ago as 1946 (in his "Second Thoughts on James Burnham"), "The Russian regime will either democratize itself or it will perish."

12

Restoration of the Fallen?

In 1938, after Stalin had publicly disposed of Bukharin and the Right-wing oppositionists, and secretly liquidated his own more senior supporters, like Kirov and Ordzhnoikidze, there was in effect no alternative government available. Except for Petrovsky (who seemed to have disappeared, but was in fact working in obscurity in a Moscow museum) and Trotsky (whose brutal murder in exile in Mexico by one of Stalin's agents was to take place in 1940), there were no living ex-members of the Politburo. The situation at the end of 1964 is quite different. Men who have held the highest positions in the Party and government, including four ex-Premiers, remain "available." It is true that they have been thoroughly smeared, but it would be assuming a great deal to conclude that they have been permanently eliminated politically. (Indeed, there are prominent figures who have not been publicly attacked at all, or only barely so, such as Andreyev and Ponomarenko.)

It would have been a very difficult undertaking for Khrushchev to try to crush the old-line *apparatchik*—and it is probably a task that, considering the Party's present state, is beyond his successors. Meanwhile, the Central Committee contains a large number of men who cannot be regarded as truly committed to Brezhnev or Kosygin or to their policies, and whose experience and prestige in the Party and State are certainly adequate to make them perfectly good alternative rulers, either as a group or even singly.

There are thirty living ex-members and ex-candidate-members of the Politburo, the Presidium, and the Secretariat (*not* counting the large Presidium of 1952–53)* who are no longer at the seat of power. Before we go on to the leaders at present in disgrace or discarded, we should note that thirteen of these thirty are still members of the Central Committee, and thus available for almost immediate recall. Except for Khrushchev, these thirteen do not include any major figures; but whatever weight they themselves carry, they are representative of a very large group of experienced Party operators whose good will any regime at present would be glad to secure, whose neutrality even would be beneficial, and whose opposition would be a dangerous threat, to be disposed of if a possibility of doing so presented itself. Among them are Nikolai Patolichev, whom Stalin made Party Secretary in 1946; Nikolai Mikhailov, Stalin's First Secretary of the Komsomol and later Secretary of the Central Committee and Head of the Agitprop Department; Nikolai Pegov, a departmental head in the Central Committee from 1946 on, and eventually (1952–53) Secretary of the Central Committee; V. V. Kuznetsov, a member of Stalin's last Presidium. In addiition, the Central Committee contains others who reached high positions in the period *after* the death of Stalin and have since lost it—four ex-members of the post-Stalin Presidium and three ex–candidate-members.

We may take as an example of typical potential material from the most experienced cadre Patolichev, who has (with one or two ups and downs) held positions immediately below

* See the following table, which gives a detailed listing of these "reserves."

THE "RESERVES"–THOSE WHO HAVE SERVED IN HIGH POSITIONS BUT ARE NO LONGER AT THE SEAT OF POWER

Full members of the Politburo or the "small," post-Stalin Presidium:	Date removed	Date removed from CC
A. A. Andreyev†	1952	1961
V. M. Molotov†	1957	1957
L. M. Kaganovich†	1957	1957
N. A. Bulganin	1958	1961
G. M. Malenkov†	1957	1957
K. E. Voroshilov	1960	1961
M. Z. Saburov	1957	1961
M. G. Pervukhin	1961	1961
G. K. Zhukov	1957	1957
A. I. Kirichenko†	1960	1961
N. I. Belyaev†	1960	1961
N. G. Ignatov†	1961	*
A. B. Aristov†	1961	*
E. A. Furtseva†	1961	*
N. A. Mukhitdinov†	1961	*
N. S. Khrushchev†	1964	*
Candidate-members of the Politburo or the "small," post-Stalin Presidium:		
L. G. Melnikov	1953	1961
P. K. Ponomarenko†	1956	1961
D. T. Shepilov†	1957	1957
D. S. Korotchenko	1961	*
Ya. E. Kalnberzins	1961	*
P. N. Pospelov†	1961	*
V. V. Shcherbitsky	1963	*
Members of the Secretariat (not listed above):		
N. S. Patolichev	1947	*
G. M. Popov	1950	1956
N. M. Pegov	1953	*
N. A. Mikhailov	1953	*
S. D. Ignatiev	1953	1961
N. N. Shatalin	1955	1956 (?)
I. V. Spiridonov	1962	*
Members of the 1952–53 "large" Presidium (not listed above):		
V. M. Andrianov		1956 (?)
D. I. Chesnokov		1956
V. V. Kuznetsov		*

* Still a member of the Central Committee.
† Has also served on the Secretariat.

the top leadership, and who still does. His evident versatility, ability to avoid permanent downgrading, and presumed acceptability to various leaderships are qualities of a possible contender. He was trained as a technical and military chemist, and so has the background for the modern economic drive. He became a candidate-member of the Central Committee as long ago as 1939, and a full member in 1941. By 1946, he had reached the high posts of Secretary of the Central Committee and Deputy Chairman of the Council for Collective Farm Affairs. After a partial eclipse under circumstances that are still unclear (but arising out of Khrushchev's struggle with Kaganovich in the Ukraine in 1947), he served as First Secretary of Belorussia from 1950 to 1956, being then demoted to Deputy Foreign Minister. He became First Deputy Foreign Minister in 1957 and since 1958 has been Minister of Foreign Trade. He has remained a member of the Central Committee throughout, and in the last two or three years has been much in the public eye. It will be seen that his seniority and availability more than match those of most members of the current Presidium, and the same applies to others on our list.

We must indeed distinguish among the current power positions of some of these veterans. Seven former high State and Party officials—including Aristov, Mikhailov, and Pegov—are out of the way, as ambassadors in various parts of the world. Doubtless, absence must make it difficult for them to become properly involved in any current intrigues. Still, such appointments are not permanent: For example, Epishev and Andropov, both Khrushchev followers, did turns in embassies for some years and yet returned to positions of power. In moments of sudden crisis, most of them would doubtless have no chance to play a part—just as Tevosyan, demoted the previous winter to the post of Ambassador in Tokyo, seems not to have arrived in Moscow for the critical fight of June, 1957. Nevertheless, this does not remove them from the arena even at present.

And any faction in a precarious position of temporary ascendancy might well make a deal with one or the other of them and recall him to the center.

So far, we have referred to figures of moderate significance who still retain a certain amount of power. But the true giants of the Soviet past are not among them. If we want to consider really formidable contenders, and ask if they have any prospects of returning to power, we must turn primarily to Vyacheslav Molotov and Georgi Malenkov.

As we have seen, the influence of these men is by no means dead. And Khrushchev's ouster, on grounds they put forward years ago, must strengthen their political reputations. Indeed, the present political tone is unmistakably "Malenkovite."

It is not impossible for a Communist leader to return to power after complete public disgrace, expulsion from the Central Committee and from the Party itself, or even imprisonment. The case of Gomulka springs instantly to mind. But we should consider the difference between Gomulka's position and that of Molotov and Malenkov. The attacks on the Polish leader were twofold—for political error on the one hand and criminal treason on the other; the criminal charges, designed to discredit him completely, were wholly libelous. The attacks on Molotov and Malenkov for complicity in the Stalin terror, on the other hand, are based on fact. It is conceivable that the Party, or rather the *apparat*, would decide that after all Molotov and Malenkov had been politically right over the past few years, just as the Polish Central Committee decided that Gomulka had been right. The question remains, Would the true revelations about Molotov's and Malenkov's pasts, which have no parallel in the Gomulka case, exclude them from any chance of a comeback? Part of the answer must be that most of the other leaders also have responsibilities for the terror, and it may be that an *apparat* reacting in the direction of tighter controls and less attention to any public feeling that had been roused might not consider the past worth bothering about. In any case, elements in the Party managed for a long time to prevent the expulsion from its ranks of any of the figures concerned, despite accusations that should have secured not only expulsion but actual imprisonment. This in itself is presumably a sign that the charges are not everywhere taken very seriously. (And, indeed, Voroshilov has been publicly forgiven after equally lurid accusations.)

On this point, we must distinguish between Molotov and Malenkov. Molotov was certainly involved in the purges as a supporter of Stalin. But he himself came close to suffering from them in 1936 and in 1953. And his involvement was in any case largely that of a supporter and accomplice rather than a principal.

The recent political concentration against Molotov makes it clear that his political views were of such an extreme and severe nature that they isolated him in the past, and doubtless still do at present, even from his closest allies. Nevertheless, this presented certain disadvantages from the point of view of Molotov's enemies. A powerful feud subsisted among a section of the *apparat* against Malenkov. Kaganovich, never a popular figure in any case, was rightly regarded as responsible only after Stalin for the Great Purge. Voroshilov, a political lightweight, even though not wholly without prestige, seems to have attracted the permanent enmity of a powerful military faction as a result of his activities during the massacre of the officers in the late 1930's. Such arguments apply to a much lesser extent to Molotov. It is true that he was Stalin's closest political ally for many years, and that he gave his approval of the purges—but even this hardly represented a greater responsibility than Khrushchev's or Mikoyan's.

In any case, whatever Molotov's political limitations, he retained the prestige of an old Bolshevik who had been the editor of *Pravda* years before the Revolution and had been briefly in charge of the Bolshevik organization in Revolutionary Petrograd. Again, in recent years at least, his stand must have seemed to the Party membership to be, however misguided, one of principle, a rare enough phenomenon in Soviet political circumstances.

None of this is to say that the partial protection he seems to have found in 1962 was due to any desire to hand over the leadership to him. Still, if Malenkov and Shepilov were able to cooperate with him with a view to forming a new anti-Khrushchevite collective leadership in 1957, there is no reason to doubt that a comparatively conservative faction nowadays might be happy to keep him as a potential counterbalance to their opponents. His maintenance of the political struggle against the new line has surely made him a potential contender for power in certain circumstances. Many of the more conservative-minded members of the leadership and senior Party members must have some sympathy with his point of view, although his outlook and attitudes have been too rigid to secure general acceptance and support even by this wing. Indeed, in 1955, on the issue of reconciliation with Tito, he seems to have been opposed by all members of the Presidium, including "Stalinist" reactionaries like Kaganovich. Yet, though such considerations might operate against attempts to give him decisive power, they would not necessarily have much significance if it was merely a question of bringing him back as an important figure in the Presidium.

We know of Molotov's "platform" only from a few hostile references. But in any case, there does exist this "conservative" program designed to appeal to the traditionalist cadres.

We may perhaps conclude that a "reactionary" leadership would face increasing difficulties, since its existence would signify an unwillingness of the traditionalist cadres to come to terms with the objective situation, while it is rather improbable that they would produce a Stalin enough in control and with the will and mind to meet the situation head-on with force. In any case, a wholly reactionary regime seems unlikely. Molotov was the only one even among the fallen leaders to stand for something of the sort. A basically conservative regime, moving rather too slowly, but more or less in control for a considerable period, is somewhat more likely. And that perspective merges imperceptibly into a "progressive" regime going a little bit faster. From the point of view of a rational *apparatchik*, controlled modernization of this sort represents the best hope of preserving apparatocracy. But it presupposes a certain stability at the political level. Our whole analysis leads us to think that this would be difficult to attain, and the incentive to add to the regime the credibility of Molotov's name might be strong, especially in circumstances that appeared to threaten chaos.

Georgi Malenkov was much more directly involved than Molotov in the 1936–38 terror. And in the postwar period he was most prominent in using the purge weapon to destroy his own political opponents—particularly in the Leningrad Case. His rise, through his control of the Cadres Administration, evidently produced many bitter enemies within the *apparat* itself. Leningraders have attacked him more bitterly than have Khrushchevites—although this is in the main doubtless an attempt to throw the stigma of anti-Party activity primarily on the "liberal" rather than the "Stalinist" representative in the group.

Yet, even Malenkov could plead that he had little more choice than any other Stalinist; that he was an agent rather than a member of the Politburo, and hence not fully a principal, during the Yezhov period; and that in the Leningrad Case, he tried (if a commonly repeated story is true) to save Voznessensky. Moreover, he is fully entitled to claim credit for the initial post-Stalin relaxation. The question that is difficult to determine is whether the mud thrown by Khrushchev has stuck—and whether, even if it has stuck in the public's view, the *apparat* might not in certain circumstances decide either to ignore it or to do whatever possible to scrape it off. We may certainly regard it as a handicap. But to assert that it has made Malenkov's return to a share of power absolutely impossible would be going too far. A more valid approach might be to say that in circumstances in which the decisive elements in the Party felt that the return of Malenkov would be of benefit to them, they might ignore his handicaps.

But what are the circumstances in which the Party might wish to recall him? It would certainly represent an important political reversal for any such question to arise. Still, we cannot regard the future variation of Soviet politics as being in principle limited to the single alternatives of a "Kozlovite" or "Khrushchevite" regime, and even such a swing as this is conceivable. Malenkov's political strength is not entirely dissipated.

From the viewpoint of the serious economists now coming to grips with the recalcitrant problems of the Soviet economy, Malenkov and his school must have some attraction—if only as people who might pursue a consistent policy. It is conceivable, moreover, that the political revolution that overthrew Khrushchev might find it necessary or useful to bring in Malenkov and his quasi-"liberal" wing as a counterweight, even if with the intention of destroying them later. In this case, he would be back in the political arena with who knows what final results.

Malenkov seems to be the only leader who, over the post-Stalin years, aroused any popular feeling of sympathy, and it is said that some of this still survives. Moreover, it took an alliance of old-line "Stalinists" and Khrushchev's own group to overthrow him, so it is evident that he also had much support in the Party. The question is whether his crimes might have been forgotten and his merits of policy and political skill remembered. At least, it must now be apparent to such of the *apparat* as admits at all the need for modernization that Malenkov's comparatively unadventurous tactics in seeking it is the superior method. Already we see that the style of a Brezhnev-Kosygin regime appears to be rather that of Malenkovian step-by-step reformism than Khrushchevian adventure. Of course, no one is going to share power unless for very compelling reasons. And the only reason why we cannot exclude the return to the center of Malenkov is that the present rulers may feel they need his skills, and, in the present vacuum of prestige, his repute in Party and country, while, on the other hand, they might feel able to take measures adequate to keeping him under control.

There are still members of the Central Committee, such as Mikhailov and Pegov, who were his associates in the past and might yet act as a bridgehead for him. And there are more important figures who, though at present in comparative disgrace, have not been expelled from the Party and continue to exert some influence—in particular, Mikhail Pervukhin and Maxim Saburov.

We should note, indeed, that Pervukhin and Saburov are figures worth watching in their own right. As highly experienced State and economic leaders from the 1940's, and members of the Presidium for a number of years, they have as much intrinsic claim to consideration for the highest posts as Kosygin has. It is easy enough to envisage them playing important roles in the years ahead. A "Malenkovite" rehabilitation which did not go so far as restoring Malenkov himself might well establish Pervukhin in the Premiership.

Thus far, we have spoken of the possibilities of a return to the public stage of the oppositionists should the right circumstances arise. Basically, such possibilities must be considered to be remote. If we can speak of them at all, it is because of the shakiness of the present leadership. It is a group carrying very little political punch. Already in 1960, the fact that Kozlov, an evident lightweight, could rise to the second position in the

Party, in succession to an oaf like Kirichenko, implied a notable lack of impressiveness. The sources of political credibility were running dry. And, even apart from the results of an inevitable and destructive internal struggle, the present coalition, with most of the elements of power theoretically under its control, might find no rallying point and simply disintegrate, unless firmer buttresses are sought.

Thus it is perfectly conceivable, in circumstances of sharp struggle between factions in the post-Khrushchev epoch, that one or the other of the contending groups may wish to play the card of the prestige and experience of some of the old leaders. Even Khrushchev found it desirable to bring in the almost ludicrously useless and unimportant Kuusinen to provide some sort of appearance of ballast. Rule by a conservative-style faction containing Molotov is much more politically "credible" than one centered on Suslov or a recovered Kozlov.

We may compare the present ruling team with that put in power by Stalin at his first triumph, in the early 1930's. Stalin was a much younger man than Khrushchev at the comparable times in their careers. If Stalin had died in, say, 1935, it would be rather difficult to envisage his Politburo successfully maintaining its grip on the Party without considerable pressure toward a political *détente* with some of the fallen leaders, more probably of the Right.

As things are, any such return to power by the oppositionists seems to be unlikely. But the succession period will certainly be one of instability—and very probably of surprises. So although we need not regard the reversals speculated upon in this chapter as very probable, we should by no means exclude them as impossible. We are not here considering the odds, but examining even those possibilities against which the odds are high. Indeed, we might ask, who in 1952 would have taken a bet that five years later Khrushchev would be the supreme figure in the State? Today the field is even more open.

13

The Army

APART FROM THE PARTY ITSELF, the Soviet Army is the one organized body in Russia with its own *esprit de corps*, professionalism, and potential ability to carry out moves to place its nominees in power. It is an old story under authoritarian regimes, where the people have no direct opportunity to intervene in political events, for the Army to consider itself a legitimate bearer of the national will, sometimes even in opposition to the government.

In any case, the problem has been understood by the Soviet rulers right from the start. They have always made an attempt to combine the not easily replaceable professional expertise of the officer cadre with strict Party control over its actions. There are political officers at every level whose responsibility is to the Party. At the head of this vast network stands the Main Political Administration of the armed forces.

The powers of the political officers have varied from time to time. What has not varied is the resentment of the genuine military at this sort of supervision. There have, as we shall see, been times when the Army has managed truly to play a political role. The initial stimulus has always been a desire to abate the nuisance of the military-political machine's intervention in

Army affairs. The Party has always fought back. And the struggle over the issue has gradually involved the Army High Command in politics to the degree that it has already—on one brief occasion at least—found itself a major force in decisive affairs of state.

The Army leaders are Communists. Almost all the senior soldiers at the present time have been members of the Communist Party longer than their political superiors.* Chief of Staff Marshal M. V. Zakharov, an officer who has shown particular resentment at the intervention of the political organs, actually joined the Party before the Revolution and served in the Red Guard in Petrograd during the seizure of power. It is true that the junior officers, and thus the officer corps as a whole, went into the service in a more formal and professional manner. Still, we must conclude that there is a good deal of truly Revolutionary background at the core of the Army: The older and senior figures at least were politically motivated in taking up careers in the Army.

But theirs was the political feeling of the Leninist Revolution, not of the hierarchical Soviet society that has emerged from it. During the 1930's and since then, Stalin and his successors did a great deal to build up all over the country a feeling among the elites that they were a highly privileged caste, and thus that their bonds were with the political leaders who had created these conditions for them, rather than with the people from whom they had emerged. The old ranks were revived, the old epaulets were restored, regiments began to receive grandiose titles, the traditions of the campaigns and command-

* The following are dates on which representative soldiers and political leaders joined the Party:

(a) Zhukov, 1919; Konev, 1918; Zakharov, 1917; Malinovsky, 1926; Rotmistrov, 1919; Rokossovsky, 1919; Chuikov, 1919; Grechko, 1928; Biryuzov, 1926; Gorbatov, 1919; Moskalenko, 1920; Meretskov, 1917.

(b) Khrushchev, 1919; Brezhnev, 1931; Kosygin, 1927; Podgorny, 1930; Suslov, 1921; Kirilenko, 1931; Voronov, 1933; Mikoyan, 1915; Shelest, 1928; Epishev, 1929; Golikov, 1943.

ers of Czarist times were again given military glory, and so on. But at the same time the Army seems to have been affected by the fact that its conscripts were mainly peasants, whose feelings about collectivization were not to be concealed from the High Command. And in any case, Stalin's purge of the Army, starting with the 1937 trial of Marshal Tukhachevsky and the others, and destroying the leading cadres of the Army down to and below regimental level, was resented even by the survivors. It is a far greater insult to a general than to a politician to murder him under false accusations of treason. Moreover, when the war broke out in 1941, a number of the generals—for example, Gorbatov, Meretskov, and Rokossovsky—who had not at that time been shot but were in labor camps, were perforce released and restored to command, thus maintaining continuity. During the post-Stalin period, the Army pressed continually for the rehabilitation of the executed soldiers and had some difficulty in obtaining it. In fact, the struggle was so sharp that theirs is the only important case in which partial rehabilitation was followed by "de-rehabilitation," with the marshals disappearing back into the world of "unpersons" during the period following the fall of Zhukov.

Certain of the soldiers appear to have been "Stalinized." But on the whole, there was, naturally, a considerable revulsion from Stalinism, and a considerable dislike of the Party control that was long administered by particularly repulsive political gangsters and police and purge veterans. In so far as the *generalitet* did begin to think of itself as a privileged class, it was with reservations about any gratitude to the Party. And in so far as some Party-mindedness did remain, it often seemed to be associated more with the pre-Stalinist Party of Civil War times. In a dictatorship, however strong the more or less automatic loyalties of the Army to its political superiors, there are also special reasons for resentment. When the political leaders appear to be producing failures and operating according to narrow, cold-blooded, and unrealistic versions of the ruling ideology, alternative ideological interpretations may arise in the comparatively free discussion held among groups that have reason to trust each other. There has been some formidable independent thinking among Army intellectuals on strategic problems: for example, Marshal Rotmistrov's well-argued theory that the Battle of Kursk, not that of Stalingrad, was decisive in the war. Such minds are capable, in private, of seeing through at least some of the third-rate political theorizing of today.

We find, at last, in the Army an important group of Party members who are not *apparatchiks* in the ordinary sense. Their professionalism, unlike that of all the others connected with any machinery of power, is intense, specialized, and difficult to master. By comparison, the special skills of the secret police are simple. When Yezhov took over from Yagoda at the end of 1936, he was able to massacre the whole of Yagoda's police cadres and replace them with his own men from the Party machine proper within months—and it would scarcely be argued that the terror of 1937–38 was a technical failure. But when Stalin slaughtered the officer corps in 1937–39, the effect (as Khrushchev tells us) was long-lasting, even though the commanders were replaced not from outside but by their surviving juniors.

The military membership of the Party, like its members in all other spheres, is represented in the Central Committee. But whereas the more or less truly non-*apparatchik* element otherwise included in that body amounts to a powerless handful of technicians, scientists, writers, etc., the marshals bring into the political arena a dangerously powerful and highly organized element.

At the end of the war, the soldiers who had achieved victory had won immense prestige with the population. It seems clear, in fact, that the public vaguely looked to them as in some way incarnating an alternative and less vicious power than that of Stalin. Marshal Zhukov, particularly, was as popular in the country as in the Army, and Stalin must have thought of him as a potential threat of considerable danger. Even during the war, Stalin had (Khrushchev tells us) sought to undermine Zhukov's reputation. With the war ended, he struck. Zhukov was expelled from the Central Committee for "faults" that have not yet been made public, and exiled to a provincial command. A number of other leading generals and admirals were cut down to size, and some of them were sent to labor camps.

However, Stalin was in something of a dilemma—a dilemma that faces any autocrat or oligarch, including the present-day rulers of Russia. He had seen the nearly disastrous results of his first military purge. He was committed (as he had not been in 1938) to a forward, expansionist foreign policy. And in the struggle for world domination which he seems to have thought would soon come to its climax, he had every need of the best military skills he could get. For some years, he compromised. His Chief of Staff was General Shtemenko, a professional officer of moderate military repute but high political loyalty, and similar officers (who were to be demoted in the immediate post-Stalin years) held a large proportion of the high posts. At the same time, some of the fighting marshals—particularly those thought hostile to Zhukov—were retained. And the whole was kept under careful control, both by the secret police, which operated the machinery that had succeeded the wartime Smersh, and by the political organs (manned by operators in the apparatus of the Central Committee), which penetrated every level.

However, in the last months of his life, when he was, perhaps, really contemplating war, Stalin to some degree reversed this trend. Political control remained tight and absolute. But Shtemenko was replaced by the veteran Marshal Sokolovsky, and Zhukov and others formerly in disgrace were recalled to the center and given key posts (Zhukov was again elected, as a candidate-member, to the Central Committee).

All this seemed to amount to little more than the oscillations bound to arise from an attempt to carry out two contradictory policies at once. In the post-Stalin period, a new element came into play. For in a succession period the temptation is bound to arise for one Party faction to play the Army card against the other.

In the first days of the new regime, when appeals were being circulated against "panic and disarray," Malenkov and Beria, backed by thousands of MVD troops, presented the Central Committee with a *fait accompli.* But even then, they felt it necessary to make Zhukov Minister of War. And although the Moscow Military District was firmly in MVD control, this was not the case in other cities. It has been suggested that one of the most important reasons that the two leaders did not seize the occasion to destroy all their political enemies was the fear that the Leningrad District under Marshal Govorov might support a different leadership by armed force.

In June, 1953, when his colleagues carried out the coup against Beria, there were reports of suspicious troop movements on both sides. And it is certainly the case that after the police chief's fall, the Commander of the Moscow Military District, the Commandant of the City of Moscow, and the Commandant of the Kremlin were replaced within a few weeks.

The Army commanders, at a special meeting, enthusiastically endorsed Beria's removal. Zhukov was promoted to full membership in the Central Committee, and, in a new departure, two marshals served on the court that tried (whether posthumously or not is at present unclear) the fallen Beria.

In 1955, at the time of the fall of Malenkov, when there was a certain amount of controversy in the press regarding Malenkov's scheme for increasing the supply of consumer goods, the Army press actively supported the anti-Malenkov line. Over the next months, when the focus turned rather to Khrushchev's disputes with Molotov, the continuing struggle gave the marshals the opportunity to extend a quiet revision of the Stalinist history of the war that had been in circulation to quite public claims that they, and not the political leaders past or present, had been responsible for the Soviet victories. The rule was plainly established: Whoever has the power to do so claims to be the victor of Stalingrad. In their turns, Stalin, Zhukov, and Khrushchev have all worn this palm.

At the Twentieth Party Congress, Khrushchev finally brought the Army, which was already showing these signs of independence, into a position where it could be truly dangerous. Zhukov was promoted to candidate-member of the Presidium. This paid off in June, 1957, for the most important element in the defeat of the attempted coup against Khrushchev, which had a big majority in the Presidium, was the opposition of Zhukov. There were reports of troop movements, and at least credible rumors that Zhukov openly threatened intervention; he certainly put the Air Force at Khrushchev's disposal to fly members of the Central Committee to Moscow under Khrushchevite supervision. And at the end of the crisis, he was made a full member of the Presidium.

But after victory, a king has less than no use for a kingmaker. Zhukov was now a menace to Khrushchev. In October, he was removed from his high positions and expelled from the Central Committee. The way this was done was significant. In every other case of a political purge, the first move has been denunciation at a Central Committee Plenum and expulsion from that Committee, followed by removal from government and other posts. In Zhukov's case, he was first (while absent in Albania) removed from the Ministry of War—that is, the post from which his real power derived—and the Central Committee expulsion followed. Whether Zhukov really intended to be a "Bonaparte," as some accused him, seems doubtful. What is perfectly clear is that his goal—and he came close to achieving it—was total victory in the Army's battle with the military-political organs. During his ascendancy, the power of these organs over the officers was cut down to almost nothing. The Central Committee itself was forced to issue, in May, 1957, an instruction accompanying an order of Zhukov's that flatly stated, "Criticisms of the orders and decisions of commanders will not be permitted at Party meetings." When he fell, this trend was instantly reversed. A precisely opposite instruction came out within days. He was accused of splitting the Army from the Party, setting up his own personal control in the Army, and "liquidating" Party leadership in the armed forces. A number of marshals who had been associated with him lost their posts at this time.

Zhukov was replaced as Minister of War by Marshal Malinovsky, an experienced professional fighting soldier without Zhukov's special prestige, and at the same time, one who had been associated with Khrushchev in the Stalingrad campaign—where Khrushchev was the leading Party representative on the local Military Council. And while Party control was reimposed, the pill was sweetened by the removal of the political nominee Zheltov from leadership of the Political Administration and his replacement by a professional officer with political connections, General Golikov.

The defeat of the Army seemed complete. Yet the logic of its professionalism and of its special internal loyalties was to bring it back into play within a few years. The Zhukov era shows how the Army can emerge into the political field during a struggle at the top, even under entirely "legal" conditions. This is a most important and significant demonstration. The Malinovsky era which followed also shows the Army offering corporate resistance to political decisions, but not as yet in so dramatic a fashion. On the other hand, this period gives us insights into the particular matters troubling the Army as we enter the Khrushchev-succession period.

First of all, Khrushchev maneuvered to secure control of the Army by promoting to high posts the "Stalingrad group" of marshals. Even in 1955, he had managed to put through the promotion of six new marshals—all men who had served on the southern front. The Central Committee's military members before 1956 had included only three Stalingraders; this figure now went up to seven (and at the Twenty-second Congress to ten—seven of them full members). The fall of Zhukov resulted in the appointment of these new marshals, and their lesser-ranking subordinates, to key posts throughout the armed forces.

This typically Khrushchevite maneuver, similar to the "Ukrainian" appointments in the Party apparatus, was equally unsuccessful in the long run. A number of the Stalingraders did exhibit servile gratitude for their accelerated and invidious promotion. But others of them, including Malinovsky himself, retained their professional attitudes. And meanwhile, a number of senior representatives of the other fronts, and of the old General Staff which constituted the alternative military claimant to responsibility for the Stalingrad victory, held certain positions.

A controversy directly affecting military professionalism was soon upon them. The argument about the relative importance of the missile forces and the orthodox ground forces had been going on since the mid-1950's. In January, 1960, Khrushchev publicly declared that the main emphasis must be on rockets, and announced the creation of a new arm, the Missile Forces. At the same time, under pressure of the extremely sharp "allocations crisis," he announced a one-third cut in the armed forces. The military budget had already been reduced, and a custom particularly irritating to the *Ofitserstvo* —their temporary employment in civilian economic posts, under control of the military-political organs—had been introduced.

There were many signs of resistance. In August, 1961, the reduction in forces was halted, and in the spring of 1962 the civilian-employment scheme stopped. But it was clear that Khrushchev was dissatisfied with the Army's attitude. In May, 1962, a key appointment was made: A. A. Epishev, the Party official from Khrushchev's Ukrainian machine who had (an additional insult) served under Stalin as Deputy Minister of State Security, was appointed head of the Main Political Administration in place of Golikov. Another Party and police official from the old Ukrainian machine, N. R. Mironov, became head of the Central Committee Administrative Organs Department, which also deals with certain military affairs. In August, Epishev strongly attacked the political attitudes of the Ground Forces and the Ministry of Defense, and continued thereafter to issue tough disciplinary and ideological instructions.

The Cuban crisis of October, 1962, seems to have produced military ill-feeling: It is clear, at least, that the military held the Party leadership responsible for the debacle. Moreover, as the crisis raged, Malinovsky took the opportunity to deliver a sharp criticism of the political organs* in accordance with the old political law that when the Soviet Army faces action, it turns against its controllers.

After the crisis, one of Khrushchev's Ukrainian marshals, Chuikov, made a massive counterattack against military criticism of political decisions and asserted that there were still many who did not truly accept Party leadership in military matters. Epishev, often accompanied by Mironov, returned to the attack in a whole series of meetings and articles. And the Stalingrad anniversary in January, 1963, provided, as usual, the occasion for a great many barely concealed expressions of

* See *Krasnaya Zvezda*, October 25, 1962.

mutual ill-feeling—with a number of marshals omitting Khrushchev's name and others of them giving him almost sole credit. Malinovsky firmly gave the Army full responsibility for the operation and even mentioned Zhukov's role very favorably. Almost open argument on these lines, covering the last war, the political organs, and so forth, went on until the middle of February. As we have noted, this was a period of dispute within the highest ranks of the Party, and there seems no doubt that it was once again a case of the military taking advantage of the lack of a single will in the political sphere.

But by the middle of March, the politicians had struck back. From then on, criticism was greatly muted. The lesson that the Army had been taught was the removal of Marshal M. V. Zakharov from the post of Chief of Staff. And this brings us to the crisis of Khrushchev's ouster, in October, 1964.

For Zakharov's role has been crucial to the Army's position right through this period. He had been appointed Chief of Staff in 1960, in succession to Marshal Sokolovsky. Zakharov is a "Stalingrader," and this had appeared to complete the victory over the other element. But, and above all, he is Malinovsky's closest follower, having been his Chief of Staff against the Germans and gone with him when he was transferred in 1945 to lead the attack on Manchuria. As one of the nonservile Stalingraders, he spoke particularly sharply in attacking the political officers. In November, 1964, after Khrushchev's fall, Zakharov was reappointed Chief of Staff. We do not yet know the role of Malinovsky in the fall of Khrushchev. But we can trace strong opposition between him and certain Khrushchevite policies; we can note that he threw his weight on the professional side in the struggle against the military-political machine; and we can see that his closest adviser was made a scapegoat at the time when the military was being silenced, and that Khrushchev's fall saw his return. If we consider the circumstances of the June, 1957, crisis, we can see that the Army is not to be despised in these difficult moments. It seems quite clear on general grounds that Brezhnev and his colleagues could not have thought of mounting their coup if there had been any question of Army opposition. The most ordinary prudence might seem to have dictated sounding out Malinovsky. And although the Marshal doubtless approved Khrushchev's ouster, he might yet have lacked enthusiasm for the newcomers and have asked for some assurance.

On the other hand, what are assurances worth? That Malinovsky was thus allowed to bring back Zakharov was certainly a great advantage; and it did him the good of acting as a striking demonstration to the Army. (We might note the circumstances, though: Biryuzov, who had succeeded Zakharov as Chief of General Staff—and was perhaps the least professionally and most politically qualified of the Khrushchevite promotions to Marshal—had died, with Mironov, in a plane crash immediately after the seizure of power, so Malinovsky was presented with an opportunity.) In the long run, however, the political leaders must resist the Army's attempts to secure independence—at the same time that they are trying to secure its good will. The immediate issue is almost certainly the role of Epishev. His removal would be both a pleasure and a triumph for the Army, and it might be thought a small price to pay for its support. On the other hand, the "Ukrainians" in the Party machine must wish to hang on to every position they can hold. And the Party leadership as a whole must anyhow wish to replace him with another politically reliable figure. A Golikov may be adequate after a severe defeat for the Army leadership, but at present such a move would be a sure formula for further trouble.

In the new period, as the succession struggle sharpens, it seems rather unlikely that the Army can be reduced to total subservience. And, as we have seen, it is a force that anybody struggling for power must wish to turn to advantage. This gives it perspectives over the next few years similar to those of 1953 or 1957. Malinovsky, meanwhile, has not built himself the extraordinary reputation and power in the Army that Zhukov had. But he is a respected veteran, and over the past years he has shown himself a firm champion of the Army and must already have some personal support in the officer cadres. In any case, his successor would face much the same situation. The problem is complicated, and so is that of the political leadership, by the inevitable strategic primacy of the Rocket Forces, of whose largely technical officer cadres it has been complained frequently that they are confident of their indispensability, politically apathetic, and lacking in military spirit. This last fault is largely due to the fact that they have no fear of civilian life, since they are always sure of good jobs—while the professional officer is always in terror of being axed and put on an inadequate pension, since he lacks the skills for any other trade, as many articles and stories in the military press have shown.

However, it is the Ground Forces that constitute a potential political threat: After all, one could hardly seize power with nuclear warheads. And although, in principle, the Army's concern in a fairly stable situation is only to preserve its own organizational integrity, it is the fact that a regiment of infantry is capable of obeying its commanding officer and seizing the Kremlin that really constitutes the political power of the Army. During political crises of the type that have occurred over the past decade, the potentiality of Army intervention has, in effect, been invoked several times. But it has always been on the side of one or the other existing political faction. We may expect to see similar moves in the near future.

But this can scarcely be separated from the question of whether there could be a clear-cut, *bona fide* Army *coup d'état*. It is partly a matter of definition. An Army intervention to put in power a given group of political figures might be effected on such terms that the Army remained the decisive force in the State, even though this did not appear in the formal ruling bodies. And again, this merges gradually into situations in which the Army more or less openly imposes political nonentities plainly of its own selection, while belatedly giving them the appearance of constitutionality through a meeting of the Central Committee held in the presence of a number of armed, uniformed figures—as in Napoleon's "legal" coup of the Eighteenth Brumaire. The real questions are more basic. Can we envisage a possible future in which the Army will retain its solidarity, while the political machine is disintegrating? Surely we can. And can we foresee the possibility of instabilities that would leave the Army regarding itself as the surviving repository of the popular—even the Party—will? Once more, why not?

Again, we see in cases of other countries and times in which the army has become a political force that it is possible for an army uprising to take place away from the center of power. In 1937–38, in Russia, it seems to have been feared, and was perhaps possible, that Marshal Blyukher's Far Eastern Army might rise and march on Moscow. It appears not at all unlikely that such a move was prevented only by the vigilance of the political officers, aided by the secret police network, with their task made much easier by the atmosphere of demoralization and terror that then prevailed—and might not in the circumstances we are envisaging.

There is another and rather different question. We have considered possible Army action in circumstances of political struggle. But what of the not impossible conditions of a return to "stability" of the Stalinist type? If such a regime were reasonably firmly in control, with no signs of effective opposition in the leading cadres of the Party and State, could the Army offer opposition? Could it, and would it, consider striking for power?

The first answer is that it would have done better, from both its own point of view and that of the country, to have made some attempt to oust Stalin in the 1930's, whatever the risks. And this lesson may perhaps have been remembered. Secondly, it is unlikely that the stability of a neo-Stalin could be anything like as impressive as that of the old original, given the new social, political, and ideological circumstances. It is quite true that any "strong" political leadership could fairly rapidly reduce the Army to complete subordination in a general way, and it would require foresight and nerve to mount an anticipatory coup. But we can add that even a small group of really determined armed men, the history of other dictatorships tells us, can seize power, given luck and audacity, so that vast and suspicious preparations are not necessarily required.

But once we reach this far, the possibilities are endless. We need only think of the histories of countries that have gone through this sort of crisis to convince ourselves that none of this is impossible. This is not to pass one way or another on its *probability*. But if the Soviet Union reaches the level of political crisis that from many considerations appears among the likeliest of future developments, then the military certainly represents one of the most formidable contenders.

As to the nature of a regime that depends wholly or mainly on Army support, we can again conceive of a variety of possibilities. Military coups in comparable circumstances have led to the transfer of power to aggressive and reactionary factions, or have, on the contrary, paved the way to the handing over of power to democratic coalitions. A period in which the military came to feel itself as embodying the popular protest might well produce democratic moods among the officers. But at present it seems that a military ruling caste would be full of simple certitudes hostile to free thought, to the genuine civilianization that is another way of saying democratization and is the opposite of elite professional rule, party or military. It is regularly reported that the intellectual rebels in Moscow view with distaste the prospects of military rule. And when we look at examples of an army embodying a nation and its revolutions—for example, the rule of the major generals in Cromwellian England—we can understand such qualms.

But meanwhile, we have to consider the dangers of a period of even partial Army ascendancy in the field of foreign affairs, which most directly concerns the West. What evidence we have implies that the soldiers are inclined to a rather more intransigent attitude than are the politicians. Zhukov seems to have been associated with a forward "adventurist" policy over Hungary in 1956 and over Turkey in 1957;* and the marshals now appear, perhaps inevitably, to be working against the transfer of funds from armaments to economic advance.

There are signs, too, that they opposed the test-ban agreement. Marshal Malinovsky did not refer to it at all in his Order of the Day on Soviet Navy Day, July 28, 1963, two days after the agreement had been initialed, and instead accused the "imperialist camp" of heightening international tension and continuing the arms race. *Krasnaya Zvezda*, the Soviet Army organ, failed to praise or comment on the agreement at a time when the rest of the Soviet press was enthusiastic. It may also be noted that the Peking *People's Daily* of September 24, 1963, pointedly quotes a Soviet delegate to the Cypress meeting of the Executive Committee of the Afro-Asian People's Solidarity Organization as drawing a distinction as follows: "The Soviet Foreign Minister, Gromyko, signed the treaty, and the Soviet Minister of Defense, Malinovsky, did not oppose it."

The military has shown signs of reluctance to accept the fact that the U.S.S.R. cannot match, or at the very least cannot overcome, the American military-technical advantage. On the

* The official accusation against Zhukov, for what it is worth, included "adventurism, both in his understanding of the main tasks of the Soviet Union's policy and in heading the Defense Ministry."

other hand, once the lesson has penetrated, it might perhaps be expected to give rise to the professional caution often to be found in military leaderships when the political rulers are inclined to aggression. For the moment, it is not so much that the military is urging adventurist policies as such. Rather, those representing the special interests of the Ground Forces, which may be thought of as the army element proper, are finding it difficult to swallow a reality in which there is little probability that they could ever play a decisive part in war. The facts, nevertheless, are likely to penetrate, particularly over a period. And if we cannot even so regard the coming to power of a military regime as necessarily implying a lessening of tension in the short run, it would nevertheless mark a stage in the breakdown of the old system and thus, though only most doubtfully progressive in itself, be something that might lead to better things.

14

The Seeds of Change

CRITICAL PROBLEMS will not cease to emerge for the rulers of Russia. As Togliatti wrote in his last "memoir," "In fact, difficulties, contradictions, and new problems are constantly arising in all the Socialist countries." But who will face them?

We have already noted that the next stage in Russia must eventually bring to power a generation of Communists younger than those who have hitherto exercised control. And we have pointed out that the "Young Turks" now put forward so hopefully are not themselves promising material. The "Young Turks," in any case, though young in comparison with the present top leadership, are not young by standards normally prevailing in periods of political change. The first Politburo, in 1917, contained only two men over forty, and none over fifty. This is not to dispute the contention that a younger cadre will eventually arise in the Party. But here again, we must ask, what are the types that are likely to emerge?

Unless great changes are made, the answer will be a depressing one. A new generation of political leaders will arise, as ever, from the Party secretaries of the lower levels. These will be the men who, in their late teens or early twenties, were the most enthusiastic of Komsomol members and at the same time the most skilled committee intriguers in their university, technical college, or place of work. This would not be very promising as a basis for future leadership within the Conservative or Labour Party in Britain, or, doubtless, in the U.S. Republican or Democratic Party. And even though we can be sure that the Komsomol is not so crudely or brutally managed a body as it was in Stalin's time, there is still plenty of evidence of the sort of thing it represents and the sort of leaders it throws up. The youth gangs who wreck the poetry readings by the Mayakovsky statue, the young prigs who publicly censure girls' hair styles or break into dance halls to stop excessive jazz: such are the activists' rank and file. As for the leaders, we may quote the complaint by the Komsomol's present First Secretary, Pavlov:

> We are amazed at the tendency of certain producers, scenario writers, and playwrights to draw comparisons between Komsomol activists and workers and so-called ordinary people (as though the former were not ordinary people). In these films and plays, the ordinary lads and girls at least bear a resemblance to normal people, but the youth leaders, the Komsomol activists, are invariably hidebound bureaucrats, formalists, and fools. . . . And really, the figure of the activist migrates from book to book, from play to play, from film to film, and always wearing the same silly mask of a bureaucrat, a colorless, stupid person.*

It does not take much imagination to see why the situation complained of here arises.

Recent controversies about "fathers and sons" are certainly significant. The notion, evidently prevalent among the genuine post-Stalin generation, that a certain conflict subsists between themselves and their elders was warmly rebuffed by Khrushchev himself. Perhaps even more interesting, it was

* *Molodoi Kommunist*, April, 1958.

pointed out that a similar controversy took place in the 1920's and was settled unequivocally in favor of the Party veterans and those younger men who accepted their line. In a formal statement by the veteran Stalin and Khrushchev spokesman V. Stepanov, the "problem of fathers and sons" was branded as a "rotten idea of Trotskyite doctrine."* In fact, none of the real young, the actual "student" types, are going to be allowed to emerge. Instead, a traditionalist Komsomol clique will filter upward.

So far, all this is negative criticism. Although it is true that the newest cadres were thoroughly indoctrinated under Stalin, it may yet be the case that they are rather more open-minded than their immediate predecessors. In the first place, they seem to have risen quickly and without painful incident, so their self-confidence is perhaps unlikely to have been sapped (at least to the extent it has been among older men) by the continual, cumulative, and finally exhausting friction of year upon year of Stalin-style defensive in-fighting. Secondly, some at least are fresh enough to have identified themselves, for factional purposes, with a forward policy. The way in which power and policy considerations operate in Soviet political minds is a complex one. But it must at least seem likely to a modernizer, to put it at its crudest, that his personal progress might not be great if he simply submitted to and supported a conservative takeover.

We have before us a clear example of the way factional and personal attachment has decided policy. In the military controversy of 1962 concerning the relative merits of the rocket and conventional forces, almost without exception the pro-rocket men among the generals were men who had served along the southern front in the war. This was not the result of some geographical or climatic influence: The point was that these were the men who had worked most closely with Khrushchev.

* *Pravda,* April 16, 1963.

So we can conclude that on a matter which was in theory solely a technical one, opinions were in fact decided very largely at least by the political or factional allegiance of the principals. We may similarly conclude that the former "Khrushchevites" among the young Party figures found themselves supporting opinions reached by the leader to whom they attached themselves, even though these opinions might not be the ones most naturally arising from their training and background. It is true, to take a simple view, that they could be at liberty to abandon these opinions now. But this would assume a pure and conscious cynicism; actually, people become sincerely attached to views with which they and their faction have associated themselves. Indeed, their original adoption of such views may often be the result of mixed motives: It is easy to attach oneself sincerely to opinions that suit one's career, and less easy to abandon them without ceremony when they seem to block it. And this is true not only for subjective reasons, but also, of course, because a man who is associated with a policy is not going to find it easy to convince his colleagues and rivals of the worthiness of his motives when he abandons it.

It is also true that the rival factional and power interests of the modernizers must impel them, by the logic of politics, into translating their struggle for position into a dispute about policies, forcing them to adopt different positions from those of their rivals. It is natural that this should mean continuance of an "anti-conservative" line. We *may*, therefore, see a continuation of the current type of "anti-Stalinism"—policies based on partial insight into the present condition of the Soviet Union and on a willingness to make part of the changes required by the objective situation. What seems unlikely is that progress by this cadre, or by any cadre one can easily see succeeding them in the next generation, will involve the truly sweeping changes necessary—such as the virtual (even if not formal) abandonment of collectivization. And what one can be certain of is that the cadre will not make the basic change of abandoning the principle of rule by the self-perpetuating apparatocracy. But the present situation in the U.S.S.R. does show all the signs that mark societies heading for revolutionary change. There is an intellectual crisis, in which those working in all fields of thought and creativity find themselves in dispute with the representatives of official theory. There is an economic crisis, in the sense that the present system, despite various adaptations, has been unable to adjust to the demands of a modern-style economy. The main question is whether the current political crisis will be extreme enough to crack the carapace of an obsolete sociopolitical form which is hampering the development of the living forces in the U.S.S.R., or whether—for a time, at least—it will be possible to repair the damage and keep the old system together for a further period. For it is impossible to predict the defeat, or at least the imminent defeat, of the *apparatocracy*. Even a very severe crisis indeed might prove to be its equivalent of 1848 or 1905, rather than February, 1917.

In considering the Soviet future, we have had two quite different questions in mind. First of all, there is evolution within the present political system—that is, within a system in which political life is conducted among (and only among) a limited number of permanent officials of Party and State. It is the problems within this sphere that must concern us for the immediate future. As for the longer term, it is possible that Party rule along present lines will continue. But one must also allow for the eventuality of evolution away from the Lenin-Stalin-Khrushchev rut.

In considering the immediate period, we have had to deal with a complicated but limited set of facts about the polity as it now exists, and about personalities, factions, and issues within it. A longer-term view involves a broader and more general examination of social, economic, and political potentialities existing now only in embryo. The tendencies themselves are often more indisputable and easier to grasp than are the particulars of current Soviet political life. But when it comes to their future development, we are obviously on uncertain ground. We must, at any rate, avoid the temptation to predict the precise outcome, especially as regards detail.

The succession situation opens up almost endless possibilities, some immediate and some to be thought of as conceivably arising as the result of a long crisis. We may start by listing schematically just the more immediate probabilities, in terms of policy:

a) Continuity or even intensification of "modernizing" policies, with the present Presidium perhaps shedding some of its more conservative ballast.
b) A more temporizing regime based on compromise between the modernizers and the old-line *apparatchiks*.
c) A regime canted further in the direction of conservatism, perhaps unable to sustain itself without reliance on the older elements.

Each of these general possibilities would either contain dangerous factional tensions within itself or be faced with a dangerous opposition, or both. And a "modernizing" regime might provoke a successful conservative reaction, and vice versa.

The generalized possibilities in the phase following this earliest settlement might be outlined as:

a) Reasonable stability with adequate progress in solving Soviet economic and other problems.
b) Reasonable stability without such progress, based simply on the power of the Party machinery—which is in theory capable of ruling even in such conditions.
c) Instability with severe factional fighting at the top, with the gradual emergence of a dominant figure or figures to restore direction and order.

d) Continued instability, not accompanied by mass unrest.
e) Continued instability, finally leading to mass unrest.

In the case of the last possibility, we may consider the further outcome to be a reaction back to pure "Stalinism"; a reaction of a centrist, Kadar-Gomulka type, unable to return entirely to the old methods; a military dictatorship; or the emergence of a truly liberal, Nagy-type Communism and the breakup of *apparatchik* rule.

We must not dismiss even what may now appear to be extravagant speculations when we try to consider the Soviet future. Whatever formal possibilities exist must be borne firmly in mind. The events of 1953–63 in the Communist bloc would have been regarded as totally fantastic if predicted at the time of Stalin's death. Russia is, in a quite basic sense, in a state of transition. And at the same time the prospects of political stability at the top are very poor. This opens up possibilities even more extreme than those which have already been realized.

What are the prospects for the disintegration, as against the stabilization, of *apparat* rule?

First of all, we may note that there are certain reserves of strength in established Soviet society over and above the success of its machinery as an organization of tyranny. An important section of the educated and semi-educated classes at least appears to accept automatically the doctrines that have been hammered into it for a generation. Among the young people, the regime, like many other purveyors of simple dogmas, can rely on the faithful support of some millions of healthy young dimwits. Among the privileged classes, the tendency to want the regime to ease off and settle down is to some extent counteracted by the feeling that it could do so only as a result of changes that would certainly involve the ruin of some of them; and some of the privileged seem to have no real interest in or understanding of the situation and to be perfectly content with their own comforts. The authorities have gained at least some slight measure of success in rousing hostility toward the Western countries' alleged preparation for a new war. Then again, in World War II, the Soviet Government was able to some extent to rally support on the basis of Russian nationalism, and this may also be the case today.

And yet, there are other social forces and tensions within the country which may, in the long run, determine its further development.

The stresses and strains of Soviet society may conveniently be considered in two main divisions: (1) those general strains manifested over the entire breadth of society and affecting great masses of the people; and (2) those operating among the sections actually in positions of political and military power.

There is no doubt at all that the peasantry is not reconciled to collectivization of the land. The Soviet press regularly presents examples of a strong tendency for the collective-farm system to be evaded. But at present the peasantry has no effective means (apart from forged quotas and so forth) of combating the government's policies.

The minority nations of the Soviet Union are, on the whole, unreconciled. And even their political leaderships are restive at excessive Russianization and centralization.*

The economic pressures and the still frequent shortages of consumer goods result in the extremely widespread system of illegal evasion by consumers. This system of *blat* is endemic, and examples are continually being denounced in the Soviet press. Workshops and factories divert parts of their output to illegal consumers and falsify their books accordingly, thus providing the consumer with normally unattainable goods and providing the organizers of the traffic with cash.

* See the following chapter, which deals with the possibility of succession states.

There is considerable evidence of widespread class hatred in the Soviet Union—of fear and envy on the part of the underprivileged toward the ruling castes. While this feeling constitutes a significant stress in the Soviet society, it is again not really directed against the regime itself. It would even be an exaggeration to represent it as a division between Party members and others, since the highly privileged are not necessarily Party members, while the Party has a considerable membership, if not in the lowest, at least in fairly low strata of society. It is true, however, that the Party membership above its rank and file constitutes a major part of the privileged group. In addition, there is a special dislike among all sections of society for members of the secret-police organizations, and this feeling is necessarily more political in nature.

The fact that the churches are still well attended and the sects still aggressive despite years of official attacks is at least indicative of widespread failure of the Soviet Government's indoctrination of the masses.

Such, in brief summary, are the social stresses affecting the Soviet future. Apart from the strains affecting the masses directly, there are those stresses, still not overtly political, which affect the intellectuals: apparently incorrigible tendencies in philosophical, cultural, and scientific circles to diverge from the Party line in the direction of "objectivism" and "cosmopolitanism." As has already been pointed out, Soviet cultural trends do not follow the lines laid down by the regime. The intellectuals provide the focus for *all* resentments against dictatorship, besides being the standard-bearers of the desire for intellectual liberty and an end to petty control by Party hacks.

The divine right of the *apparatchik* to rule in general, and to have the final say in all decisions in every walk of life, has not been challenged—as yet, anyway—by any faction within the Central Committee, even the most "liberal." So it is natural and inevitable that the intellectuals should be the focus for all moods tending away from the regime. The rivalry for the lively minds of the new generation has been clearly expressed. In his speech of May 8, 1963, to the writers (attacking the notion put forward in the "artists' letter" of December, 1962, that various art forms must be allowed to exist), Khrushchev denounced the poet Rozhdestvensky, who had written that "the sentiments of our young people are expressed only by a group of young authors." Khrushchev retorted: "That is certainly not so. Our youth have been brought up by the Party and see in it their teacher and leader."

It is true that we cannot at present be too sanguine about even certain of the apparent "liberals"—Rozhdestvensky seems to have reached an accommodation with the regime; and this will remind us that there is no more effective supporter of an establishment than the former "young rebel." Thus a temporary comparative tolerance may pay off. Even the fairly careful treatment of less easily corrupted "liberals," like the much more significant Yevtushenko, may pay the ruling group. Such flexible attitudes in cultural matters have in any case had a particularly powerful effect on the international Soviet image, and this has been reinforced by the visits to the West of Yevtushenko and others. The young poet and like-minded fellow writers, when actually in the Soviet Union, have engaged in a continual struggle with the obscurantist elements, which still retain so much power and may at any time reassert their full authority. In attacking actual abuses in Russia, as Yevtushenko did in his poem "Babi Yar," the young writers are showing considerable courage and perhaps, in the long run, taking considerable risks. When they go abroad, they are bound to protect their flanks by saying nothing in the least hostile to the Soviet establishment, which they criticize so outspokenly at home. To do otherwise would be to make themselves extremely vulnerable to counterattack on their return to the Soviet Union. And apart from this obvious calculation, some of them doubtless feel general loyalty to a political abstraction called the Soviet Union and to an ideal Communism which does not resemble what actually exists, but whose image is perhaps more powerful in their minds than the reality. This again is natural enough and applies to some extent to all forms of patriotism. Kipling could write:

> If England was what England seems,
> An' not the England of our dreams,
> But only putty, brass, an' paint,
> 'Ow quick we'd drop 'er! *But she ain't!*

For all these reasons, the picture of the Soviet Union given by Yevtushenko when he writes or grants formal interviews abroad is much more favorable than one would gather from his poetry. But one would not want to give the impression that this reflects simply cold calculation on his part. Yevtushenko appears to be a perfectly honest man, and when he presents a different picture abroad, it represents an adjustment of tone so natural that it is, perhaps, hardly a matter of conscious thought. Moreover, by letting him out of the country—in addition to permitting publication of his poetry in the first place—the Soviet authorities provide incarnate proof of their tolerance.

Notwithstanding all that can be said in Yevtushenko's favor, it is fairly clear that he is not—and perhaps none of such writers is—representative of any general principle of freedom. His enthusiasm for Castroite Cuba, a sentiment now fashionable in young Moscow circles, is perhaps an attempt to return to revolutionary dynamism and verve, but it is scarcely a demonstration of enthusiasm for civil liberty. As a matter of fact, his poem about the anti-Communist demonstrations in Helsinki during the 1962 World Youth Festival is on the lowest Stalinist level—referring to the demonstrators as "Fascists" who "chew gum." Of course, one cannot expect a comparatively humanist and nonpolitical poet like Yevtushenko to involve himself in spheres that do not interest him. It is just that we should not fall into the error of thinking of him in an unrealistic way. To talk about him in terms of Pope's "The rights a court attacked, a poet saved" is going a little too far.

There is an element in "official" Communism that is progressive up to a point, but which it would be naïve to identify with genuine liberalism of the Nagy type. Yevtushenko may be regarded as representing the more progressive wing of the "Khrushchevite" tendency—influenced by humanist ideas, but still tied to the principles of the regime. It is conceivable, indeed, that the poet and others like him would evolve in a crisis, as so many did in Budapest. Moreover, there are certainly writers now who have been much more consistently libertarian—not even taking into account those who cannot get published—and are persecuted for that very reason. And these represent a far wider feeling both inside and outside the Party.

Yet, at every level it is plain that there is an insensitivity at the core of the Party mind, even at its most "liberal," which cuts it off from the essential aspirations of any new generation. This can be seen even in the area of economic reform. The Stalinist regime implied a siege economy: a rickety agriculture and an inadequate consumer-goods industry supporting a heavy industry far beyond the stage of the country's natural evolution. The need to maintain the economy in this state of stress was one of the motivations, and excuses, for the terror. The disproportion still exists, though it is notably less than it was ten years ago, and the Soviet economy at least shows some tendencies toward normalization, toward being able to stand alone, without the eternal buttresses of force. Yet the Party program and economic plans presented to the Twenty-second Party Congress show a curious lack of imagination. What was promised, in fact, was material prosperity approaching that of the United States in fifteen years or so. Leaving aside the question of how far doubts about the fulfillment of such promises may affect the Soviet people, it is clear that a good many of their aspirations would in any case remain totally unanswered, even by the fulfillment of the plans. It was no accident that the title of the most popular (and the most censured) book of the 1956–57 "thaw" was *Not by Bread Alone*.

The Soviet population is offered, with some vagueness, a standard of living approaching that of the West. Yet it has heard for years how the rulers of the West have not created happiness. What is more, the tales of crime and corruption in America which are the staple of much Soviet propaganda are matched in the people's own experience by the immense increase of "hooliganism" at home and in the general apathy and discontent of the younger generation.

If genuine "liberalism" carries no weight at present in the higher councils, there is an important sense in which the opinions of the writers and students are *potentially* much more significant. In every great established empire with an entrenched bureaucracy and police system, the opposition view—and that is to say the potential revolution—has been carried initially by intellectuals without access to the political machinery. A study of the Austro-Hungarian Empire and of Czarist Russia in the nineteenth century shows this clearly. It is true that these old legitimisms gave rather more scope for oppositionist organization than is the case in the present-day Soviet Union. But, although overt organization in opposition to the regime is no more possible in Moscow now than it was in Budapest in 1955, one must assert that even a totally unorganized and inchoate stratum of intellectuals can be the seedbed of future change.

The question is, rather, whether the forthcoming succession crisis will give these possibilities any chance to develop. The first and natural response is a resounding No. The momentum of the bureaucracy can certainly be expected to keep the current form of state wholly intact even during a phase of great shakiness at the top. The crux of the matter, however, seems to be how long that phase can last. A series of crises, one following quickly on the other, with second-rate and third-rate men miscalculating and wildly scrabbling for power, might give time for opinion to become truly "hardened" if it went on long enough. For if the mechanism of political rule deteriorated to this extent, we might find in the *apparat* itself that crumbling of self-confidence on the part of the ruling class which Lenin speaks of as being one of the conditions of successful revolution. It is possible, for example, to imagine in certain circumstances an ill-considered conservative coup, such as that planned by the Natolin group in Poland, which would provoke a popular outburst. Alternatively, such conditions might lead to the opposite—a military dictatorship which, however, would lack the underpinnings necessary for its viability unless it came to terms with some form of political leadership.

The great obstacle to any evolution of the Soviet Union toward greater liberty has been the inconceivability that any members of the Central Committee would be less than totally devoted to the preservation of the present system of self-perpetuating *apparat* rule. It is bred in their bones to an extent far exceeding anything in Poland or Hungary or even the other East European states. But, to draw an admittedly imperfect parallel, none of the theologians engaged in the great religious disputes of the sixteenth century had the slightest intention of allowing freedom of conscience or thought, or of abdicating the right of a priesthood to impose an ideological monopoly. Yet, as a by-product of the struggle, freedom of conscience emerged in Europe.

The factions in the Presidium are well aware of this danger. They heard Khrushchev say of the Hungarian Revolution that it might have been prevented if a few writers had been shot in time. But the logic of the struggle itself might again prevent a faction which (however two-facedly) had put forward the libertarian slogans from moving promptly and decisively against the monster of democracy, which such tactics might awaken.

Distant prospects? Perhaps. Carrying speculation too far? Surely not. For without the full range of perspectives, one is confined to a short-range view that, in effect, distorts even the immediate picture. And once we free ourselves from preconceived notions, it seems clear that among the conceivable Soviet futures democratic development is a clear and hopeful possibility. It is not attachment to any democratic mystique, not any notion of the inevitability of the Western style of political rule that leads us to such a conclusion. It is rather the evident lesson of the past decades, in both West and East, that a democratic system is better suited than a closed oligarchy to cope with the problems of a modern society.

15

Succession States?

A CONSIDERATION of the succession problem in the last years of Habsburg rule would not have been regarded as very adequate, however accurately it predicted a Social Democratic Republic in Vienna, if it omitted the point that Vienna's control would shrink from the Dniester to the Neusiedlersee. Multinational empires may give rise to succession states as well as succession regimes.

In the postwar world, one of the most insistent problems that has faced the advanced countries has been the demand for independence on the part of peoples previously ruled from the metropolitan centers. The Soviet Union has no more been able to escape this confrontation—as opposed to delaying it by the sheer use of power—than it has any of the other problems facing a modern state.

There is no shortage of material from the Soviet press proving that nationalist sentiments continue to subsist at the popular level, and among the literary and other intelligentsia in the peripheral republics. This has great relevance in that it shows that there are potentialities waiting to be tapped, ready to emerge in circumstances of change in the Soviet Union. But we should concern ourselves not merely with the a priori argument that in a disintegrating Soviet Union, a collapsing Communism, nationalist movements would automatically be thrown up.

Even in much less catastrophic conditions, national feeling may play a major part. The point is that a certain rebelliousness is already evident in the leading cadres of the national republics themselves. Just as in Eastern Europe, there are elements in the leadership of the republics that could cause considerable upheaval even without the question of the disintegration of Communism as such entering into the picture.

In fact, with weakness or schism at the center, it is not improbable that moves might be made by the leaderships of some of the peripheral union republics to increase their power, and perhaps even to effect virtual or even overt secession from the U.S.S.R. When we consider the Soviet future, we should bear in mind the possibility of some such breakup of Stalin's old empire. At the very least, there is no doubt that "nationalism," in the sense of a desire on the part of the local *apparat* for freedom from Moscow control, exists at the highest levels in the minority republics.

It must naturally occur to a First Secretary in Tashkent or Vilnius that his local Party and nationality have as much claim to independence as those of countries like Hungary or Mongolia. But while devolution is now the rule in Soviet treatment of the once rigidly controlled dependent states of Eastern Europe, within the U.S.S.R. itself the official line has lately been running strongly against this trend. At just the time when the local Communist leaderships on the Dvina and the Syr Darya have appeared to be envious of the position of their colleagues on the Danube and the Vistula, Moscow has been coming out strongly in favor not only of practices but also of theories tending to the destruction even of those national distinctions which remain in the U.S.S.R.

The last couple of years, in fact, have seen a change in the official Soviet attitude to the nationalities problem—a change that cannot but trouble all members of the local nationality and even of the local Party. For it amounts to a theoretical justification for the gradual transformation of the U.S.S.R. into a unitary state. It is true enough that the country is, for practical purposes, highly unitary already. But at present there exist at least shadow institutions manned to some extent by members of the local nationalities. And so long as such exist, there is always the distant prospect of their phantom rights being transformed, as the result of some crisis, into real ones. After all, the independent status of Poland and Hungary was never intended, when it took its present *form* in the 1940's, to provide more than a cover for Soviet rule. Yet events made it possible for these institutions to be exploited to gain some measure of local control. The situation in Latvia or Azerbaidzhan is not the same; nevertheless, a potential, even if a lesser one, does exist.

For even the present formal conditions of autonomy have on occasion been utilized as real vehicles for attempts at increased local control. And, all in all, the prospect of further centralization and further reduction and restriction upon local institutions is one that must be resented—going, as it does, against not merely the whole trend of relations between Russia and the nations of Eastern Europe, but also developments in free Asia and Africa, which cannot fail to remain attractive in the minds of the Soviet minorities.

The denationalizing tendency is in accord with the following view, flatly stated in one of the national republics: "To combine national interests and the interests common to all the peoples correctly means always to bear in mind the overriding importance of the interests common to all the peoples."*

But the declared aims of the Party are not simply the overriding of minority interests, but, in the long run, their total

* *Kommunist* (Lithuania), No. 12 (1962).

suppression. One of the most authoritative organs of the leadership, *Party Life* (December, 1962), carried an article on the national question in which it stated flatly that Marxists must oppose "the perpetuation of artificial preservation of national differences." This view is, of course, to be found in Lenin. But it has been usual to keep it in the background and to lay stress on the Soviet claim that national cultures flower particularly under the system in force in the U.S.S.R. The article went on to call for "ruthless struggle" against survivals of "every form of nationalism and chauvinism, against tendencies to national narrow-mindedness and exclusiveness, against any idealization of the national past"; it openly spoke of national traditions and customs which "run counter to the Socialist system" and called for their elimination.

Nationalist tendencies, the author maintained, might be "a serious hindrance to the building of Communism." He spoke of the need to eliminate "local patriotism in the solving of economic questions, in the choice of personnel, or in the development of national cultures," and the "forcing of parents against their will" to register their children in the schools of the local nationality even though Russian was their "second mother tongue" and the children would have been better off in Russian schools. Other local authorities were accused of refusing to allow people to take any subscription to Russian newspapers unless they took local-language papers as well.

The point about the language issue is that the School Reform Law makes the language of instruction voluntary, from the parents' point of view, as against the previous principle that both Russian and the national language were to be taught in all schools. The practical effect is that local parents wishing advancement for their children are inclined to choose Russian-language schools rather than those of their own nationality. The Russian schools are, in any case, of higher quality. A practical result from the nationalist point of view is an increasing

Russification and a shrinking of the effective scope of the local language.

A most significant article in *Voprosy Filosofii* (June, 1963) listed three main elements "discovered in recent years in a number of republics and sternly condemned by the Party" as currently marking the cruxes of local resistance: "opposition to the expansion of other-nation population; to the exchange of cadres; and to the voluntary principle in the study of national languages."

As we shall see, these are precisely the issues on which the intraparty struggle in Azerbaidzhan, Latvia, and Kazakhstan has taken place over the past few years. In demonstrating the sharpness of the disputes on these matters, we are showing the power of "nationalist" revolt within the local leaderships.

The present Party Program (adopted at the Twenty-second Congress in 1961) is a wide-ranging rebuff to such local aspirations and stands as a constant provocation to them. It expresses in the most formal way (in Section IV, "The Tasks of the Party in the Field of National Relations") the intention gradually to dissolve the separate republics. At the same time, it flatly asserts the assimilationist case in all the other issues in dispute. On the basic issue, it says:

> Full-scale Communist construction constitutes a new stage in the development of national relations in the U.S.S.R. in which the nations will draw still closer together until complete unity is achieved.

On the influx of Russian *colons*, it maintains:

> The appearance of new industrial centers, the prospecting and development of mineral deposits, Virgin Lands development, and the growth of all modes of transport increase the mobility of the population and promote greater intercourse between the peoples of the Soviet Union. . . . The boundaries between the Union Republics are increasingly losing their significance.

On the imposition of Russian cadres, it asserts:

> The growing scale of Communist construction calls for the continuous exchange of trained personnel among nations. Manifestations of national aloofness in the education and employment of workers of different nationalities in the Soviet republics are impermissible.

And on the language issue it states:

> The Party is called on to continue promoting the free development of the languages of the peoples of the U.S.S.R. and the complete freedom for every citizen of the U.S.S.R. to speak and to bring up and educate his children, in any language. . . . The Russian language has, in effect, become the common medium of intercourse and cooperation between all the peoples of the U.S.S.R.

We are, in fact, faced with a policy of merging the nations of the U.S.S.R. into a unitary state, in which the old boundaries have lost their significance, Russians infiltrate the republican apparatus without even the old residual concern for local sensibilities, and the overt linguistic Russianization of the local population is pushed through against all national objections. And the point central to our analysis is that resistance to these moves has been met with "in a number of republics" among the local leaderships. In 1959, Azerbaidzhan was purged. The condemned First Secretary, Mustafeev, was accused at the Plenum of the local Central Committee on June 16–17, 1959, of "causing bewilderment in the completely clear language question." Another secretary of the Azerbaidzhan Central Committee was charged with "artificially differentiating between native and nonlocal officials." Later, the Chairman of the Council of Ministers was obliged publicly to confess to the same deviation. The authorities took all this extremely seriously. The sending of the head of the Party Organs Department (Union Republics), Semichastny, to take over the key Second Secretaryship in Baku was strictly a crisis move.

In Latvia, the signs were even more striking. In July, 1959, it was announced that E. K. Berklav, Deputy Chairman of the Latvian Council of Ministers, had been dismissed.* Among the accusations against him, it was alleged that he had made "persistent attempts to direct the development of the republic in the direction of national limitedness and exclusiveness," particularly on the economic side, by opposing heavy manufactures and advocating emphasis on the light and food industries, "whose products are mainly consumed within the republic." This analysis was made in September, 1959, by the new local First Secretary, Pelse. He also attacked "certain comrades" who had "tried artificially to hold up the process of population movement specifically called for. In their speeches they repeatedly stated that in Riga, for example, the mechanical growth of the population by a single person must not be allowed." Their motive was said to be "a false and groundless fear that the Latvian Republic would lose its national features."† The Prime Minister, Lacis, although not directly accused of belonging to the "hostile group," was criticized and replaced in November, 1959. He had declared in favor of compulsory Latvian in schools.‡

Berklav was not isolated. During the ensuing weeks, the purge struck at many others of what came to be known as Berklav's "nationalist group." *Sovietskaya Latvia* (November 18, 1961) named as members of this group the editor of the main local-language paper (*Cina*), the Minister of Agriculture, and the Minister of Education. Among others disposed of were the local Chairman of the Trade Unions, a Deputy Chairman of the Planning Commission, the First and Second Secre-

* *Sovietskaya Latvia*, July 16, 1959.
† *Kommunist Sovietskoi Latvii*, No. 9 (1959).
‡ *Pravda*, November 29, 1959.

taries of the Komsomol, several high officials in the Riga City Soviet, and the Director of the Institute of Economics. A. E. Voss, a Secretary of the Latvian Central Committee, in even stronger terms recalled the "unmasking of the anti-Party actions of the former Party and State leaders." (And it may be noted that even this did not have adequate results. In January, 1962, the local Ministers of Culture and Education were dismissed after attacks for mistakes of a nationalist character.)

There seems little doubt that these purges of "nationalists," of which there were less striking examples in other peripheral republics, were taken very seriously in Moscow. It is plausible that the fall of Kirichenko in early 1960 was due at least in part to alleged softness on nationalism shown over this period, when he was Secretary in charge of cadres for the Union Republics.

A more recent case is equally striking. On December 25, 1962, a Plenum of the Kazakh Central Committee was held. It was attended—that is, conducted—by Kozlov in person. In an important shakeup, the local Prime Minister, Salkan Daulenov, was dismissed from his State and Party posts. The accusations referred to April, 1962; the main charge was that during drinking bouts with other Kazakhs, senior officials in the Party and State, he "made nationalist statements" and was rude to certain local officials. It was made clear that this was a case of anti-Russian Kazakh nationalism, and there were speeches denouncing Daulenov's behavior in powerful terms. One of the Kazakh officials accused with him was the "former" First Secretary of the Chimkent Provincial Party Committee, together with the head of the local state administration in that province.

Meanwhile, in Moscow, the main ideological organ of the Party, *Kommunist* (December, 1962), came out with the general statement that "the opinion of certain comrades concerning attaching certain districts to a given republic . . . only because the majority of the population is of persons belonging to the basic nationality of the given republic, also will not withstand criticism." What this referred to was soon revealed. In January, 1963, territory from Kazakhstan was transferred to the Uzbek Republic on the grounds of economic efficiency in the cotton industry.

This was made the occasion for a powerful attack on nationalism in the local press. *Kazakhstanskaya Pravda* on January 16, 1963, for example, attacked the "national narrow-mindedness" which manifested itself in the fact that "certain people still harbor old notions about territorial community and the administrative frontiers between republics. They do not want to understand that in the period of the building of Communism, economically and politically motivated frontier changes between republics, with the aim of creating the best conditions for the development of the national economy, are becoming natural and comprehensible"–linking this directly with the transfers and explaining them on economic grounds.

In fact, one finds here, both as a definite assertion and as a practical example, the policy that the ethnographical basis of the Soviet forms of "national autonomy" is no longer even to be given the formal status and priority it has had for many years. In particular, the emphasis on the "national"–i.e., U.S.S.R.–economy and its overriding interest is typical of the current Kremlin reaction to nationality problems.

Meanwhile, Kazakh grievances against the Russianization of the northern part of the republic had also roused even Party circles. The local *Party Life of Kazakhstan* (No. 1 [1963]) links nationalism in the Party with opposition to the Virgin Lands development:

> Certain comrades even lament the fact that the Virgin Lands Territory receives so much attention from the Party and the government. Such people do not understand or do not want to understand . . . that the wealth and resources of the Virgin Lands Territory are the property and pride of the whole Soviet

> people. Nationalist narrow-mindedness and egoism prevent these people . . . from . . . seeing the role of the new territory in bringing together the nations.

It went on to generalize the whole issue by pointing out that there were still people "who do not wish to take account of such a natural phenomenon as the growing rate of influx of cadres, as a result of which the republic's population is becoming progressively more mixed in its national composition."

Most recently, in the highest forum—at the June, 1963, Plenum of the CPSU's Central Committee—both Rashidov, First Secretary in Uzbekistan, and Yusupov, then First Secretary in Kazakhstan, attacked nationalism and defended the influx of Russians. Rashidov, in fact, boasted (along the lines of the new formula) that the population of the Soviet republics was becoming ever more mixed in its national composition. The issues are clear. The Moscow line is forthrightly stated. As we have seen, nationalist resistance within the Party has shown its strength and its potential.

There are signs that the post-Khrushchev regime may institute some tactical relaxations, or at least not push the denationalization program so bluntly and offensively. But there are no indications of real concessions to the national leaders. Nevertheless, in the period before us, one faction or another in Moscow might well make a play for nationalist support, as Beria did during his bid for power in 1953. As one of the products of the political struggle, comparable to attempts to seek other forms of popular backing during circumstances of political difficulty, such a development must mark an important stage in the evolution of the whole Soviet system.

Whether the Soviet Union faces centralization, devolution, or dissolution, we should note that in this sphere, too, the Chinese may play a part. They implicitly maintain their territorial claims in the Pacific Coast area and on the Kazakh frontier.

And, less explicitly, their new attitude implies a revival of their claim on Outer Mongolia, and with it a threat to at least the Buryat area. (In fact, Soviet attacks on them have charged them with supporting the historical aims of Genghis Khan.)

It is true, on the other hand, that Chinese imperialism must have very little attraction for the nationalities of Central Asia; that the Turki peoples of Sinkiang actually have even fewer rights than their fellow nationals over the border. The Russians can, therefore, play the Turki card against China with about equal plausibility, and they have begun to do so.* But even so, in conditions of crisis, Chinese support might well be usefully forthcoming for secessionist movements in Soviet Central Asia, and might be thought worth accepting, on the same principle that induced Burmese nationalists (for example) temporarily to support the Japanese against the British.

The Chinese weapon is appeal to anti-white feeling. The CPSU's letter of July 14, 1963, to the Chinese Central Committee makes the point that the Chinese had

> . . . come out against the participation of representatives of Afro-Asian solidarity committees of the European Socialist countries in the Third Solidarity Conference of the Peoples of Asian and African Countries in Moshi. The leader of the Chinese delegation told the Soviet representative that "the whites have nothing to do here." At the journalists' conference in Djakarta, the Chinese representatives followed a line toward preventing Soviet journalists from participating as fully fledged delegates on the plea that the Soviet Union was not an Asian country.

Again, the Chinese managed to exclude the Uzbek delegation from the meeting of the Afro-Asian Economic Organization held in Karachi in December, 1963, on the grounds that the "independence" of Uzbekistan was questionable. And they

* See, for example, *Komsomolskaya Pravda*, September 20, 1963.

have regularly prevented Soviet attendance at Afro-Asian meetings on the same grounds.

These are examples of an overt stand for an Asianism in which the Soviet Union can play no part, and one that carries an obvious threat to the whole Soviet presence in Asia. For the only justification for Moscow rule in Kazakhstan or Azerbaidzhan is precisely the theory that these territories are equal components of a union. To call the U.S.S.R. non-Asian is to assert that Soviet Asia is simply a possession or colony of a European power. It is easy to see where this train of thought leads.

As to the institutional possibilities of secession, as guaranteed by the Constitution through the machinery of local "governments" and Supreme Soviets, we know that they were never intended to be taken seriously. But they exist in form, and we can see how they might be used in a real crisis. In addition, the nationalities of the peripheral republics are represented in the Central Committee in Moscow. They are few in number, and their political weight has in recent years been almost negligible. Those who have carried weight have been large groupings like the Ukrainians, who are plainly not at present to be considered as in any sense representing anything more than one denationalized faction within the CPSU as a whole. The representatives of Central Asia, promoted and demoted from year to year, have been lightweights. Yet we can perhaps envisage circumstances in which the votes even of the Asian periphery might count for something, and might be cast with a view to improving the independence of the local *apparats*.

But even in the Ukrainian case, it is perhaps not totally excluded that the present lot could, in a crisis of a particular type, be forced into the position of attempting to hold Kiev against an anti-Ukrainian wave in Moscow, and fall back into a territorial schism that would in practice amount to nationalism. Kazenets or Kirilenko invoking the secession clause of the

Soviet Constitution against a Molotovite *revanchist* government in Moscow may be an astonishing and extravagant conception. Just the same, who would have imagined Hoxha standing out for independence? Not, one hastens to add, that the differences are not enormous. But so might the crises be. For if we look back at the origins of the various national Communisms, we note that not all of them were originally associated with revisionist tendencies. The Titoite secession was begun as essentially the revolt of a local *apparat*, itself then just as anti-popular and "Leftist" as–indeed, in a sense even more "Leftist" than–that in Moscow. In fact, it was precisely the future leaders of Yugoslav revisionism, like Kardelj, who immediately after the war were urging the annexation of Yugoslavia by the U.S.S.R.

Thus there are potentials within the Party for a breakup of the U.S.S.R. into national Communist states–just as in conditions of lesser crises than those we have adumbrated the Soviet empire in Eastern Europe crumbled in an earlier decade. If trouble grew more intense still, the national *apparats* might not even come into play, but instead might be overtaken by the far more powerful feelings of the national citizenry.

Meanwhile, we may note that if the Soviet Union is to deal with its colonial problem in even the most superficially adequate way, it has no real choice but to turn itself into a genuine federation. But if the unity so created were voluntary, it might be temporary and precarious. The present rulers would certainly make no move in such a direction if they could possibly help it. But they may yet find themselves constrained by forces outside their control to make concessions–which could only lead to bigger demands, put forward from positions of increased strength. The question is critical, and not only is it unsolved, but it is probably insoluble under the present system. That is to say, it is one of the elements in the present general crisis of the Soviet system, and one that could lead to future changes which may now appear remote and extravagant. Here, again, we should remember that the Soviet future is unlikely to comprise an easy and evolutionary development, and that any too cautious or conservative view of its potentialities is certain to be wrong.

16

Chinese and Other Communisms

WHEN WE WRITE of the Soviet Union and its possible evolution, it is clear that we cannot deal with even that vast country in isolation. The outer world manifests itself in two types of pressures: There is the external and ideologically hostile pressure posed by the mere existence and preparedness for self-defense of the West and the lesser non-Communist powers. And there is the weapon created by Lenin to ruin these hostile regimes (a weapon that, however, has now got out of hand)—the international Communist movement. In this context, of course, the hostile doctrines and powers of Mao Tse-tung present the greatest present challenge.

This is a vast and complex subject, and only some of the effects on Soviet policy can be dealt with here. The mere existence of two rival centers—even if the motives of both of them are simply the establishment of their own variety of thought control over the international Communist movement—is bound to lead to revolt against all types of thought control.

This is a long-term consideration, a vector that is now established in the movement but whose fullest and most general results will not emerge in the immediate future. For the present, we may view the Chinese issue as it presents itself on the stage of internal Soviet politics.

As early as July, 1963, Chinese intervention in the Soviet struggle for power was being openly alleged by Khrushchev (in his speech at the Soviet-Hungarian Friendship Meeting):

> Some comrades—know-alls—think that if they appeal to our people and our Party on the grounds that the Twentieth Party Congress' decisions on Stalin were not acceptable, and that condemnation of the personality cult was not right, the Party will promptly dismiss the Central Committee and instantly, so to speak, truth will triumph.

Who these comrades were was stated clearly soon afterward: "The C.P.R. Government . . . seeks in its statement to set the Soviet people against the Soviet Government."*

The Chinese had, in fact, justified this analysis in a letter from their Central Committee to that of the Soviet Party on June 14, which said: "If the leading group in any party adopts a nonrevolutionary line and converts it into a reformist party, then Marxist-Leninists inside and outside the party will replace them and lead the people in making revolution." And there has since been no doubt of Chinese opposition to Khrushchev or, after a brief sounding-out, to his successors.

It is sometimes implied that if a dogmatist "pro-Chinese" faction came to power, Soviet foreign policy might then swing to a position close to that of Peking. But, leaving aside for the moment other considerations which affect the whole question of the possibility of a genuine "pro-Chinese" faction in the Kremlin, the matter is not as simple as that. In the first place, Russia, unlike China, is an industrially developed country with even its consumer standards well beyond the desperate, starvation level. So, to put it simply, the Soviet Union has much to

* Soviet Government statement, August 3, 1963.

lose, as Soviet spokesmen have long been careful to point out. Remarking that half the world's population would perish in a nuclear war, a Soviet commentator, Major General N. Talensky, wrote pointedly: "Moreover, the most active, capable, and civilized portion of mankind would be wiped out."*

This is, in fact, to recognize a community of interest with the other developed powers in preventing the outbreak of nuclear war. But for the Chinese, atomic warfare, however devastating, would on the whole mean the destruction of other people's power and production. It would be expected, in fact, to bring the whole world down to the Chinese level. This is not a prospect the Russians could possibly wish to face. Even assuming that no major political upsets took place, it would mean, apart from anything else, that within the bloc China would be more powerful than Russia. Thus, *any* faction—indeed, any sort of conceivable regime in Moscow—must take a different view from Peking's on the whole question.

Heterodoxy has throughout history attracted more hatred than has disbelief. The Protestant Sea Beggars who freed Holland from the Duke of Alva had as their badge a crescent with the words "Better the Turk than the Pope." But, while there is no real reason to think of the present Soviet leadership as in principle more tolerant of Chinese ideology or more amenable to Chinese pressure than the last, it may show greater reluctance to press to extremes, a greater tendency to keep the remaining bridges to Peking in existence, however tenuously, in the hope of improvement—perhaps arising as a result of the forthcoming succession crisis in China.

In any case, it is as obvious to the Soviet leaders as it is to us in the West that the Chinese would prefer *any* faction that took a tougher line on international affairs than Khrushchev's, and that within the current leadership they prefer those who

* "The Character of Modern Warfare," *Mezhdunarodnaya Zhizm*, No. 10 (1960).

have sponsored the "hard" periods in the last two or three years over the state of affairs prevailing in mid-1963. The way is therefore open for "softer" men to brand any more or less Leftist opposition as, in effect, "Chinese" as well as "Trotskyist." And from what we have seen in unofficial accounts of meetings of the Presidium and the Central Committee, we can be reasonably sure that no epithet suitable for branding opponents goes unused. It has been suggested that an assumption by the Chinese that Khrushchev was about to fall early in 1963, and their too enthusiastic approval of the idea, became Khrushchev's most powerful weapon in the ensuing struggle. In any event, it is reasonable to conclude that Chinese support is the kiss of death for any faction on which it is inflicted.

The Chinese Party has its own special characteristics, distinguishing it from the CPSU and rendering it quite alien to the Moscow *apparat*. These are not merely doctrinal. Indeed, in *some* respects the Chinese appear to be more "liberal" than the Soviets—to take an obvious example, the Chinese publication for their people of the Soviet side, as contrasted with the Soviet withholding from their public of the Chinese case. Although this, like many other points, may appear anomalous, the conclusion to be drawn is perhaps not so much that there is a certain illogicality in one or another position as that long-established local customs—such as the Soviets' dislike of publishing any criticism of themselves—become so deep-rooted as almost to appear as a law of nature to the *apparatchik*. It is this habitual-mindedness, this inertia of thought and custom, which is the real essence of conservatism in any policy or community. It is important for us to bear in mind the immense drag of tradition on any change or progress in the Communist countries, and not only in this context.

When we speak of the possible effect of Chinese intervention at present, this is not the same as considering what might happen at a time of extreme crisis. If the situation became very fluid and self-confidence were lost at the top to any considerable extent, the Chinese might conceivably play a more positive role. This would, even then, depend upon whether the Sino-Soviet breach had meanwhile been made total and absolute, or whether some sort of *détente* between Peking and Moscow, even if only formal, had been effected. The Chinese card is one that *might* be played by a faction within the leadership, just as the card of reconciliation with Tito was played by Khrushchev against Molotov in 1955 and later. If the right atmosphere were created, it is not impossible that the "liberal" faction in the Soviet leadership might be held responsible for a dangerous breach.

If things in China remain precisely as they are, and if the Chinese continue to employ the same clumsy and doctrinaire tactics, all this would doubtless be rather unlikely. But it cannot be assumed that affairs will remain just the same. Mao Tse-tung is seventy-one, and we are soon likely to see a succession crisis in Peking. Surprises are possible. Moreover, in the event of simultaneous power struggles, a faction in Moscow might well be tempted to strengthen its hand by intervention in Peking, and vice versa.

Meanwhile, despite the various and very strong motives that make for solidarity in the face of the outer world, the two regimes are obnoxious to each other, and there is no doubt that each would use any possible means to secure the other's overthrow. There is little prospect of a real compromise. Two pike in a pond is one too many.

The cool correctness of Chou En-lai's reception in Moscow in November, 1964, represented such a change from the personal virulence of the previous phase of Sino-Soviet relations that there was an inclination to view it as warmer than it really was, or at least to wonder if it foreshadowed a further *rapprochement*. But the visit saw clear Russian announcements of policy, domestic and foreign, on lines basically unacceptable to

Peking, and an ostentatious refusal to applaud them by Chou and his entourage. So the amenities may be better preserved, and the Soviet side may believe that the tactics pursued by Khrushchev were unsuccessful, but everything points to the doctrinal dispute becoming, if anything, deeper unless further changes take place in Moscow—or in Peking.

And, of course, it is not simply a matter of doctrine. Chinese policies are always involving the Communist world in foreign dangers without the consent or approval of Moscow. Soviet criticism of Khrushchev condemned his ostentatious arming of India during the Chinese invasion, yet said nothing that could be taken either as approval of the Chinese attack or as a change of Moscow's policy of friendship with India. When the power issue is also taken into account—not merely the struggle for the leadership of world Communism, but also the active Chinese intervention in Soviet internal affairs—the corporate chauvinism of the CPSU forbids retreat.

Moreover, the policies which, under Khrushchev, the Chinese branded as a "restoration of capitalism" have demonstratively been taken a step further. As we have seen, within days of the coup in the Kremlin, the Liberman economic proposals were scheduled for application on a large scale. In the first agricultural announcement of the regime, the peasant's private plot was given special guarantees. Such an approach is anathema to Peking.

It is as plain to the Russians as it is to ourselves that, in *their* internal policies, the Chinese leaders made calculations even more erroneous than Stalin's. They seem to have thought that after a decade of indoctrination the population would support them in all circumstances. In 1957, freedom of criticism was allowed. It was even announced that the works of bourgeois authors like Keynes would be published. (This never did happen.) But the result of the relaxation was the opposite of what Mao had hoped. Everywhere the thinking sections of the population and of the Party called for an end to the dictatorship and development toward something like a social democracy. As soon as the leaders realized the position, they restored order by a gigantic purge. Since the country, if given the freedom to choose, would evidently choose wrong, this freedom was withdrawn. And, no doubt as a result, Mao swung violently to the opposite extreme. A regimentation was imposed that went far beyond even what Stalin had done in Russia. The Maoist deviation might be described as a military one; politics in the original sense was forgotten in favor of administration. The communes regulated every aspect of the peasants' lives. They lived, ate, and slept there, and family life was destroyed.

This extreme regimentation, along with the plan to produce steel in the villages (regarded by the experts in the outside world and, evidently, by many in China, too, as totally unrealistic), was eventually abandoned. In fact, such a scheme could not have been put forward in Russia even in Stalin's time. The Chinese have developed a notion of Marxist economic methods that in Russia is considered to be a Leftist, "adventurist" deviation. Here we may perhaps see, as is often apparent in other Communist countries, a national tradition influencing doctrine—the Chinese tradition of absolute and centralized administration in all things. Economic retreat had to be made, but the administrative grip became harsher. And meanwhile, the second conclusion, drawn by Mao from the instability of his regime, was that the only hope of success on a world scale was war. These decisions—an increase of terror internally and a stepping-up of aggression externally—came just at the time when the Soviet leaders, in both fields, were tending in the opposite direction.

The Soviet assessment demanded controlled relaxation inside the Communist countries, and diplomatic negotiations outside. It is true that these tactics could not have passed for anything much in the way of democratic and peaceful behavior in a normal world. Nevertheless, they were, within their limits, pushed ahead in a way that Mao seems to have regarded as fraught with disaster for the Communist movement. The ideological dispute that ensued was accompanied by a struggle for power in the international movement. There had always been tensions between Peking and Moscow, simply because one was not under the other's control. But now the breach became overt. The Communist world was divided by a major schism.

This was the most important, but not the only, crack in the Communist monolith. "Polycentrism" is a term that began to be used in the Italian and other Communist parties about 1956 to imply devolution rather than fission. The idea was of a Communist movement still wholly united in principle, but decentralized in regional groups based on the most powerful or experienced Party in the given area. But this has now been officially repudiated almost everywhere in favor of "equality" among the parties—that is, a more complete decentralization still. All this is very theoretical. Regional and other groupings existed even under Stalin—when the French Party was responsible for stamping out deviations in the American Communist Party, the British for transmitting instructions to the Communist Party of India, and so on. In the Communist movement, the formal ties have not necessarily reflected the realities of power.

The present situation is different. There is no doubt that the Italian Party has, in practice, put itself forward as leader of West European Communists. This does not, on the face of it, involve much departure from complete coordination, ideological and practical, with the Soviet Communist Party. But Italian Communist spokesmen have gone very much further in criticizing the Stalinist past than the Russians have so far done. If the more progressive wing of the Italian Communist Party firmly captures the leadership, the Party will be well over the edge of heresy more intolerable than that of Albania or Yugoslavia—or of China. Even its mere printing of the views of "liberals" like Terracini, who openly blame Stalinism on the lack of freedom of expression in the Soviet Party dating *from the 1920's*, was notably unorthodox. The condemnation of Soviet artistic repression in 1963 took things further. And Togliatti's "memoir" has provided a gospel, only semiliberal as yet, but notably deviant from any Kremlin view and strongly condemned by the Soviets. I have spoken of the Italian case first because of the way it shows how even the most partial swing to independence automatically produces the seeds of schism. And, central to our view of Russia itself, developments in other Communist parties may give us some idea of the possible directions of development in the CPSU, and of the types of pressures and problems likely to affect such development.

The first true split in the Communist movement, the expulsion of Yugoslavia in 1948, was coped with by Stalin by the rigid enforcement of unity on all those remaining in the fold. The Yugoslav case was made a test of loyalty, and any who refused to see Tito as a fascist and a former Gestapo agent were ruthlessly cut down. In those circumstances, the existence of a single heretic was in a sense useful to the centralizers. Now things are different. There are three main hostile centers of power and doctrine: Belgrade, Moscow, and Peking (with its European office in Tirana). But, in addition, the more flexible tactics of Khrushchev resulted in such phenomenons as the Italians and the Romanians.

The Gomulka regime is not considered heretical or schismatic only because the formal definitions of heresy and schism have been dangerously relaxed. It is not so much that Gomulka is, in principle, undictatorial. He is rather, perhaps, an *apparatchik* who has seen the practical failure of the extreme rigors of *apparat* rule. The lesson of the 1950's in Poland was that Stalinism, or even the sub-Stalinism of present-day Russia, was a dead end to any progress whatever being made in converting the population to an acceptance of the regime. The ten years of Communist rule had been worse than wasted. Moreover, with all Gomulka's undoubted acceptance of the present principles of Communist rule, he saw that a rigorous adherence to political preconception had led to economic disaster. It was not simply that the plans had been faulty; it was far more the fact that no one had been able to question them. And yet, although he understood this, Gomulka has never shown the moral and intellectual insight required for a clear break with dogmatism and the search for a new path.

Both organizationally and ideologically, Soviet relations with Eastern Europe have been in a state of ferment for nearly a decade. Thus far, no total retreat from Eastern Europe would seem to be likely (except in quite unforeseeable circumstances) and a more probable outcome might be the acceptance of *comparatively* unreliable and heretical buffer states which would still be an adequate defense zone. Indeed, it seems reasonable to assume that such a system would, in present circumstances, do more to encourage the spread of some sort of Communism, or at least neutralism, in Western Europe than any severer pressures could. Taking a long-range view, there might even be some prospect of reducing these newly proliferating moderate Communist regimes to order at a later date, just as Stalin was able to purge the Communist regimes of Eastern Europe, *after* they were fully established, of genuine revolutionary and national elements which had been necessary during the takeover of power.

The most obvious difficulty, of course, is presented by East Germany, where Soviet withdrawal would certainly lead to the total collapse of the Communist regime. Soviet military objections to a reunited Germany are obvious. Although the German Democratic Republic is a great nuisance to the U.S.S.R., withdrawal and the presentation of the area to Bonn on any terms at all would be hard for it to swallow. At an earlier stage, it might have been possible to trade the G.D.R. for an all-German neutralization. Such a possibility may hardly exist now, but when it did, some members of the Soviet leadership seem to have seriously considered the abandonment of the Ulbricht regime. It appears that Khrushchev and Adzhubei, in their last phase, were toying with the idea of some deal. The lesson is perhaps that only a firmly established regime in Moscow could rid the world of the East German ulcer, and that if such an offer is made to the West, we should clinch it on any reasonable terms before the next coup in the Kremlin.

But this is not the place to discuss all the varied possibilities of an unpredictable international situation; there are more than enough imponderables to handle in connection with Soviet internal politics alone. In that context, it is worth noting that the difficulties arising from the devolutionary policy in Eastern Europe tend to discredit such a policy among the Soviet *apparatchiks* and hence to strengthen opponents from the conservative wing at present comparatively dormant.

Meanwhile, heretical currents in the satellite and other Communist parties cannot but have some effect on the thoughtful in the Soviet Union. And practices hitherto condemned in Russia, but now in operation in Yugoslavia and elsewhere, are, when successful, bound to affect Soviet economists. The same applies, for example, to the devastating analyses of orthodox Communist economic policy which have been appearing in Czechoslovakia.*

One of the results we may hope for from the current breakdown of Communist centralization is the progressive disintegration of the effective political challenge to the democratic

* For example, that of the Vice-Chairman of the Czechoslovak Academy's Economic College, in *Politicka Ekonomie*, No. 5 (1964).

world. There may be another equally important probable development. In Yugoslavia, doctrine has evolved under pressure to the point that the Titoites no longer officially regard the Communist method as suitable to the entire world, and no longer even view the "capitalist" societies of the West as lacking in progressive and evolutionary features.

The original Yugoslav revolt was simply that of one *apparat* against another. The truly democratic tendencies which took the opportunity to show themselves and are implied in the thought of Milovan Djilas and his call for political liberty and a multiparty system never got very far. Nevertheless, the national *apparatchiks* themselves learned by experience, so that now the economic measures are adjusted to the real situation of the country rather than to dogma, and the view has been officially abandoned that only Communist parties can introduce Socialism and that the social systems of the West are simply "capitalist" without redeeming features. That Marxist-Leninist doctrine can evolve under pressure is a cheering fact. We have to consider what the pressures are under which Soviet doctrine itself might improve. The answer seems to be: on the one hand, the arising in Soviet society of increasingly powerful aspirations for a different life, and on the other the military power of the non-Soviet countries to prevent the expansionism to which dictatorships facing troubles naturally tend.

Even Yugoslavia, it is true, remains a one-party state, so that developments in the direction of "liberalism" have nowhere reached a crucial point internally. But there are voices in the Communist movement—in Italy particularly, but also among Polish official theoreticians like Schaff, and elsewhere—that call for at least a measure of true political freedom. Nor is it only a question of theorists: The pressures for evolution in broad strata of society even in Russia are obviously powerful and are going to become more powerful. It cannot be other than a long and painful process. But there is at least *some* prospect of an evolution within Communist parties that would turn them into organizations like the one Nagy almost succeeded in creating in Budapest in 1956. That is, while retaining their social and political objectives, they would abandon the two points that make them intolerable in the world community—desire for world conquest and refusal to accept democratic verdicts. This is a long-term prospect, and one that (in spite of the deeply ingrained Rightism of the intellectuals and others, as shown in 1957) seems to be a nonstarter in China. In the Soviet Union, the solidarity of the *apparatchiks* is a very formidable obstacle. Yet the mere possibility of such a long-term change is something we should not fail to take into account.

17

The Role of the West

GEORGE ORWELL, writing at the height of Stalin's power, said that although the way Stalinism would end could not then be predicted, the inevitability of its end was clear enough. Viewing the situation after more than a decade, we can see and begin to interpret the trends and tendencies that were not manifest in Orwell's time. Our interest is not simply academic. Nor is it only a matter of humanist sentiment, of wishing to extend to the subjects of the Communist world the liberties available in the democracies. The question is even more vital. In our nuclear age, it is of urgent interest to us that a doctrine of irreconcilable hostility against all other beliefs and systems should cease to be a military threat to the populations of the world.

The Communist regimes, as they are constituted at present, are objectionable on moral grounds, and at the same time they are a menace to world peace—a menace because of the basic principle of Stalinist megalomania. They are not the only regimes that are morally objectionable, nor do they constitute the only threat to peace, but in both spheres they are much more basically menacing than anything else—simply as the most powerful, the most intransigent, and the most expansionist of the dictatorships now in existence. Yet, even within the Communist sphere, there are better and worse governments in this respect. We must distinguish. And we must see what possibilities of further improvement exist.

We may ask what the criteria are for a real peace in the world—not a Utopian condition of total fraternity, but a relationship among all countries at least no more hostile than that now prevailing among the non-Communist states. The question is worth asking not simply on theoretical grounds but because the criteria for such a genuine peace must exert a natural and logical attraction to those with progressive minds, even within the Communist parties. They are bound to come to much the same conclusions as ourselves, and in fact some of the criteria presented here have already been formulated by certain Communists.

Such a peace would involve a settlement of outstanding individual disputes, particularly the German problem, and would imply the control and inspection of armaments. These points are obvious, and even the most Stalinist of the Russians at least claims to be working for them. But genuine peace implies more than this. *Pari passu* with progress in these international fields must go a relaxation of Soviet internal conditions which are partly a result of international tension and partly the cause of it. In the first place, there can never be genuine peace until what amounts to the state of siege in the Soviet Union has ended and there is a free influx and efflux of ideas and travelers. And this would imply the end of the Soviet siege economy, freedom for decollectivization of the land, adequate autonomy for national minorities, freedom of trade-union organization, and the reduction of heavy industrialization to a tempo acceptable to the population. It will be noted that none of these points has any bearing on the question of altering the essentials of the Russian social system, in so far as these may be described as Socialist (except, in one view, on the farms—but even here there are Communist countries where the Russian methods have been abandoned, as in Yugoslavia and Poland, without the social structure being thereby revolutionized).

For what most people object to about Communist regimes and the Communist movement as they are presently constituted has nothing to do with the type of society the Communists claim to be constructing. Far from being a social objection, it is a political one pure and simple. It is concerned with methods of rule, and for this purpose quite similar objections would be brought against a Conservative or Cao Dai government that used the political techniques and made the political claims in question.

If the Communist regimes are to remain virtually unchanged, then there is nothing to be done. We are in for a struggle *à l'outrance*. Their claims are total and their appetites insatiable, as a matter of principle, and we can in the long run expect from them nothing but subjugation or nuclear war, or —at best—continuous and dangerous stalemate. But they are *not* unchangeable. Certain changes have already taken place.

It is easy to say that if the Communist countries were converted to Western democracy and the Communist parties were to disappear, the problems would no longer arise. But this seems rather beside the point. We have asked ourselves what changes in a Communist state—however much one still disagreed with its principles and practices—would make it an acceptable or at least tolerable part of the world community. But secondly, we must ask, are such changes possible? With all the reservations that need to be made, we may yet conclude that such changes are possible; that the Communist countries can remain "Communist," retain their current social structure and (except perhaps in certain cases) rule by a Communist Party with the same social program, and yet cease to be a threat to world peace and in a continual state of strife against their own populations. Even Tito's one-party Yugoslavia, with its modification of the notion that only Communist parties are in principle legitimate rulers, and of some of the more extreme pretensions in internal matters, has rendered itself more or less tolerable (even though, while power remains in the hands of a self-perpetuating *apparat*, this is not irreversible).

Meanwhile, our objectives are twofold. If we take the long-range view, only a fully liberalized Russia can be a tolerable member of the world community. This, as we have said, is not for idealistic reasons, but for the pragmatic one that a state based on an ideology with pretensions to world rule and organized on a siege basis is automatically a permanent threat to peace. It is possible to imagine a state still Communist in some general sense which would have abandoned most of this. In the more immediate view, though, it is our overriding interest, pending any such radical improvement, to prevent the outbreak of nuclear war with the Russian State of the present and near future. These objectives may not necessarily harmonize on all occasions. There might be circumstances in which a ruler who seemed—objectively if not subjectively—to be helping the progress of the U.S.S.R. toward true liberalization might yet be more of an immediate threat to world peace than a stand-pat Stalinist. Even Napoleon may in a sense be thought of as a liberalizer and at the same time an aggressor; and we can, in any case, recall a far closer lesson from the French Revolution itself, when it was the extremist Jacobins who were the peace party and the moderate Girondins the war party.

Again, another factor affecting a Soviet leader in any tendency to foreign adventure must be his assessment of the power of his country. The optimist who believes that the economy is, or shortly will be, in fine shape is at any rate more inclined to an expansionist policy vis-à-vis the "capitalist" world, and less likely to play for time than the pessimist, even though the latter may be basically more hostile to us. It is worth remembering that Stalin totally abandoned foreign adventure and expansionism during the whole decade up to World War II.

In fact, we must distinguish between hostility and aggressiveness. The most dangerous move of the last ten years—even, perhaps, of the last twenty years—was the installation of Soviet missiles in Cuba. While the precise argumentation about this at the top Soviet level cannot be investigated, we know it happened in a period when Khrushchev appeared to be in a very strong position—and, indeed, one during which his "liberalization" within Russia was at its height. Khrushchev's style of leadership (as we noted earlier) was associated with maneuvers combining *élan* with the appearance of giving vast profits on the cheap. The Cuban intervention had many of the stigmata of this style. It was an "adventurist" risk far greater than any run by Stalin.

Even the Chinese censured it. And when we consider a dogmatist wing in Russia, we are thinking of something a good deal less extreme than anything in China. Even from the point of view of Stalin, Mao and his associates would be considered Left adventurists, the communes an "infantile" deviation, and the attack on India an absurd miscalculation. If we take Molotov as the most "dogmatist" of the Soviet figures, and allow the possibility that he, or men like him, might return to power, we must still remember the type of foreign policy he stood for in his heyday. The Stalin-Molotov line certainly involved aggression where it was thought aggression would pay. But it also involved a good deal of prudence. When a real military threat to Russia was building up in Germany before the Nazi-Soviet Pact, Stalin acted with the greatest circumspection. And although, with German connivance, he made territorial advances in the following years, it is notable that the Nazi-Soviet Pact—which was backed on the non-Soviet side by a powerful military weapon—was the only treaty the Soviet Union never broke.

Even after the war, when the Soviet forces were by far the most powerful in the world, the forward policy in Europe was pursued rather circumspectly. The Berlin blockade was never really allowed to get out of hand, and defeat there was accepted. Stalin wrote off the Greek rebellion, telling Djilas that it was quite hopeless since the Americans and British would never allow Greece to fall into Communist hands. Similarly, after Stalin's death, the policy Molotov advocated was certainly extremely anti-Western, tough on atomic weapons, wholly unwilling to make any concessions whatever—but there is no sign that he proposed anything in the nature of aggressive risks.

If we ranked the three leaders who have contended for power in recent years in this light, we would probably now decide that in the long view, Molotov was the least liberal in domestic affairs, Malenkov moderately "progressive," and Khrushchev the most "progressive." If we looked at their foreign policies, we would find Molotov most hostile to the West, but probably very prudent in his hostility; Malenkov most inclined to come to a settlement on the basis of the *status quo;* and Khrushchev somewhat inclined to "adventurist" acts.

Even before Beria's fall, the post-Stalin regime had already initiated certain measures of a comparatively peaceable nature, such as the negotiations leading to the Korean armistice. But Beria's fall did not mean the end of a certain relaxation. (Rakosi, who thought it did, was swiftly rebuked by the surviving colleagues of the police chief.) Malenkov is now accused, along with Beria, of wishing to pursue a policy of surrender over the German question.* And at the time of his fall from the premiership, in 1955, he was also strongly attacked† for his statement, in his speech to the Supreme Soviet on March 13, 1954, that "a fresh world carnage, given modern methods of

* See Khrushchev's speech of March 8, 1963.
† See *Kommunist,* No. 4 (1955).

warfare, means the ruin of world civilization." It seems possible that if he could have defeated the Khrushchev-Molotov coalition ranged against him in 1954–55, he might have brought to a fruitful conclusion certain ideas of disengagement. An interesting piece of evidence was the use of one of the usual Communist peace meetings in February, 1955, as a sounding board for the open advocacy of the acceptance of the Eden plan for Germany.* Nothing more was heard of this after Malenkov's demotion, which took place that same month.

There is a further consideration. Different conditions obtain when a person or faction is firmly in power from those prevailing when a struggle of particular intensity is taking place. Stalin could afford to accept defeat. He could either prevent all further discussion of the subject or (if so inclined) could blame some more or less innocent subordinate. When a major struggle is taking place, things are obviously different. If there is a defeat, the leader of the moment can be blamed for it, unless he has managed to involve the opposition in the project. And—even if it is their project which he has reluctantly accepted—members of the opposition can perhaps blame him for vacillation in execution. In these circumstances, a contender may press for a dangerous policy originally as a debating point in the struggle for power, and press it too far for either faction to accept responsibility for a retreat. In a general sense, the point is obvious. The question is rather how substantial such a danger is.

We are arguing, of course, at a time when the nuclear rocket is an absolutely decisive weapon. But even in these circumstances, there have been Soviet pressures, as in Cuba and Berlin, that have entailed risk—despite the fact that the Russian leaders seem aware of the extreme dangers of a nuclear war and reject with horror the Chinese notion that the mutual

* See *Trybuna Ludu*, February 9, 1955.

destruction of the Russian and American populations and industrial achievements would be a price worth paying for world Communism. If we are viewing the problem over a long period, though, we must at least bear in mind the possibility of developments that would considerably lessen the decisiveness of present weapons. A real breakthrough in the antimissile field, for example, might produce a situation in which the temptation to war could be just enough to swing the mind of a comparatively expansionist and belligerent Soviet leader, and just not enough to convince one who was of a more prudent turn of mind.

We should consider, also, what relation of forces *between* the Communist states is of the greatest benefit to us. It might be argued—though perhaps with excessive sub-Machiavellian cunning likely to rebound against its sponsors—that since it is in the democratic interest to ensure a schism between Moscow and Peking, everything possible should be done to see that a "revisionist" ascendancy in one capital should be balanced by a "dogmatist" regime in the other. In fact, if Mao's death were followed by the triumph of one of the "Rightist" factions which have shown themselves in recent years, our interests would (on this argument) be best served by the return to power of a "Leftist" group of rulers in the Kremlin. Viewed this way, the argument seems dangerous. The Soviet Union is the true repository of modern military power in the Communist world, and it is presumably our basic interest in all circumstances that the least aggressive regime available should control it. Even a Sino-Soviet bloc reunited on a moderate basis would, one imagines, be preferable to a dogmatically aggressive Russia. But taken the other way, with a Maoist China and a "modernizing" Russia, the point is considerably less clear; it may well be argued that the present situation is better in the short term at least than a Communist bloc united on a Soviet basis. And, in any event, we have to consider the extent to which the Khrushchevite type of Communism is genuinely nonaggressive—a question to which we have been unable to give an entirely positive answer. (A *truly* "revisionist" regime in both capitals would certainly be the most acceptable development in every respect.)

Such a point is not susceptible of easy answers. It may suggest a maneuver too sophistical for a real policy. And it does not raise any issue on which the evidence as such is relevant, and so cannot be pursued further. But, with all these reservations, it represents a train of thought that should perhaps not be entirely dismissed.

The divisions in the Communist world are extremely relevant to our attitude to the prospects of nuclear war. One sees it argued that it would be better to surrender to the Communists than to have such a war. Now, naturally this is not in any case the choice as it really presents itself—for the multilateralist case is that a refusal to surrender is also our best chance of avoiding atomic catastrophe. But the thesis contains, in addition, a totally unjustifiable hidden assumption—that a world which had surrendered to the Communists would at least avoid nuclear warfare.

There has already been one war between governments headed by Communists—the short Hungarian-Soviet conflict of October–November, 1956. A Soviet-Polish war, at the same time, was barely averted; the Chinese tell us that they managed to deflect the Russians at the last moment, but the troops of the two sides were already facing each other, and it was clearly a near thing. Ironically, the decisive factor seems to have been that the Poles, though not strong enough to defeat the Russians themselves, were strong enough to strike into Eastern Germany and produce the world war they would have preferred to capitulation. In fact, the effective deterrent to a bigger intra-Communist conflict was the existence of the Western powers and their rockets. In a world wholly under Communist rule, there is no doubt that the Russians would have struck at Warsaw. That this might have led to Chinese intervention is a reasonable speculation.

Other wars within the bloc have at least been planned: For instance, we are told by the British leftist Konni Zilliacus (on the authority of the Czechoslovak Vice-Premier, Z. Fierlinger) that Rakosi was considering an attack on Yugoslavia. It is clear, in any case, that if such things can occur even within a Communist group of states that considers itself menaced by the democracies, *a fortiori* they would show up on a much bigger scale in a 100 per cent Communized world. Moreover, apart from the counterdeterrent, the main inhibition upon the free employment by the Russians of their atomic weapons is the existence of a non-Communist political opinion which they are concerned not to alienate. This would not apply in a Communist world. And we can envisage a series of frightful clashes with neither side inhibited in any way either by humanity or by public opinion. Those who now advocate surrender would find that they had paid the price of accepting totalitarianism without even receiving the *quid quo pro* of peace.

The nature of Soviet international motivations is crucial to the understanding of the fearful world problems facing us. Yet study of it, or even serious attention to it, is amazingly neglected even by people seeking rigorous analysis of, for example, the nuclear question. For example, Professor P. M. S. Blackett has written* of disarmament in a way that purports to be rigorously logical and is backed by careful quantitative analysis of the effects of nuclear weapons. But when it comes to the political question on which all the rest is dependent, he lapses into vagueness, with "any sane government" being deterred from striking first by the prospect of 10 million or 100 million deaths. The whole question, of course, is the extent to which that vague word "sane" applies to the Soviet

* *Scientific American*, April, 1962.

rulers in this context. (As it stands, Professor Blackett's remark is evidence only of his, and presumably other liberal and democratic, opinions, and hence may tell us something about the attitudes of the governments of the Western democratic culture.) The Soviet Government has certainly done things in the past that *we* would regard as insane—Stalin's execution of the majority of his officer corps, for example. No one would deny that the present sanity quotient of the regime is higher than Stalin's. But how much higher? Ideology, the notion that it is the Party's duty to rule the world, is itself a paranoid compulsion. And we have noted other elements of irrationality in the *apparatchik* mind.

In any case, the Soviet motivation cannot be penetrated by vague "common-sense" notions. (And Professor Blackett's own inadequacy on the point is strikingly demonstrated by his curious theory that Stalin's political *gleichschaltung* of Eastern Europe was motivated *militarily*, as a defense against the American postwar atomic monopoly.) Soviet foreign policy emerges, on the whole, as clumsy, awkward, and often muddled as to immediate objectives. But its basic characteristic is that it is always (and for essential doctrinal reasons) "forward." That is, it is concerned to force situations. The astonishing thing is that certain Westerners who would be horrified at the West's promotion of self-determination in Soviet Asia, for example, find little to reprobate in armed Communist adventures in the backward areas of the rest of the world.

Although the present Russian leaders have (as the Chinese have not) understood much of the danger to themselves of any possible nuclear war, they continue to engage in this kind of peripheral trouble-making, which is inevitably dangerous. And this is especially true when the information upon which they act is so often plainly defective. Litvinov used to warn foreigners in his last years, at considerable risk to himself, that the members of Stalin's last Politburo were absolutely and dangerously ignorant of the realities of the outer world. Looking at the current Presidium, we may wonder which of them is much superior in this respect to their predecessors. As Burke put it, "A great empire and little minds go ill together."

In Anatole France's *Thais*, the Prefect's secretary remarks, "There are forces, Lucius, infinitely more powerful than reason and science." "What are they?" asked Cotta. "Ignorance and folly," replied Aristaeus.

Conceding that this is a cynical, short-range attitude, and that in the longer run those who are mad will be destroyed, we might yet point out that we have seen great nations possessed by rulers of maniac delusion whose power has been enough to ruin whole continents. This is to take the most pessimistic view possible. It is much more probable that any rulers arising in Russia over the next years will at least be sufficiently prudent about atomic war. Yet, though probable, it is not certain. There is no institutional guarantee against another Stalin—and one perhaps less prudent than the old dictator. We have seen already that the *apparat* is not an adequate reservoir of men of good sense. Nor is current doctrine a source of good will to the non-Communist world. There may be no need to worry ourselves unduly about the rise of a truly belligerent ruler in Russia. Nevertheless, until there are institutional guarantees against such a development, we cannot exclude it completely. If the internal situation in Russia deteriorates, we should be vigilant. A combination of characteristics that have already been seen in the supreme leadership—say, Stalin's paranoia and Khrushchev's irresponsibility—would be hard to cope with. And there are circumstances when a hard-pressed *vozhd* might consider a thousand hydrogen bombs straddling the Northern Hemisphere preferable to even a single bullet in his own neck.

We may ask if it is, in fact, possible for Western policy to have any effect on the outcome of a conflict within the Presidium. This question can be considered in terms of general policy, on the one hand, and specific intervention, on the other. Since we cannot particularize with any great probability about the future, we must look instead at one or two examples from the recent past.

It is obvious that Western foreign policy is one of the components of the world in which the Soviet leaders operate, and one of which they are continuously aware. And it can be said straightaway that the mere existence and maintenance of the military power and the world alliance of the West is a powerful pressure upon the Russian leadership. If this pressure were substantially slackened, encouragement would certainly be given to the more aggressive elements in the Kremlin.

One assumes that no substantial change is going to take place in our policies as such. For it seems plain that the best way to encourage any "progressive" faction in the Kremlin is to offer the most powerful and indisputable evidence of complete determination to resist any aggression, and at the same time complete willingness to settle all problems in a peaceful manner. And, in addition, there is the economic effect, in that the U.S.S.R. is not economically equipped to compete with the United States in a modern armaments race and at the same time to do anything serious toward settling its internal economic problems. So that, again so long as the West maintains and modernizes its armaments, there is continual pressure on Russian leaders to call off the race or else to abandon the economic reforms they themselves may consider to be essential. In the process, the competition is exacerbated between advocates of aggressive expansionism (and certain inadequately politicalized sections of the military) and more realistic elements.

The general lines of Western policy are not, in fact, in question. And in this context all that one can urge is that the goal of encouraging and strengthening that section of the leadership most inclined to seek compromise with the West should always be borne in mind in the making of speeches, the drafting of notes, and all other activities of a foreign-policy nature.

How the West might more directly influence any of the crises in the leadership is another matter. We may consider past cases. First of all, it seems to be established that, in the U2 incident of 1960, the Presidium must originally have voted for Khrushchev to go through with the Paris summit, and that President Eisenhower's acceptance of responsibility for the flights was decisive in producing a vote forcing Khrushchev to wreck the meeting. This is not to say that the particular decision of the President was (or even could have been) decisive in itself in a struggle for power at the time, but it might have turned out to be the last *banderilla* necessary to get the First Secretary in position for a moment of truth later on. Nor are we arguing that considerations of the effect in Russia should have been the only ones taken into account by the President. There is substance in the idea that if he had failed to take responsibility, this would have strengthened the false and dangerous Soviet image of the Pentagon as a bunch of suspicious warmongers actually operating along lines contrary to the policies of the U.S. Government. All the same, it seems doubtful that the possible effect in Russia was adequately considered, and it certainly shows that Western actions can influence the vote in the Presidium.

We may next consider a case in which no action was taken by the West, when the Presidium was in disorder and seems to have voted its final decision by a narrow margin which suitable Western policies might possibly have modified: Eastern Europe in 1956, and specifically the Hungarian intervention.

The West clearly had done no adequate contingency planning in advance to cope with such situations as the ones that arose in Warsaw and Budapest in October, 1956. Even with the unfortunate diversion of Suez, it seems conceivable that a Western diplomatic initiative during the last days of that month might have changed the whole situation. Without trying to suggest the precise detail of a policy for the occasion, one can imagine that a firm and public offer of neutralization for the whole of Allied and Communist Central Europe, perhaps coupled with an implied threat of intervention in Hungary and Poland, might either have swung the Presidium into acceptance of the Nagy Government or, as a lesser objective, at least have diverted and confused it long enough for the Hungarian Revolution to be stabilized as a *fait accompli.*

The arena in which this would have been settled would have been the Presidium in Moscow, and every move made by the West would, in effect, have been a pressure on the minds of its members. And once Moscow's policy had been decided, either way, the struggle for power would clearly have been notably affected. As it was, Khrushchev was in difficulties with his colleagues for the rest of the year even though he could claim to have won a partial defensive victory. Unmistakable defeat might have had a different result—not necessarily ensuring the triumph of Molotov, but, on the contrary, perhaps making it necessary for Khrushchev to destroy his opponents even more quickly.

Cases in which we actually know that Western action has had some effect on a struggle for power in the Communist countries are bound to be rare. If only for this reason, it is worth referring to the Swiatlo case. There is no doubt that the revelations of this high-level official of the Polish secret police, coming at just the right time in 1955, played an important role in the development of the inner-Party crisis in Poland during the following year. Swiatlo was, of course, a windfall, and the West will be lucky to get anything like him again. Nevertheless, there have been other leakages of confidential information. Khrushchev's "secret speech," distributed by the U.S. State Department in 1956, had no direct effect in the Soviet Party, where its contents were already known, but indirectly, through the international Communist movement, a shock wave was set up that was soon reflected back to the Presidium, with momentous effects.

Indeed, we must be careful not to misunderstand the way in which even Swiatlo had his results. It can hardly be thought that his revelations about secret files kept on Polish Politburo members by Berman and his police organizers could have come as very much of a surprise to the local top leadership itself. It was at a slightly lower level, but probably including many members of the Central Committee, that the information provided a useful shock; and thereupon it became usable against the Stalinist "Natolin" faction in the top-level struggle itself.

Such things, in any case, are useful weapons, and the timing of their employment can to some extent be adjusted to suit any hopes we may have of influencing a struggle for power. Any really firm information (such as that provided by the Smolensk Archives against the unfortunately not very influential Korotchenko) might have an effect if properly utilized.

If any sort of disintegration of morale were to set in in Moscow during a succession crisis, it would perhaps increase the likelihood of this type of material becoming available, and we can at least hope that the Western leaders have that possibility in mind. And it might, in any case, be feasible to concentrate what firm information they already have, but which is not available in the U.S.S.R., and have it ready for specially planned campaigns rather than dissipate it piecemeal.

We may note that the immediate effect of Stalin's death was to produce an atmosphere of crisis. The public appeal of the ruling bodies called openly for the avoidance of "panic and disarray,"* as if these were to be expected in the absence of strong counteraction. This period of fear and insecurity at the top was one in which it is conceivable that the West might

* *Pravda*, March 7, 1953.

have taken advantage in some way. Even some direct approach or implicit promises of support to proponents of suitable policies at such a critical moment might have been possible.

When Stalin died, some sort of relaxation of foreign and home policy was doubtless to be expected. But his control of his subordinates' overt thinking had been so strict that there was little to go on in judging which of the new leadership would incline most strongly to policies of *détente*. What evidence there was, however, might have prepared us to expect Molotov to be the advocate of a tough, old-fashioned, Stalinist line; Malenkov to be a pragmatic, nonfanatical, and (in a sense favorable to ourselves) unprincipled ruler; and Khrushchev, perhaps, inclined to ill-considered adventurism, as with his 1951 *agrogorod* scheme. But the general assumptions actually made by the West do not seem to have been accurate enough. Malenkov, as the ruthless bureaucrat, and Beria, as the ruthless police chief, were looked upon with particular suspicion. Yet it seems certain that Beria's plans envisaged a considerable disengagement in Europe (including perhaps even the abandonment of the G.D.R.) and measures of relaxation in the Communist bloc. A further though quite different argument for backing Beria is that if he had come to power it must have been in circumstances that would have made the Soviet state extremely unstable; and it is at least arguable that such a condition might produce a highly desirable result.

However, Beria went quickly. And the circumstances of his overthrow are such that it seems most unlikely that the West could have influenced matters either way. (The Berlin rising, which probably played a part in bringing him down, was the only relevant event in which the West might have had any influence whatever.) One can perhaps envisage similar events in which the West's influence would be stronger. Clearly, in a similar crisis, there would be many other considerations before us than simply speculation about what effect our actions might have on the fortunes of a Soviet faction supposedly favorable to us. Nevertheless, it is a point that needs to be borne in mind, and strongly.

Meanwhile, it seems extremely important to keep a vigilant watch on political events at the top Soviet level—including the minute details of the struggle—since, whether we can influence them at a given moment or not, they will certainly create changes that the West should not fail to recognize and to exploit. We may conclude with Colonel G. F. R. Henderson's comment on Stonewall Jackson: "The motive power which ruled the enemy's politics as well as his armies was always his real objective. . . . Every blow struck in the Valley campaign, from Kernstown to Cross Keys, was struck at Lincoln and his Cabinet." As a generality, this is probably always recognized; but it seems doubtful that it is borne in mind with adequate concreteness in day-to-day diplomatic planning.

Such, in any case, are the short-run considerations—none the less urgent for that, from the point of view of avoiding war. All the same, the firm establishment of world peace—and a reasonable life for the Soviet peoples—depends upon the evolution of Russia toward a genuine liberalism.

18

A Liberal Future?

ALTHOUGH THERE ARE no real portents of any relaxation of the grip of the *apparat* (whether in "progressive" or "conservative" hands) on the instruments of power, nevertheless, as we have noted, there are stirrings or tendencies in more than one field which may be taken as the harbingers of a saner society. If the best came to the best, it might well be that the Khrushchev era would rank with other attempts to combine despotism with relaxation—which are seen later as symptomatic of the end of autocracy. Even economically—if, roughly speaking, we view a free economy as a pyramid held together by natural laws, and Stalin's economy as an essentially unstable structure held together only by the iron cables of main force—we may think that any turn toward stability must automatically render such extraneous trusses less necessary, and thereby hasten their decay. But, despite signs of hope, there is a long way to go yet even in this field.

What we seem to see at present is partial and interrupted progress by a wing in the apparatus that can be described as "concessionist" only in comparison with its opponents. As in many other historical cases, the argument of the "concessionists" is that extreme repressive measures of the Stalinist type are likely in the long run to prove more dangerous to *apparat* rule than more permissive tactics. These were the ideas found in the France of Turgot and Necker—and, indeed, in the France of Mirabeau—in the late eighteenth century. And, again, the transformation of Napoleon III's regime into the "Liberal Empire" in the last year of his reign was similarly motivated. The trouble is, of course, that although repression leads autocracies into great difficulty, so does concession.

There are certainly elements that would prefer a less oppressive method of rule. But, as Tolstoy said of the "liberal" Russian landowners in Czarist times, they would do anything for the peasant except get off his back; and a similar comment would seem to apply to the "liberal" *apparatchik*.

For even a benevolent despotism is not, in any sense whatever, a democracy. Moreover, it can very easily give way to a malevolent despotism. Chateaubriand, in his *Etudes Historiques*,* deals with the early years of the Roman Empire. After considering the faults of the bad emperors, he goes on to examine the good ones. He points out that they had every sort of merit, and were in positions of such power that they could do what they chose:

> Yet what was achieved by this despotism of virtue? Did it bring about a reform in morals? Did it re-establish liberty? Did it save the Empire from its downfall? No. Human nature was neither improved nor changed. Firmness reigned in Vespasian, moderation in Titus, generosity in Nerva, greatness in Trajan, the arts in Hadrian, and piety in Antoninus. Finally, with Marcus Aurelius, philosophy itself was placed on the throne; and yet this fulfillment of a sage's dream brought no solid benefit. For nothing is durable or even possible when everything comes from good will and nothing from the law.

This absolutely vital point, which has not been properly grasped by many middle-of-the-road liberals in the West, was

* Vol. I (Paris: 1833), pp. 134–204.

clearly stated by the left-wing Italian Socialist leader Pietro Nenni. On October 25, 1964, his newspaper, *Avanti*, published an exchange of letters between Suslov and himself from the period following the first denunciation of Stalin in 1956. He had written: "It was impossible for the Congress—and its Central Committee—not to have been aware that they were not only destroying the Stalinist myth but also calling in question the juridical and political structure of the State, the very idea and practice of one-party government and the conduct of economic and social affairs—in short, the entire system."

He found the fault to lie not in Stalin's or Beria's personal tendencies, but in "the absence of any system of juridical guarantees against abuses of power. . . . What is more, despotism and abuse have become systems of government, and one cannot but fear that despotism and abuse will rear their heads again tomorrow as they did yesterday, if the denunciation of the 'shameful facts' of the Stalin era is not followed by a full and complete restoration of democracy and liberty."

Commenting on this exchange to the weekly *Espresso* (November 1, 1964) after the fall of Khrushchev, Nenni remarked: "It is now possible to draw the moral, which is that the good will and good faith of human beings, even those endowed with exceptional personalities, are powerless against the vices of a system. There is no doubt that Khrushchev was an exceptional personality, but his limitations, in many ways, were symptomized by the fact that he never managed—or even intended—to change the system. That being so, it was inevitable that he should be crushed."

In fact, no liberalization is secure until it is fully institutionalized. We see the example of Poland, where things looked extremely promising in 1956, but where a great many of the liberties have been whittled away and there is clearly nothing to prevent their total destruction unless it is calculation by the rulers that over the long term this might produce revolt.

Today, as under Stalin, the citizen of the U.S.S.R. has, in practice, no political rights. His vote means nothing. His "national autonomy" is meaningless. On paper, though, this is not the case. This is the essential point when we consider present Soviet institutions. Those carrying out the will of the State as against the individual are real, and full of life and power. But there exists side by side with them a phantom set without any practical significance, designed to give the impression that the citizen has rights over the State. The motions are gone through. Elections are held. The Supreme Soviet meets—only for a few days each year, to be sure, as against the months its supposed opposite numbers in the parliaments of the West are in session. The Soviet Constitution is full of provisions for the guarantee of civic rights, and for ensuring the smooth working of the supposedly supreme governing bodies in case of a voting deadlock. In practice, the rights do not exist and the votes are unanimous.

The present constitution came into being in 1936, at the very time when the dictatorship was clamping down most strongly. In appearance, it is an instrument of democracy. In practice, of course, it was devised simply and solely to give a respectable look to the Russia of Stalin, Yezhov, and Beria. Starting at the bottom, the actual ballot paper in Soviet elections gives instructions to the voter on crossing out the names of those candidates he does not wish to vote for: indeed, the very word *vybor*, like the English "election," signifies a choice. But there is only one name on the ballot.

In general, as far as appearances are concerned, the Soviet Constitution reads like one of those model liberal documents that were so often in the nineteenth century voted into being in Latin America and elsewhere to cover the shame of dictatorships. (It is true that even among the hundreds of articles in the Constitution itself, there is one [No. 126] that refutes all the rest: It provides for the leading role of the Communist

Party in the State. While the other articles amount to nothing, this one is absolutely in accordance with the facts. You can have either the rest of the Constitution or Article No. 126. The Party has naturally preferred the latter.)

As we distinguish between a genuine set of institutions (those making up the rulers' chain of control over their subjects) and a false one (those claiming to be the means by which the people control the rulers), we may note one very interesting and significant fact. While there have been many minor adjustments in the administrative machinery of oligarchy, there have been virtually none on the "democratic" and "electoral" side. The system of soviets, the autonomous republics, and all the rest of the paraphernalia are just the same as they were under Stalin. And naturally so, for they were then already perfectly adequate in appearance.

Yet this "democratic" machinery, though now quite ineffective, might at least conceivably be turned to democratic purposes. It is difficult to imagine an easy evolution to the rule of law in Russia. But in the event of the disintegration of the ruling group, there are already in existence, at least, these "ghost" institutions of the Stalin constitution. Although meaningless now, they could conceivably provide the mechanism for making the transition to a sane society comparatively peacefully and legally; in short, they could be utilized as the vehicles of change.

But the first moves cannot be made in these bodies. Until the Party itself has been forced to concede a certain degree of real substance to the soviets and of choice to the electorate, the fulcrums of reform must be in the Party's own institutions, even if some of the pressures are applied from outside, from the universities, or factories, or elsewhere.

If we wish to consider the passing of the present type of Soviet rule into a state of extreme crisis, we must go for parallels—incomplete though these may be—to Poland and Hungary in 1956. These are, so far, the only occasions on which the grip of a conservative *apparat* on the elements of power has been broken or severely shaken. We have, indeed, to eliminate from our consideration of the Soviet Union an element that was quite relevant in both satellite countries—the various pressures of a more powerful Communist neighbor.

In the Hungarian case, a moderately liberal "centrist" regime under Imre Nagy from 1953 to 1955 had been replaced by a return to reaction under Rakosi (though not to the full extremes of the earlier Stalinist period). So far, this is not an impossible thing to envisage in the Soviet Union. The troubles, primarily economic and intellectual, produced by this reaction led to a clumsy attempt to make concessions, too few and too late, and to associate with the regime first a purged wing of the *apparat* (Kadar and others) and finally a Nagy who had now become genuinely liberal, in the hopes of their sharing its odium and propping it up. We may again say that such a thing is not quite impossible in Russia—of course, only in parallel circumstances of intellectual ferment, reaching far down among the populace. This seems unlikely to the degree it occurred in Hungary, unless preceded by a much longer and more obvious period of political instability at the top. And even then we should perhaps envisage things not going so far. Two essential points are relevant, however: first, that a second-rate "conservative" leadership can make enormous and provocative miscalculations; and second, that a wing of the *apparat* driven into opposition can make common cause with the genuine progressives among the non-*apparatchik* youth and intelligentsia. Moreover, these are precisely the factors the Hungarian situation had in common with the Polish. Gomulka and his centrist faction of the *apparat* came to power on the basis of mass demonstrations led or sparked by the students and by the non-*apparat* intellectual element within the Party—in each case reflected in votes in the Central Committee, where the shocks and pressures of the outside movement produced disarray and retreat even among old operatives.

Things went further in Hungary. The Communists supporting Nagy faced the facts. Georg Lukacs, the *doyen* of European Marxist scholars, gave an interview to the Polish press just before the final Russian intervention. He said that he and many of the other Hungarian Communist leaders now recognized that to stay in power by force and fraud alone was useless. The population remained unconvinced, simply waiting its chance to overthrow such a regime. In the circumstances, he said, the Hungarian Communists must start again. They must allow free elections, with the full knowledge that this would result in their defeat. He hoped that a new Communist movement might be started by some of the intellectuals and young people. It would at first get only 10 per cent or so of the vote and would have to go into opposition. But in the long run this would be better for the Communist ideal. For in this way it might be possible, over a period of years, or "even decades," to gain the trust of the population and come back to power on a democratic basis. The path of repression, the only alternative, could not but lead to permanent estrangement between people and Party.

The Russians chose repression. But throughout Eastern Europe, "revisionist" moods were at work among the younger members of the Party. In East Germany, the Party intellectuals supported such views as those for which Professor Harich, a correspondent of Lukacs, was imprisoned early in 1957. He stated that the "Socialist Germany" for which the Communist Party was allegedly working, could only be attained in a united Germany, by democratic means and in alliance with the Social Democratic Party, in which the workers placed their main trust.

Throughout the Soviet bloc, the writers proved to be the strongest center of revisionism. Those of Czechoslovakia were denounced by the Prime Minister for tacit "demonstrations against the Party." In Russia, the Central Committee struggled in 1957 and 1963 against "rotten liberalism"; recantations were few. In December, 1957, the Bulgarian Communist writers publicly defied the orders of the Party. All these writers denied the Party's claim to order a made-to-measure literature from them. Many of their works went further and attacked the whole Party-police-bureaucratic system. Nor could the Party forget that the Hungarian Revolution was sparked by the meetings of the Communist writers' Petoefi Club.

And intellectual agitation can lead to political change. The Hungarian writers had close connections with political leaders like Nagy. And there were denunciations over the period 1957–63 of high-ranking revisionists in the Romanian and Bulgarian Communist *Party* leaderships, and elsewhere. They, too, were accused of basing their bids for power on an appeal for greater freedom of discussion and election in the Party.

For the essence of the new revisionism was the demand for discussion, for the chance to judge for oneself. Unlike earlier "deviations," it criticized not merely particular policies, but the right of the leaders to impose policies at all without the consent of the governed. The view that the Central Committee may merely order what it wants and that "democratic centralism" involves obeying blindly has been shaken to its foundations. Yet freedom to know, to discuss, and to judge are incompatible with totalitarian rule. The new epoch of struggle between the old Party apparatus and the fresh and young forces of revisionism would be full of bitter and complicated struggles. The old ruling caste has been able to reimpose thought control partially, but on the whole it seems that we are in the presence of a phenomenon similar to that which split Europe in the 1840's. After decades of sporadic and individual resistance to the absolute monarchies, the whole educated class, and eventually the workers, became rapidly and irrevocably possessed with a thirst for greater liberty of thought and action. From then on, the bureaucrats and dogmatists of legitimism were doomed, even after their apparent victory in 1849.

It will be noticed that these revisionists, even those who fought Soviet troops in Budapest, had no objections to the social policies of the Communist parties as stated in the Party program. They looked forward to the creation of Communist states without secret police, with freedom of discussion and publication, and with political democracy. If, in the long run, they attain these goals, the irreconcilabilities which now endanger world peace will be removed and Communist and non-Communist states will truly be able to live together in "peaceful coexistence" and "peaceful competition."

The Hungarian and Polish revolutions were both in a sense failures, though in different ways. In Hungary, even the Kadarist section of the *apparat* lost control, but was reinstated by foreign help. In Poland, once the Natolin Stalinists had been defeated, the Gomulka *apparat* group was able to contain and subdue the genuine progressives. Even so, it is probably fair to say that neither in Hungary nor in Poland has it been possible in the long run wholly to expel the entire thinking public from the polity, and the potential for further development remains. Meanwhile, we may note that although the "objective" conditions for a true liberalization were better in Eastern Europe than they are in the U.S.S.R., the decisive force which —either in action or in potentiality—finally prevented a democratic evolution was the external threat from a counterrevolutionary Soviet Union. This consideration would obviously *not* apply to similar movements in Moscow itself.

On the other hand, it should be noted that in the Polish, Yugoslav, and Hungarian cases a powerful element came into play which could not, as far as one can see, be of such importance in Soviet (or at least Russian) conditions—the immense force of nationalism, which led in all these cases to a rallying around the reformers by elements who might otherwise not have done so, and probably demoralized any opposition. It is clearly true that support for the Khrushchevite and post-Khrushchevite policies has been greatly strengthened by nationalist resentment against the Chinese. And this may perhaps be regarded as a constant. All the same, it is unlikely to be so effective as the similar anti-Russian feelings in Eastern Europe.

If unrest were to reach the stage it came to in Hungary and Poland, there is of course no doubt that it could be put down, physically speaking, by the Army and the MVD. But we must assume in any case that no such mass movements could take place unless and until a considerable disintegration had set in at the top, and this could imply two things: first, factional strains of such intensity that one or the other contender might be prepared to try to use the masses against his adversaries in the *apparat;* and second, a considerable degree of uncertainty about the advisability of concession or repression.

One Communist Party (in Hungary) did briefly and precariously fall into the hands of a leadership prepared to abandon the monolithic state. But it should be noted that the progressive element that events brought into prominence came very largely from the intellectual, journalistic, academic, and student sections of the Party, and very little from its *apparat*. *Apparatist* authorities have, under extreme pressure, abandoned —or rather shelved—collectivization, as in Poland and Yugoslavia. But they have never given up the dynastic claims of the *apparat*.

The relaxation that took place in Russia in 1956 and in China in 1957 may be seen as based on the idea that after so many years of Party rule a return to considerable freedom of expression would show that the vast majority supported the regime in all essentials. Things did not work out quite that way. In Russia, intellectuals, students, and representatives of the minority nations produced a lively public opinion highly critical of much government activity. In China, the great bulk of the intellectual classes, on which the regime had relied, showed themselves to be "Rightists"—i.e., urging a more democratic Communism. The Chinese Government's reaction was one of panic repression. In Russia, things did not go that far. One reason was that over the years a comparatively stable society had evolved, whose resentment and resistance to full-scale terror would quite evidently be powerful. A prominent member of the Soviet bureaucracy, Assistant Procurator-General Kudryavtsev, said that "if it becomes necessary, we will restore the old methods. But I think it will not be necessary."

This is not a particularly reassuring attitude. And it seems plain that the bureaucracy regards its right to power as coming before all ethical principles. But it is important to remember not only that the Russian bureaucracy at least realizes that repression has long-term effects which may be unpalatable to it, but also that the bureaucrat, though he may be the typical Communist ruler, is not necessarily a typical Communist. The important developments of the last eight years in the Communist movement have been possible because there is always this other dream in the Party—because the initial idealism has never disappeared. Lukacs in Hungary and Harich in East Germany both urged abandonment of the theory that all non-Communists were in the long run enemies. In Poland, the Communist philosopher Leszek Kolakowski denied that "the criteria of the moral evaluation of human conduct can be deduced from the knowledge of the mysteries of the *Weltgeist*" and defined a non-Socialist country as one where the writers and professors say the same thing as the politicians and generals, but always *afterwards.* This intellectual ferment was found throughout the Communist world, from North Vietnam to Albania. Nor was it confined to intellectuals. Imre Nagy, one of the oldest and most senior of Communist politicians, attacked the degeneration of power and the "moral crisis," drawing particular attention to the "violent contrasts between words and deeds . . . rocking the foundations of our society and our Party," even before he came to power on a program calling for the restoration of political democracy and collaboration with other Socialist forces.

None of these tendencies attained immediate political success, but their influence did not disappear, and they were revived notably in the 1962 "thaw." And we must remember that Soviet achievements, even when they can be attributed in part to the ruthlessness of the government, depend also upon devoted scientists and social workers who consider themselves "Communists" like the bureaucrats, though not equally bound to a dogmatic interpretation of the Party line. Since their views are more in accordance with reality, there is excellent reason to hope that on some future stage their voices will count for more.

For there are certainly within the Party, if only at lower levels, genuinely "liberal" elements who "have not spoken yet." Or rather, who have spoken only in previous moments of stress, and then only sporadically: *Kommunist*, in July, 1956, spoke of opinions "objectively directed toward unseating the leadership chosen by the Party masses themselves, and toward discrediting the Party cadres." These had "nothing in common with a correct Leninist understanding of the role of leadership. Such opinions have been expressed by individual, insufficiently mature Communists in discussing the results of the Twentieth Congress." The same organ the following year (December, 1957) was more explicit:

> When, at the meeting of the Party organization of a scientific laboratory, a small group of workers, under cover of a discussion about the personality cult, tried to exploit inner Party democracy for slander against the Party and attacks on its policy, the Central Committee of the CPSU took a stern de-

cision, not only against that group, but also against the Party organization as a whole, which did not repulse the slanderers.

As to the actual possibility of a genuine ferment in the Soviet Union in time of political crisis, we must consider events of the same period. The huge, enthusiastic meetings of students at Moscow University—when all the catchphrases were questioned, when official speakers were greeted with slogans of "Democracy—from below," when illegal magazines proliferated and reports of foreign news broadcasts were posted on the bulletin boards—showed that a great potential reservoir of liberal thought and action exists in the capital, and elsewhere, since similar phenomena were reported from universities all over the Union.

At the same time, the ferment had begun to reach the workers. Factory meetings openly jeered at members of the Presidium for their high salaries. And the continued existence of an easily roused resentment among the workers can be seen in such scattered incidents over the past few years as the riots in Temir Tau and elsewhere. In addition, of course, there have been nationalist demonstrations on a mass scale in Lithuania and Georgia. To dismiss the potential of intellectual and mass movement in the U.S.S.R. might be a mistake.

In principle, the wind of change in the U.S.S.R. might manifest itself outside or inside the Communist institutions and forms of thought. The former would be as the result of explosion after long repression. The latter is the more peaceful alternative—and perhaps the more probable.

Any real change in Communism must involve an evolution of ideology and, with it, of institutions. Ideologies do evolve. They evolve under pressures. And if we ask ourselves what the relevant pressures are in the Soviet Union, we see that they are twofold. In the first place, there is the pressure of what may be thought of as the permanent economic crisis. The whole tendency of society in the U.S.S.R. is to break out from its present lines. The high-capitalization programs are kept in operation only by restricting the demands of the consumer. Some concession is already being made to him, but it is not much of a concession except in comparison with the past; housing, particularly, remains a major complaint. Then again, it is only continual political effort that keeps the collective-farm system going. It is contrary not only to the desires of the peasantry but even to the interests of higher production. In short, the economy is kept in its present form only by an extreme and continual application of ideologically motivated power from above. The "natural" tendencies of society in economics imply continued pressure on the regime. So do the natural desires for "democratization" among many members of the Party itself, to say nothing of the population. In the past, they could be countered because Stalin had created an apparatus whereby a single will could impose itself against these pressures. The apparatus is still in being. The single will is not. As a result, there is already considerable halfheartedness in the operation of the Stalinist machinery.

The other pressure on the ideology is the international situation. It is not simply that the ruling group is faced with powerful states fully determined to prevent expansionist adventures. It is the fact that is generally penetrating the consciousness of the Soviet leadership, that the risk of war is one that cannot be seriously taken with modern weapons. But if war cannot be risked, and the non-Communist powers are prepared to fight rather than retreat, very little possibility of political expansion abroad will exist, despite Lenin's statement that the world would eventually become Communist after a series of "frightful clashes." The Soviet leaders (though not the Chinese) have already revised Lenin on this point, as well they might. Thus a Western foreign policy of "containment" is the best way of securing one or the other of the two alternative possibilities—the disintegration or the democratization of the Communist movement. It could usefully be supplemented by more frequent and higher-level references to the peaceful world community which could emerge if the Communist regimes instituted the minimum necessary modification of their insistence on the principle of permanent conflict against other nations and against their own subjects.

No system of human thought, or of human organization, is immutable. The Communist movement, arising out of Lenin's interpretation of Marxism, has seen radical changes. And to some degree we can trace the causes that have produced those changes in the past (as well as those producing them at present) back into the history of Marxism. For, while it is true that for many years one-man dictatorship flourished not only in Russia but over the Communist parties as a whole, it was not based on a full-blooded *Führerprinzip*. On the contrary, Marxism contains many other elements, and it was never possible to eradicate these from the body of ideas in the minds of the thinking members of the Communist parties, or even to avoid dealing with them officially. The result was what we have come to know as double-think. Instead of a frank repudiation of the freedom of thought which Marx held to, recourse was had to the argument that state monopoly of ideas was the highest form of freedom. Nonsense of this type could only be kept going by force. As soon as the force relaxed, the voices of the older Marxists were bound to emerge with the old lessons, providing a link with the past and a theoretical justification for the natural aspirations of the younger generation.

More than fifty years ago, many young men were attracted to the Bolsheviks (and to the new Communist parties founded in imitation of them) as the most militant of the Marxist factions, while at the same time they harbored notions of a Socialist democracy that could be introduced after the Revolution. Many of these were, so to speak, trapped in the movement by their slowly deteriorating hopes. Some degenerated into terrorist bureaucrats. Others never wholly gave up their old ideas even when abjectly silenced. Lukacs, for instance, was Commissar for Education in the 1919 Communist regime in Hungary, and survived to be Nagy's Minister of Culture in 1956. And he is still alive.

Marxism, in fact, contained two strands. On the one hand, it was rationalist and humanist. On the other, there were the seeds of authoritarianism: Revolution is—however briefly—an act of power, and the government produced by it must, at least temporarily, act in an authoritarian manner. There is also in Marx a tendency to political amorality, to expediency, rather than the application of general principles, in tactics. This was greatly exaggerated by Stalin, for Marx actually took for granted that there were ethical limits beyond which expediency provided no excuse, while Stalin did not. When the Communists had been entrenched in power for over a generation, it became increasingly difficult to keep up the theory that "revolutionary" necessities justified gross breaches of truth and decency. When Stalin died, it became practically impossible. The long-suppressed, but never destroyed, arguments of Marxist humanism rose again to the surface.

At the end of 1964, we see the Communist movement beset with heresy and schism. We see within it tendencies toward freedom of thought, toward liberation from the various antihumanist dogmas that have poisoned it for more than a generation. The progress that libertarian ideas have so far made should not be exaggerated. But the fact that they are there, ready to emerge, even after the long years of Stalinism, is heartening proof that they are ineradicable. Even the partial disintegration which now besets the movement provides circumstances in which the mind and the heart begin to exert their influence on the Russian Communists. It is still far too early to say definitely that the movement, or even an important part of it, may yet be reclaimed for humanism. One does not readily see the Soviet Central Committee, possessed by a new spirit, assembling like the French nobility of the eighteenth century in some *jeu de paume* in Moscow and handing over its rights to an enthusiastic Russian "third estate." The forces of reaction within the Communist movement are still powerful. It may be that they will triumph yet. Even so, in the long run, there is at least a genuine possibility that the movement and the countries it controls may be reclaimed for civilization. Among our present perils, this is a heartening prospect.

The present political leadership fails to carry conviction. Kosygin and Brezhnev, Shelepin and Podgorny, Suslov and Polyansky are not the men to rule a great country beset by general crisis. Russia, that sleeping giant, is already straining half-consciously at the bonds that hold her.

But whether, and to what degree, the new forces find expression through Party and Soviet channels, we may at least expect a tough political struggle. At some stage, in any case, the power of the bureaucratic integument which at present prevents development to sanity must be eroded or broken. For the moment, we may conclude that almost the entire tendency of Soviet society is toward a more comfortable and less aggressive and revolutionary state of affairs; that the machinery of the Soviet State is, however, highly organized for imposing on that society the will of an unrepresentative group at the top; and that the grip of this machine could at present only be shaken by a decisive split at the highest level, either within the Presidium or between it and the Army High Command, or a combination of both. We might conclude that some such development—and in the fairly near future—is not too unlikely.

Index

Adzhubei, A., 118, 227
Aliger, Margarita, 61
Andreyev, A. A., 135
Andropov, Yu. V., 29, 134, 163
Aristov, A. B., 126, 134, 156, 163
Arzumanyan, A., 88, 92

Bacon, Francis, 123
Beria, L. P., 23–24, 43, 58, 125, 127–28, 136, 176, 212, 246, 250–51
Berklav, E. K., 209
Berman, J., 245
Biryuzov, Marshal, 182
Blackett, P. M. S., 239–40
Blyukher, Marshal, 184
Brezhnev, L. I., 3, 4, 9, 20, 30, 99, 107, 117–19, 125, 129, 131–33, 135–39, 142, 149–51, 153–54, 156, 161, 182, 264
Bukharin, N. I., 14
Bulganin, N. A., 69, 128, 134

Chateaubriand, François René de, 249
Chesnokov, D. I., 126
Chou En-lai, 221
Chuikov, Marshal, 180
Chukovsky, K., 100
Churayev, V. M., 29, 120

Daulenov, Salkan, 210
Demichev, P. N., 31, 133, 158
De Sapio, Carmine, 26, 74
De Sismondi, J., 49
Djilas, Milovan, 228, 235

Efremov, L. N., 30, 133
Ehrenburg, Ilya, 100
Eichmann, A., 56
Eikhe, R. I., 113
Einaudi, Giulio, 91
Eisenhower, Dwight D., 243
Engels, Friedrich, 14, 21
Epishev, A. A., 29, 163, 180
Erlich, Victor, 62

Farkas, M., 56
Farley, James, 26
Fedin, K., 100
Fierlinger, Z., 239
Finlay, George, 57, 121
Franklin, Benjamin, 73
Frunze, M. V., 115
Furtseva, E., 117, 158

"Gavrilov, Nikolai," 131
Gibbon, Edward, 43, 52
Golikov, General, 180
Gomulka, W., 164, 194, 225, 226, 256
Gorbatov, General, 173
Grishin, V. V., 30, 90, 133
Gromyko, A. A., 186

Hanna, Mark, 74

Harich, Wolfgang, 254, 258
Hitler, Adolf, 17, 34, 49, 56, 66, 71, 122–23
Hoxha, Enver, 145

Ignatiev, S. D., 126
Ignatov, N. G., 28, 98, 107, 134, 156
Ilychev, L. F., 29, 84, 132, 134

Kadar, J., 48, 194, 253
Kaganovich, L. M., 96, 99, 106, 163, 165
Kalchenko, N. T., 156
Kapitonov, I. V., 157
Kardelj, E., 215
Kazenets, I. P., 214
Kennedy, John F., 74
Khrushchev, N. S., 3–5, 11, 15, 18–20, 23–24, 29, 34, 38–39, 42–44, 48, 62, 68–71, 75–76, 79, 81–83, 85, 87–88, 91–92, 96, 99, 100, 104–5, 107, 109–23, 124, 131, 135–36, 140–41, 143, 151, 156–60, 163–65, 174–75, 177–79, 190, 201, 218, 220–22, 225, 227, 234, 241–42, 244–45, 248, 250
Kirichenko, A. I., 68, 117, 134, 141–42, 149, 210
Kirilenko, A. P., 30, 107, 119–20, 132, 149, 153, 214
Kirov, S. M., 44
Kolakowski, Leszek, 258
Kolushchinsky, 97
Korotchenko, D. S., 46, 156, 245
Kosarev, A. V., 142
Kossior, S. V., 113
Kosygin, A. N., 3–4, 9, 20, 30, 99, 105, 107, 118, 129, 132–33, 139–40, 153, 156, 161, 264
Kozlov, F. R., 5, 47, 93, 102, 107, 114–16, 132, 149, 151, 156–57, 170, 210
Kudryavtsev, 258
Kuusinen, Otto, 170
Kuzmin, I. I., 139
Kuznetsov, V. V., 161

Lacis, V. T., 209
Lange, Oskar, 79
Lenin, V. I., 12–14, 21, 61, 106, 201, 206, 261
Leontiev, L., 84
Liberman, Professor E., 83–85
Litvinov, M. M., 240
Lukacs, Georg, 254, 258, 263
Luxemburg, Rosa, 58
Lysenko, T. G., 52, 63–64

McKinley, William, 74
Malenkov, G. M., 69, 76, 78, 81, 87, 96, 99, 103, 105–6, 110–11, 125–27, 129, 134, 149–50, 157, 164–69, 176, 235–36, 246
Malinovsky, Marshal, 178–83, 186
Mao Tse-tung, 39, 217, 221–24, 234, 237
Marr, N. Y., 52
Marx, Karl, 8, 12, 14, 19, 58, 262–63
Mazurov, K. T., 30, 133
Melnikov, L. G., 126
Meretskov, Marshal, 173
Merkulov, V. N., 24
Mgeladze, A. I., 126
Mikhailov, N. A., 126, 161, 163
Mikoyan, A. I., 9, 27, 30, 99, 103, 107, 132–33, 149
Miller, Margaret, 84
Minc, Bronislaw, 87
Mironov, N., 120, 180
Molotov, V. M., 24, 69, 96–97, 99, 103, 106–7, 111, 129, 134, 164–67, 177, 221, 234–35, 246
Montesquieu, Baron C. de, 72
Mustafeev, I. D., 208
Mzhavanadze, V. P., 30, 133

Nagy, Imre, 48, 116, 199, 229, 244, 253, 255, 258, 263
Nenni, Pietro, 250
Nicolaevsky, Boris, 111
Novikov, V. N., 156

Olshansky, M. A., 63
Ordzhonikidze, G. K., 115
Orwell, George, 7, 159, 230

Pashkov, A., 87
Pasternak, Boris, 46
Patolichev, N. S., 161, 163
Paustovsky, K., 65
Pavlov, S., 189

Pegov, N. M., 161, 163
Pelse, A., 209
Penkovsky, O., 115
Pervukhin, M. G., 134, 169
Petrovsky, G. I., 160
Podgorny, N. V., 30, 99, 107, 117, 132–33, 140–42, 153, 155, 264
Polyansky, D. S., 28, 30, 89–90, 99, 107, 133, 144–45, 150–51, 153, 264
Ponomarev, B. N., 29, 134
Popov, A. I., 156
Poskrebyshev, A. N., 126
Postyshev, P. P., 113

Rakosi, Matyas, 56, 239
Rashidov, Sh. R., 133, 212
Rodionov, N. N., 97, 156
Rokossovsky, Marshal, 58, 173
Rotmistrov, Marshal, 174
Rozhdestvensky, R., 197
Rudakov, 119, 134
Rykov, A. I., 44
Ryumin, M., 126

Saburov, M. Z., 134, 169
Schaff, Adam, 228
Schapiro, Leonard, 105
Secchia, Senator, 47
Semichastny, V. E., 28, 120, 154–55, 209
Serdyuk, Z. T., 28, 120
Serov, I. A., 143
Shamil, 124
Shatalin, N. N., 127
Shaumyan, L., 44
Shelepin, A. N., 24, 28, 30, 107, 128, 132–33, 142–44, 150–51, 154, 264
Shelest, P., 30, 107, 119, 132–33, 153–54
Shepilov, D. T., 106
Shikin, I. V., 156
Shtemenko, General, 175
Shvernik, N. M., 30, 99, 107, 132–33
Solzhenitsyn, A., 62, 100
Sokolovsky, Marshal, 175, 181
Spiridonov, I. V., 97, 156
Stalin, J. V., 5–6, 8, 10, 13, 15–21, 23–24, 26–28, 33–34, 36, 38, 40, 42–44, 46, 48, 54, 70, 103, 110, 112, 118,
Stalin, J. V. (*Cont.*)
125, 130, 135–36, 140, 151, 160, 174–77, 189–90, 194, 218, 224, 226, 230, 233–34, 240–41, 243, 250–52
Stepanov, V., 102, 190
Stolypin, P. A., 122
Strachey, Lytton, 69, 121
Suslov, M. A., 27, 30, 99, 107, 131–33, 146–49, 150, 153, 170, 250, 264
Swiatlo, 244–45

Talensky, Major General N., 219
Terracini, Senator, 112, 225
Tevosyan, I. F., 163
Tito, Marshal, 34, 221, 225, 233
Titov, V. N., 119, 134, 153
Togliatti, Palmiro, 39, 46, 68, 188
Tolstoy, Leo, 249
Trotsky, L. D., 44, 160
Tukhachevsky, Marshal, 173
Tvardovsky, A., 100

Ustinov, D. F., 86, 134

Vorobiev, G. I., 156–57
Voronov, G. I., 30, 89–90, 99, 107, 132, 145–46, 151, 153
Voroshilov, K. E., 106, 165
Voss, A. E., 210
Voznesensky, N. A., 81, 134, 139

Weissberg, Alexander, 130
Wells, H. G., 33
Woroszylski, W., 130

Yagoda, H., 174
Yesenin-Volpin, A. S., 48
Yevtushenko, Yevgeny, 8, 43, 56, 61, 66, 93, 100, 197–99
Yezhov, N. I., 23, 174, 251
Yusupov, 91, 212

Zakharov, M. V., 172, 181–82
Zhdanov, A. A., 23, 63, 75, 139
Zhdanov, Yu. A., 126
Zheltov, A. S., 178
Zhukov, G. K., 128, 134, 145, 175–79, 181, 186
Zinoviev, G. E., 22, 44, 54